the food of spain & portugal

the food of
spain &
portugal

a regional celebration by elisabeth luard

kyle cathie ltd

In memory of my beloved
husband Nicholas

First published in Great Britain 2004 by
Kyle Cathie Limited
122 Arlington Road
London NW1 7HP
general.enquiries@kyle-cathie.com
www.kylecathie.com

This paperback edition published 2007

ISBN 978 1 85626 712 0

Project editor Caroline Taggart
Designer Geoff Hayes
Photographer Jean Cazals
Home economist Janie Suthering
Props stylist Penny Markham
Maps ML Design
Copy editor Robina Pelham Burn
Proofreader Ruth Baldwin
Index Sarah Ereira
Production Sha Huxtable and Alice Holloway

A Cataloguing in Publication record for this title is
available from the British Library.

Colour reproduction by Colourscan
Printed and bound by Star Standard, Singapore

contents

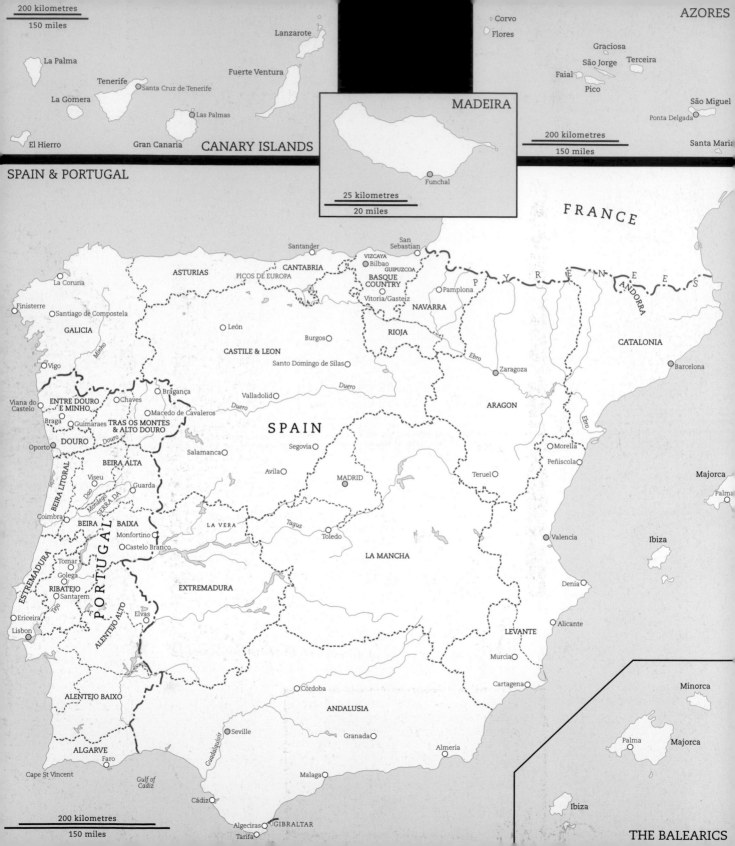

Close your eyes and imagine yourself under the shade of an olive tree with the shores of the Mediterranean just over the curve of the hill. Imagine, too, that someone – a native of this land – is preparing your meal. What shall it be? The choice is wide. Creamy white beans from the slopes of Asturian hillsides, slow-simmered with garlic and olive oil, flavoured, perhaps, with a ham bone – nothing much, you might think, until the cook explains with shining eyes that this particular ham bone is from a particular breed of pig and is cured in a particular way which makes it like no other ham in all the world. Or perhaps you might choose a dish of rice from the wetlands of Valencia, coloured and perfumed with saffron grown in the red earth of La Mancha. Or chickpeas cooked to a nutty sweetness with the deep crimson peppers cured in the smokehouses of Old Castile. Or pork and shellfish seasoned with fiery chillis cooked in a cataplana – Portugal's shell-shaped cooking implement which gives its name to the recipe. Or, if the sun is high and the breeze is cool and you have a mind to stay in the shade, you might choose a thick-crusted speckle-crumbed loaf to eat with the sheep's cheese of La Mancha, or cornmeal bread with the soft-centred cheeses of Tras-os-Montes.

Shall I go on? These are just a few of the good things to be found in this land under the Iberian sun. And in every village, town and city there are the sweet things which are, in homage to their origin, considered ladies' treats: made to please the beauties of the seraglio long before they became convent sweets, the province of Christian nuns. Custards and cakes rich with almonds and honey, halvas and egg-yolk confections sweetened with Turkish sugar and perfumed with the scents of the souk. Phoenicians, Greeks, Celts, Romans, Visigoths and finally – and most importantly in matters of the kitchen – the Moors, all have left their print on the land and the people. Their presence can be read not simply in the ingredients they brought or the recipes which still bear the names they gave them, but in the shape of the cooking pot, in every spice the cook

throws in the pan, the application of heat, the moment at which to add salt, the pause when a decision is taken to use either onion or garlic in a recipe but not both.

When you ask the reason for anything, you will be met with a smile and a shrug: 'Because that's the way it's done.' Gerald Brenan, observing life in the 1950s in the Alpujarras, a remote region south of Granada, explained the secret ingredient: 'Trevelez, the highest village in Europe, has a reputation for witchcraft, and it is even said that the famous hams that come from there owe their particular flavour to the spells said over them.' Influences were not one-sided: the smell of frying fish, he said, frightened the silkworms, the housewives' cash crop, which immediately stopped spinning their cocoons and snipped the thread, spoiling the silk.

The inhabitants of the lands of the Mediterranean, blessed with a year-round growing season, have the advantage over northerners obliged – traditionally at least – to spend half the year storing up food for the other half. Easy access to fresh produce from land and sea has had a profound influence on culinary style. The recipes which emerged from this happy situation – dependent on perfect raw materials and the knowledge to recognise their excellence – could not, until modern times, be reproduced successfully outside their land of origin. Refrigeration and modern methods of transport have changed all this – but mainly in reverse, since the passionate fish-connoisseurs of Seville are more likely to be feasting on Orkney oysters or Hebridean lobsters than Scotland's meat-eaters are on the exquisite flat-fish of the Ebro delta.

Every Iberian native will tell you it's the territory which makes the dinner. The idea of a *cocina del terreno* in the way that France has her *cuisine du terroir*, would be perfectly understood. The notion of haute cuisine – that it took a chef's skill to raise home cooking to high art – was unknown until modern times. These days, while the chefs of

Madrid and Barcelona as well as those of Seville, Lisbon, Oporto and Bilbao – not forgetting the tiny village of Rosas – have achieved international recognition, it is rarely without a regional identity as part of the baggage. When it comes to home cooking, the pueblo – a word which means both the village and the nation – knows what it likes. And what it likes is pretty close to what mother makes.

While it's only in the more isolated mountain districts that rural households still grow their own food, raise poultry, feed the household scraps to the pig – nevertheless, when, for economic and social reasons, people move to the towns and cities, they still expect to market daily. The home cooking of Iberia, as distinct from restaurant or festive food, is market-dictated: call it reaction-cooking. That is, no one cooks out of season unless there's a very good reason.

The scent curling under the kitchen door at midday is most likely to be from one of the thousand varieties of boiled dinners – one-pot dishes served first as a soup and then as a main dish (sometimes this too is divided into vegetables and meat). These, while always based on one of the pulses, are so place-specific that they can be used to distinguish one region, population or even single village from another. If the pot includes a joint of a well-flavoured boiling fowl, a piece of pork, a length of sausage, so much the richer and more delicious. Quality is valued above quantity. If the olla lacks meat but the flavouring-bone is Ibérico ham, the dish can be considered fit for a king.

Bread and water are always on the table – no one would think of eating a meal without bread, or taking wine without drinking at least as much water. Preserved pork products – chorizos, ham, bacon, lard, pig extremities from the salt-drawer – are the traditional store-cupboard meats. Eggs and cheese remain an important source of protein, with fresh meat still considered something of a luxury. There used to be a saying in Andalusia that anyone who can afford to eat fresh meat twice a day is either greedy or a politician or a lawyer – or all three. Olive oil is used not simply for frying and dressing a salad, but also to enrich and thicken a broth. Fish is eaten several times a week even by those who live far inland – if not, there's still a ready market for salt-fish.

As for technique, it's the small things – an understanding of how food behaves when it goes into the pan, a subtle hand with the seasonings, a knowledge of what makes food delicious as well as nourishing – which guide the hand of the instinctive cook, as every cook must be when following an oral tradition. A culinary habit which depends on the way a certain cook in a certain place chooses and treats those raw materials which come to hand is not easily reproduced. It's an attitude of mind. Certain things give pleasure because they are what they ought to be: they taste good and they do you good. Few of us now live the way our forefathers did; still fewer would want to. Then again, some things are too good to lose. And cooking inspired by a sense of place – seasonal, regional, using traditions and techniques our grandparents would have recognised – is surely one of them.

We – those of us who live in the developed world – are affluent as never before. We are mobile. We can choose what we eat and when and where we eat it. As no generation before us, we travel, both practically and culturally. The ingredients come to us when we can't get to them. What we find on our supermarket shelves – where most of us these days do our shopping – is no longer limited by what we can grow in our fields, nor, however familiar, can we be sure of its provenance. Bacalhau is now imported from Canada to Portugal and the land of Basques, home of the salted cod; fresh chickens are transported by air from Brazil to the spit-roasters of Lisbon and Oporto; pimentón grown and milled in Hungary is sold in Spanish supermarkets; pig-hams destined for the serrano-salters of Spain are trucked in from Germany. Certain species of fish have dropped off the menu for ecological reasons, and rightly too – far better to allow stocks to recover and use farmed fish whenever we can. If that were not confusion enough, fruits and vegetables which were once entirely seasonal are now available all year. We no longer experience famine years, terrible times whose memory is buried in prejudice against certain foods and in favour of others. Nor do we, unless from choice or conviction, use food as a direct expression of moral or religious allegiance. All these things change the way people cook.

I have had to make hard choices while compiling this by-no-means comprehensive collection of the regional recipes of the Iberian

Fishing for shellfish in the waters near La Coruna, Galicia

peninsula. Not wishing to leave out information which might help to illuminate how and why a particular regional tradition has developed, I have mentioned, but not always given recipes for, dishes which were the product of necessity and which people might not want to prepare if they had a choice. Certain of the bread-based dishes – gazpachos, migas, açordas – have excellent credentials, but may only taste good to those who have known them since childhood. Others such as the curious goose-barnacle of the coast of Cantabria, the lamprey of northern Portugal, are so local that it's only useful to describe them in general terms and give, if appropriate, suggestions for substitution. Still more are somewhat repetitive – there are, for instance, as many variations on the bean-pot as there are cooks to prepare it, each one subtly different, each with a fair claim for inclusion in a book such as this.

You can't have it all. For this reason – as well as my natural inclination as a home cook rather than restaurant chef – I have tried to keep a loose hand on the garage-manual aspect of the recipes. Measurements, at least for non-baking recipes, are deliberately inexact – a glass of wine, a spoonful of oil – bearing in mind such things as that you need more cinnamon to flavour a

dish if the spice has already been on the shelf for a year. I offer suggestions, no more, as to timing: there is no way of knowing the exact moment when a bean will tenderise or meat will begin to brown, or how a particular oven will treat a particular cake.

My criterion for selection has been not only that the dishes should be authentic, but that they should taste good too. Above all, what comes to the table should look appetising and deliver what it promises – something delicious to put in your mouth. The pleasure of cooking lies not simply in following a set of instructions – ingredients, utensils, method – but in the delight of not following a recipe to the letter, of using your own good sense, following your instincts, trusting your judgement. In other words, exactly what every cook has always done from the moment someone's cave-dwelling granny had the bright idea of boiling the bison with a handful of thyme just because that was what came to hand. The aim, after all, is the preparation of good food in convivial company for the enjoyment of all who take their place at the table. We have bread, we have oil, we have wine. Welcome to the feast.

OVERLEAF: *View of Zaragoza*, early sixteenth century, by Diego de Velázquez

spain

Behind the Spain of the tourist resorts, the sea and sand of the Mediterranean beaches, any observant visitor will be aware of older traditions, of hilltop villages shaded by Roman-planted olive trees, of a sea-horizon sparkling with the lights of wooden fishing boats night-trawling out of ancient ports whose jetties may have been thrown up by Phoenician sailors, of rice paddies watered by Moorish irrigation systems. These are the raw materials for the culinary traditions of the real Spain.

The Spanish menu, I learnt when a young housewife in the Andalusian seaport which was, for twelve years, my local market town, begins in the marketplace. By ten o'clock of a morning Tarifa knew what to expect of its day's rations. If the butcher had had a delivery of young beef from the Cadiz bull-ranchers, that evening the town's earthenware cooking pots would fill the air with scented steam from a thousand tomato-rich stews, wafted through the open doorways on whose whitewashed stoop all southern dwellers sit on warm evenings to watch the world go by.

When the local fishing boats came in with a particularly fine haul of silvery sardines or purple-tinged clams, or the tuna-fish were running though the Straits on a spring tide, the breeze carried a different flavour. Then the frying pans would breathe sea scents tinged with the sharp tang of the sherry in which the shellfish are put to open, or the rich fruity olive oil which Spaniards, whenever they can afford it, use for frying and saucing their plentiful sea-harvest.

Vegetables and salads, at their best when they have been gathered and taken to market that same morning, are usually presented as a separate course before the meat. Otherwise they are included as an integral part of a one-pot meal, of which Spain has a wide variety, mostly based on one of the pulses. Chicken – the small farmer's favourite meat – and wild game are stewed with vegetables in Asturias; in Catalonia they're served in a sauce thickened with nuts; in Galicia on the northern Atlantic coast they come baked in an empanada, the flat pie which demonstrates the same skill in baking as enjoyed by the rest of the Celtic peoples, whose basic language the Galicians share. Eggs are particularly imaginatively treated in the Spanish kitchen, and the sleight of hand needed to turn out a perfect juicy potato omelette is acquired by every country girl at her mother's elbow.

The strength of Spanish cookery lies in good raw materials simply and skilfully prepared. The Spaniard likes his food recognisably itself, without too much complication and addition: meats are preferred sauced with their own juices, fish and shellfish are prized for tasting of the sea. The best and freshest in the market is prepared quite simply, but in harmony with the three most important ingredients of the Spanish kitchen: the pure juice of the olive, healthiest of oils; wine, purest of all flavouring broths; and garlic, most aromatic of pot-herbs. From the hot plains of Castile to the cold uplands of the Basque country, the orange groves of Seville to the granite uplands of Galicia, each region has its own specialities.

The culinary legacy of the Moors in Andalusia combined with a strong tradition of communal eating led to the pleasurable and peculiarly Spanish tradition of dropping in to the local bar for tapas – that is, a doll-sized portion of the house speciality, offered on a tiny plate or a square of bread as the free 'cover' for a glass of wine. In the little ventas of rural districts this can be as simple as a dish of home-pickled olives, a slice of spicy chorizo or a nugget of the local cheese, a fan of fried fish, a dab of the stew that is on the menu that day, a little dish of cooked vegetables dressed with mayonnaise. Pride is taken in never offering the same tapa twice to the same customer. In large cities such as Madrid, Seville and Barcelona, the browsing population will stroll from one tasca or bar to another, sampling the company and the cooking of each with equal enthusiasm. Although this delightful habit is now under threat as the bars, particularly those in tourist regions, have to improve their profit margins, the habit of taking 'something to pick' has not. The tiny individual tapa is today being replaced by a full or half 'ration' of a dish which is shared between friends as an appetiser with a glass of wine – either red, perhaps with a splash of fizzy lemonade – *gaseosa* – to make a simple sangría, or, more traditionally since the habit spread from Seville to the rest of Spain, a copita of chilled dry sherry, the house wine of Andalusia.

Spain has such an abundance of fruit all the year round that meals are usually concluded with something seasonal: a bunch of grapes, a ripe orange, a juicy custard apple. Somewhat perversely, tinned fruit in syrup was – in rural areas still is – considered the great treat. The Moors introduced cane sugar to Europe both directly during their occupation of Spain and indirectly via the returning Crusaders. Sugar cane was planted both in Andalusia and in Portugal's Algarve to satisfy the Arab taste for sweetmeats and syrups. By the time Ferdinand and Isabella finally took Granada and the Moorish occupation was over, the imported taste was centuries old – and centuries-old habits die hard.

The Spanish and Portuguese convents in particular continued with the tradition of sweet-making. Confections were made with egg yolks left over from the whites used when baking communion wafers (the whites only are also used in sherry-making areas for wine-clarification, and were once a binding agent in mortar for building). The sale of these confections, specialities of feast days sacred to the Virgin Mary and other female saints, provided an income for the convents. Another survivor of the Moorish kitchen taken over by commercial interests is turrón, a delectable almond and honey halva which resurfaced as the traditional Christmas treat. In these more affluent and well-travelled times, white and black nougats and several varieties of marzipan have been added to the range. The best is still made with honey and almonds, though peanuts and sugar creep in whenever expense is a problem.

The influx of vegetables from the New World was the last major influence on the Spanish table. Since then, the regional cookery of Iberia has remained virtually isolated, snug behind its barrier of the Pyrenees, aloof from the fads which enthused the rest of Europe. Instead, she concentrated on perfecting her own native ingredients and culinary methods. Until, that is, the last twenty years, when an explosion of creativity in all the arts followed the reign of General Franco. A period of fallow, as any ploughman will tell you, cannot help but be followed by a flowering. Spain has come into her own. Her restaurants draw gourmets from all over the world and in her kitchens are to be found the most influential chefs on the planet

Terraced fields on the Majorcan coastline

Andalusia is Spain's most southern region, the closest to Africa both geographically and to some extent in spirit. Jebl Tariq (Gibraltar) is less than 20 miles (32km) as the stork flies from Jebl Musa, the edge of Morocco's Rif plateau. These twin mountains form the Pillars of Hercules, which guard the approaches to the Mediterranean. Portugal lies to the west while the steep lip of the high central plateau, La Mancha, forms the northern boundary.

The land and the people keep the print of seven centuries of Muslim rule. Granada, last redoubt of the Caliphs of Al-Andalus, fell to the Christian armies of Ferdinand of Aragon and Isabella of Castile in 1492. From their Arab overlords, the people inherited a peripatetic Middle Eastern way of eating, a tradition which survived the Reconquista and later developed into the tradition of taking tapas, tiny dishes of something good which can be said to provide a lid or sop – the 'tapa' – for a glass of wine. This pleasant habit spread to the rest of Spain, becoming a feature of the life of the towns and cities, particularly those with universities.

The landscape is varied: mountainous and forested in many of the inland areas, irrigated throughout its heartland by the mighty Guadalquivir, bordered by the Mediterranean on the east and the Atlantic to the south. Year-round sunshine and a reasonable expectation of winter rain make for a land which is both fertile and productive, with wheatfields, citrus groves and vineyards on the southern plains and olives cropped for oil in the uplands. Sherry is the native tipple, Moorish pastries provide the treats. Vegetables and fruit of all kinds grow with ease; goats are the traditional producers of milk and meat; in earlier times, a long sea coast provided ample fish and shellfish for coastal dwellers who also supplied those villages of the hinterland that lay within a day's donkey-ride.

The inshore fleets have access to both Atlantic and Mediterranean fishing grounds for shellfish, crustaceans, tuna, sardines, anchovies

The rest of Spain, not given to praising the culinary skills of what was once the land of the infidel, say no one fries fish like an andaluz. In the seafront bars of Cadiz and Malaga, Sanlucar, Huelva, Puerto Santa Maria and the riverside quarter of Seville, the perishable and least-saleable of the fishermen's catch – small sardines, anchovies, baby cuttlefish, small squid – are left whole and ungutted, flipped through rough-ground flour and sea salt and fried to crisp perfection in olive oil.

The vega, the irrigated plateau of Granada, is famous for artichokes and fava beans (cooked with mint, a Moorish flavouring). The wheatfields of the Guadalquivir provide the raw materials for Andalusia's excellent bread. Leftovers go to make *migas* (breadcrumbs soaked and fried), and hot or chilled *gazpachos*, a generic name for bread soups of which the familiar version based on tomato juice is a modern refinement. Of these, the most interesting and delicious – to my mind – are Granada's sophisticated almond-milk gazpacho blanco and Cordoba's rich, tomato-based salmorejo. Seville and Cadiz are bull-ranch territory: bull-ring meat is sold off cheaply to make stews and tripe dishes. In the old days this was the only fresh meat the poor ever tasted. The prosperity of the cities of the coast depended to a great extent on trade; meanwhile the rural population were (and to some extent remain) smallholders and herdsmen, capable of self-sufficiency when freed from the demands of the landlord or the violence of war. Want has never been far away. Few people owned their land – Andalusia was almost entirely in the hands of the latifundios, the big landowners who lived in Seville and Madrid – and even for those who had their own patch of olive trees or wheatfield, war emptied every store-cupboard – worse still

when the war pitted brother against brother. Gerald Brenan, living in the remote Alpujarras, the hills below Granada, in the late 1950s, wrote of the aftermath of the Civil War: 'Many people did not like to be observed when eating, and if compelled to so in public would sit in a corner with their backs to the room. One must expect such feelings to arise in a country where for many people food is scarce and any sort of eating an act of daring and extravagance.'

For seven years, while my young family attended local schools, I marketed every Saturday in Algeciras, where the marketplace, a Moorish tent of curved concrete, served the prosperous citizens of the industrial centre of the province – a prosperity funded from Madrid as a counter to the attractions of British Gibraltar, visible even on days when the industrial smog lay heavily over the bay. For all other necessities, including the fish we ate almost every day, I turned south towards the little port of Tarifa, its sheltered harbour out-of-bounds to all but authorised visitors since the area was, in Franco's time, under military rule. The fishermen found ways to land their catch, and we were never in want of fresh sardines, sparkling blue-flashed anchovies, spider crabs which hide in wrecks to shelter from the winter storms, pale pink shrimp and prawns of astonishing deep carmine known as *carabiñeros*, policemen, since the law always wore a red face. The pick of the catch, the swordfish and the mighty tuna which migrate through the Straits, went directly to the lorries from Madrid or to the canning factories, as did octopus, cuttlefish, yellow-patterned conger-eel, mackerel, hake, bream for the oven. Shellfish – *conchas* – were priced according not to size but to excellence – delicacy of flesh and flavour. Everyone knew exactly what was good, checking the chalked-up prices and arguing with the sellers.

The people of our valley had many stories of the deprivations of the war, but these were mostly of ingenuity and cunning – the renting out of a ham bone, a tradition of stealing rather than paying for the

Abandoned farmhouse, Andalusia

salt which came from the Cadiz salt-flats, a father who set his son to watch an eagle-owl's nest so that he might rob it of the rabbit the parents had brought to feed the nestlings. When a family has four children to feed – as we did – every little helps, and we were shown the abandoned orchards where figs and pomegranates were to be had for free. The children were taught by their schoolmates how to catch crayfish in the stream, where to gather wild asparagus in the spring and mushrooms in autumn. We kept rabbits for meat and exchanged them with a neighbour who kept egg-laying chickens.

We ate very little meat. The rest of the time we ate eggs and bean stews fortified with the salt-cured meats of the annual *matanza*, pig-killing. For this, too, we had our own supplies. We, along with our neighbours who taught us what we needed to know, kept a sty-pig of the lean, red-bristled, grey-skinned breed which has to be fattened on cork-oak acorns. Our hams had to be sent to the mountains to take the cure, but after that they made the best hams in the land.

aceitunas aliñadas
green olives in brine

The dry, pale, unfortified sherry wines of Jerez and Montilla are at their best partnered by the roughly cracked, garlic-scented, green olives prepared in the little cortijos of Andalusia – a pleasure to be savoured under the silvery leaves of an ancient grove, the twisted roots of the olive trees anchored in the red earth of the Serrania de Ronda. The first fresh olives, freckled bright emerald, begin to appear in the markets in October, ready to be pickled for Christmas. Later in the harvest they ripen and darken to a full soft plum. The early bitter green ones are most appreciated in sherry country.

Makes 2kg (4¹/₂lb)

2kg (4¹/₂lb) green olives
225g (8oz) rough sea salt
1 tablespoon dried oregano
1 small bunch of dried thyme
1 tablespoon herb fennel stalks
2 lemons, cut into chunks
2 whole heads of garlic

Spread the olives out on the kitchen table, and pick out any shrivelled ones and any odd bits of leaf and stalk. Hit each one with a small hammer or heavy rolling pin, so that the flesh cracks but the olive remains intact. Put all the crushed olives into a deep crock and cover them with fresh water. Leave them to soak for a week, changing the water every 2 days. These little green olives are very bitter – if you taste the water, you will find it gets progressively milder as it is changed.

At the end of a week, drain out all the water. Make a brine by dissolving the salt in about 5 litres (8 pints) water and pour it over the olives. They should be completely submerged. Add the herbs and lemons. Hold the whole heads of garlic over a flame and char them (the scent is wonderfully evocative of Spanish peasant kitchens), then put the garlic in with the olives. In Seville very bitter little oranges, unpeeled but quartered, are used to flavour the olives.

They will be ready to use in 2–3 weeks. The olives become steadily less bitter as the year wears on. If they begin to ferment a little (the olive, after all, is a fruit), change the brine: they will not keep indefinitely.

If you cannot obtain fresh olives, drain a can or two of green ones in brine and put them to marinate for a few days in a jar with fresh olive oil, a sliced clove of garlic, a few sprigs of thyme and a chopped whole lemon. But look out for the fresh ones: they are much more interesting than the bland, commercially prepared variety.

Richly decorated Andalusian church

gazpacho blanco
white gazpacho

A sophisticated summer refresher from Granada, this infusion of almond milk heavily impregnated with garlic owes its pedigree, as so often in Andalusia, to the sybaritic Moors. For the Middle Eastern version, look no further than drinking yoghurt. Serve this gazpacho in small quantities, o dilute generously with iced water as a refreshmen in the heat of summer. Be warned: it has a kick like a mule.

Serves 4–6

1 slice of yesterday's bread, crusts removed, torn into pieces
50g (2oz) blanched almonds
2 fresh new garlic cloves, skinned and roughly chopped
1 tablespoon olive oil
1 tablespoon white wine vinegar
1 teaspoon salt

To finish
Small white grapes

Put all the ingredients into a blender or processor with 600ml (1 pint) water and process thoroughly. Add enough water – about as much again – to dilute it to the consistency of thin milk. Taste and season. A little more vinegar? A pinch of sugar? Drop in some ice cubes and whizz it up again.

Serve in small tumblers, well chilled, with a sliver of grape floating on top and a handful on the side – the sweetness balances the fieriness. Don't forget to warn people about the garlic: looks are deceptive. Perfect for sipping, diluted with snow-water, on a summer's day in the gardens of the Alhambra. As an appetiser, serve one white and one red gazpacho (the Cordoban gazpacho below), both in small chilled glasses.

samorejo
cordoban gazpacho

The traditional Andalusian gazpacho is a poor man's dish, a fortifying bread-porridge eaten hot in winter and cool in summer, its only enrichment a trickle of oil with a few slivers of garlic for flavour and maybe chopped tomato. In its modern incarnation it is an elegant chilled tomato soup and as befits the sophisticated citizenry of Cordoba – in the days of the caliphates, the cultural centre of the western world – the Cordoban gazpacho comes closest to this. For an authentic Cordoban samorejo, look no further than the Bar Los Arcos near the Mezquita.

Serves 4–6

1kg (2lb) ripe tomatoes, scalded, skinned, halved and de-seeded
225g (8oz) robust country bread, torn into pieces
2–3 garlic cloves, skinned and roughly chopped
1 tablespoon wine vinegar
6 tablespoons olive oil
Salt and pepper
1 teaspoon sugar (optional)

To serve

75g (3oz) serrano ham, diced
2 hardboiled eggs, peeled and chopped
Diced bread, crisped in olive oil

Put all the ingredients in a liquidiser and process to a purée, or pound the tomatoes, bread and garlic to a paste in a pestle and mortar, then work in the vinegar, oil and seasonings (you'll only need the sugar if the tomatoes are not sweet enough). Leave in the fridge for a couple of hours for the bread to swell and absorb the juices, until the soup is thick enough to coat the back of a spoon. Taste and adjust the seasonings and ladle into bowls. To convert to a drinking gazpacho as a summer refreshment, dilute with chilled water. Hand round the hardboiled egg, serrano ham and fried bread croûtons separately, for people to add if they wish.

alcachofas rellenas
artichokes stuffed with spinach

A sophisticated dish from the market gardens of Cordoba. The raisins and pine-kernels add a touch of Middle-Eastern sweet-and-sourness, while the cooking broth is the dry golden wine of Montilla, one of the wines produced by the solera system, the method used to make sherry.

Serves 4

4 large or 8 small artichokes

The stuffing
450g (1lb) spinach, blanched and finely chopped
2 tablespoons diced serrano ham
2 canned anchovy fillets, crushed
1 tablespoon raisins, soaked to plump
1 tablespoon toasted pine-kernels
1 egg

The sauce
3 tablespoons olive oil
1 small carrot, finely chopped
1 small onion, finely chopped
1 stick green celery, finely chopped
1 garlic clove, skinned and chopped
1 thyme sprig
1 bay leaf
2–3 mint sprigs, stripped from the stalks
  and chopped

To finish
1 glass Montilla wine or dry sherry
Salt and pepper

Trim the hard outer leaves from the artichokes. Slice off the top of the inner leaves so that most of what is left is tender enough to eat. With a sharp knife, nick out the hairy choke. Combine the stuffing ingredients and form the mixture into four large or eight small balls. Pop the balls into the space left by the removal of the choke.

Warm the oil in a heavy frying pan and fry the chopped vegetables and herbs gently until they take on a little colour. Arrange the stuffed artichokes in the pan and leave to stew gently in this aromatic bath, lid tightly on, for 20–30 minutes. Test for tenderness with the point of a knife. When the artichokes are nearly ready, pour in the wine and the same volume of water. Put the lid on again and give everything another 10–15 minutes. Take out the artichokes. Boil the juices rapidly to concentrate the sauce, then taste and season if necessary. Serve the artichokes at room temperature, bathed in their sauce.

tortilla de espárragos trigeros
green asparagus tortilla

In Andalusia in the spring a prickly tangle of feathery branches reveals the places where wild asparagus can be gathered. The springtime wild-gatherings which can be incorporated into a tortilla include tagarninas, the basal leaves of a tall, yellow-flowered member of the thistle family, *Scolymus hispanicus*. When stripped of their thorny margins they look like small green octopi, and the flavour is like that of the artichoke, a close relative. Wild shoots – the first crop of edible greens – are greeted with pleasure and combined with eggs, for they appear just as the barnyard birds come back into lay. When making a tortilla, the proportion of egg to other ingredients should be roughly equal.

Still Life with Chocolate, seventeenth century, by Francisco de Zurbarán

Serves 2–4 (or 1 very hungry person)

Large handful thin green asparagus, trimmed
4 tablespoons olive oil
4 large eggs
Salt and pepper

Chop the asparagus into short lengths.

Warm the oil in a small frying pan (the one you usually use for pancakes or omelettes). Sprinkle in the asparagus pieces and wait until they turn bright green – a couple of minutes. Remove and transfer to a sieve over a small bowl to catch the drippings.

Whisk the eggs lightly with a fork – don't overmix – and return the drippings to the pan. Reheat until a faint blue smoke rises. Tip in the egg mixture – it should form a thick layer. Lift the egg up in the middle to allow as much as possible to come into contact with the heat. As soon as a few curds form, leave it alone, turn down the heat and cook gently for 6–7 minutes, until the base is set and the middle is beginning to firm up (you can put a lid on loosely to encourage the process).

Remove from the heat and flip the tortilla over onto a clean plate – be brave: it's easy. Reheat the pan-drippings and slip the tortilla back into the pan, cooked side uppermost. Allow another 2–3 minutes to set the other side, then slide it out onto a plate. Pat with kitchen paper to remove the excess oil.

Serve at room temperature, cut into wedges.

pinchitos morunos
moorish kebabs

In Algeciras, where my four children went to school, feria – the city's annual festival – was at the end of June, and it always rained for at least two of the five days. Each year the same fez-hatted pinchito man took up residence alongside the bodega and kept his meat in a bucket beneath the table. Meat was deftly threaded on steel knitting-needles (which we were honour-bound to return) and cooked to order. The tip of the skewer was then thrust into a hunk of bread. The trick was to pull the meat off the red-hot metal before it cooled, using just the bread and your thumb.

Serves 4

450g (1lb) boned pork or lamb, trimmed and diced
    into pieces no bigger than a hazelnut

The marinade
2 tablespoons olive oil
1 teaspoon cumin seeds
1 tablespoon hot pimentón
1/2 teaspoon turmeric
1/2 teaspoon dried thyme
1/2 teaspoon freshly ground pepper
8 long skewers or steel knitting needles
1/2 teaspoon salt

To finish
Chunks of country bread

Mix together the marinade ingredients in a roomy bowl and add the meat. Turn thoroughly to coat, cover and leave in a cool place overnight.

Thread the meat on the skewers – allow 6–7 per skewer. Light the grill or barbecue. Grill the pinchitos over a very high heat, turning them frequently, until well-browned but still juicy. Sprinkle with salt and serve hot on their skewers, with chunks of bread speared on the end of each.

perdices con naranjas
partridges with oranges

A dish from Seville's hinterland: partridges from the vineyards casseroled in a jammy, sweet-sour sauce – perfect for birds of uncertain age and tenderness. If you can't get wild birds, this sauce will give a flavour of the wild to baby poussins or a jointed free-range chicken.

Serves 4

4 partridges or poussins or chicken joints
4 bitter Seville oranges or 1 lemon and 3 small
    juice-oranges
4 cloves
75g (3oz) serrano ham (including the fat),
    or pancetta, finely sliced
Thyme sprigs
4 tablespoons olive oil
450g (1lb) pickling onions or small shallots, peeled
1 glass dry sherry or manzanilla
Salt and pepper

Wipe the birds and trim off any stray feathers. Scrub the fruit and cut into rough chunks. Tuck a chunk of orange stuck with a clove inside each bird, reserving the rest. Roll the ham in little bundles and secure with thyme stalks.

Heat the oil in a roomy casserole. Fry the onions and remaining fruit for 5 minutes, turning to brown all sides, and push aside. Fry the birds in the hot oil, turning them until they brown a little all over.

Remove half the onions – they should be tender by now – and half the fruit, and reserve. Add the wine and a glass of water to the casserole. Let it bubble up, adding salt and pepper, then pop the bundles of ham on the breasts of the birds, turn down the heat, put the lid on tightly and leave to simmer gently for 40–60 minutes, until the birds are perfectly tender. To check if they are done, wiggle the drumsticks – they should move easily in their sockets.

Remove the birds and keep them warm, along with the reserved fruit and onions. Boil up the rest of the juices, mashing the fruit until the sauce is jammy and thick.

Serve each bird with its sauce on a thick slice of country bread dry-fried in a pan in a very little olive oil, then rubbed with garlic. Eat with your fingers – with plenty of napkins to hand.

The typical pueblo blanco of Andalusia

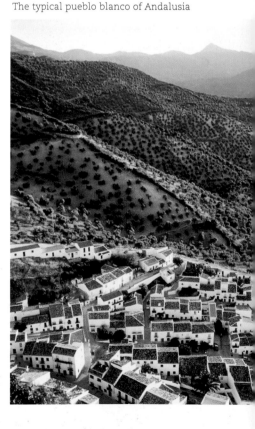

papas gaditanas
new potatoes with saffron and pine-kernels

Small potatoes – the first of the year from the sandy soil of the delta of the Guadalquivir – cooked with saffron and finished with a handful of toasted pine-kernels, just as they like it in Cadiz. This dish tastes even better with a plateful of baby cuttlefish fried whole, still with their crunchy little cuttles, the powdery bone much loved by caged canaries.

Serves 4

1kg (2¹/₄lb) small new potatoes (waxy yellow for preference)
1 large Spanish onion, slivered into half-moons
3 garlic cloves, skinned and chopped
4 tablespoons olive oil
3–4 large, ripe tomatoes or 1 x 450g (1lb) can tomate frito (Spain's equivalent of Italy's passata)
A dozen saffron threads
1 glass sherry or manzanilla
1 teaspoon rock salt
2 tablespoons green or black olives

To finish

2 tablespoons pine-kernels
1 tablespoon olive oil

Scrub or scrape the potatoes to remove the papery skins, or peel if they're a little on the mature side. Drop them into cold salted water to await attention.

Gently fry the onion and garlic in the olive oil until softened – don't let them colour. Pour boiling water over the tomatoes, if using fresh ones, to loosen the skins, then peel and chop them. Add the tomatoes and saffron to the onion, fry for a minute, add the wine and bring to the boil. Then turn down the heat and let it all bubble gently to a thick purée. Add the potatoes, salt and enough water barely to cover. Bring to the boil, remove the lid and turn up the heat to reduce the sauce to a thick slick. Add the olives, and simmer for another 5 minutes to marry the flavours.

To finish, toast the pine-kernels in a little oil in a frying pan until they brown, removing them as soon as they change colour. Pile the potatoes in a warm dish and sprinkle with the toasted nuts.

Two Children Eating a Melon, seventeenth century, by Bartolomé Murillo

riñones al jerez
kidneys with sherry

This is a speciality of Jerez, the sherry-makers' town, where fighting bulls graze the unproductive land between the vineyards that produce the venerable wine, bearing the town's name. The same dish can also be made with lamb's kidneys or chicken livers – nicest when still pink, so take care not to overcook them.

Serves 4 as a tapa

1 veal or beef kidney, skinned and cored
1 tablespoon sherry vinegar, for soaking
2 tablespoons olive oil
1 clove garlic, skinned and crushed with a little salt
1 teaspoon pimentón (optional)
1 tablespoon chopped parsley
1 generous glass dry or oloroso sherry
1 tablespoon fresh breadcrumbs
Salt and pepper

Slice the kidney thinly and put it to soak for 30 minutes in water mixed with the vinegar to rid it of the taste of ammonia. If you are in a hurry, just sprinkle the kidney slices with vinegar and then scald them with boiling water.

Warm the oil in a shallow casserole. Add the garlic and let it soften for a moment. Add kidney slices and turn them in the hot oil. Stir in the pimentón and parsley. Pour in the sherry and let it bubble up so the alcohol evaporates. Add a glass of water, season with salt and pepper and bring back to the boil. Put the lid on tightly, turn down the heat and simmer gently for 15–20 minutes, until the kidneys are tender. Stir in the breadcrumbs and bring all back to the boil to thicken the juices. Taste to check the seasoning. Serve as a tapa with bread and the fat, freckled green olives of Seville, or as a main course for two, piled on a heap of crisp chips fried in olive oil.

habas a la rondeña
fava beans with ham

This slowly cooked stew, aromatic with wine and herbs, is my own favourite vegetable dish. I first tasted it in its home territory, the fortified hill town of Ronda. The evening air is always cool in these mountains, even in summer, and many of the local dishes are traditionally simmered over a shallow brazier which did double duty in my house, and my neighbours', as central heating under the table.

Serves 4 as a starter (2 as a main course)

900g (2lb) young fava beans in the pod
2–3 tablespoons olive oil
2–3 garlic cloves, skinned and cut in slivers
1/2 mild onion, chopped
1 heaped tablespoon diced serrano ham
1 teaspoon fresh marjoram leaves
Small glass dry sherry
Salt and pepper

To finish
2 eggs
1 tablespoon chopped parsley

If using tender young beans, use the pods as well as the beans: top, tail and de-string the pods before chopping them into short lengths, following the swell of each bean. When older but still tender, the beans must be podded; at the end of the season, skin them as well.

Warm the oil in a casserole or heavy pan. Fry the garlic, onion and ham for a moment without allowing anything to take colour. Add the beans, marjoram, sherry and a glass of water. Season and bring to the boil. Cover and stew gently for 1 1/2 hours – this can be done in a gentle oven at 170°C/325°F/gas mark 3. Check now and again and add boiling water if necessary. When the beans are tender, let the stew boil uncovered for a moment to evaporate the liquid – it should be juicy but not swimming.

Mix the eggs and parsley together with a fork. Remove the pan from the heat and stir in the eggs – they'll set lightly and thicken the juices. Or, if you prefer, thicken the juices with breadcrumbs and serve the eggs hardboiled and quartered. Taste and add salt if necessary.

almejas odonienses
huelva clams

The people of Huelva are known by their Phoenician name, *odoniense*, a choice which reflects an independent turn of mind. As a self-governing *pueblo del conde* – people of the county – they remained under Moorish protection long after the Reconquista. This long association is reflected in their cuisine: the local bread is an unleavened flat-bread much like the Arab pitta, and coriander is used as a flavouring herb, a Moorish taste shared with the cooks of southern Portugal but found nowhere else in Spain.

Serves 4–6 as a starter

900g (2lb) clams on the shell
6 tablespoons extra virgin olive oil
2 garlic cloves, skinned and chopped
2 tablespoons chopped fresh coriander

Rinse the shellfish thoroughly in plenty of cold water, picking over and discarding any which are broken or whose heaviness tells you they're filled with sand.

Heat the oil gently in a large frying pan. Add the garlic and fry for a moment until it softens, then add the shellfish. Cover with a lid, shaking the pan to redistribute the shells so that they all have a chance to cook. If you have no lid, keep them moving with a draining spoon. It will take 3–4 minutes for all the shells to open – any which remain clamped shut should be picked out or avoided. Remove from the heat, stir in the coriander and serve them just as they are, in their own aromatic juices, with soft flat-breads for mopping. Don't reheat them or they'll be rubbery.

Hams on display in a Sevillan grocery

tortillitas de camarones
shrimp fritters

At feria time, these crisp little fritters, traditionally made with chickpea flour, are sold hot from the frying vat on every street corner of the windswept port of Cadiz. You can now also buy them ready-made and frozen. The raw materials are the tiny, clear-bodied shrimps netted in the long, sandy shallows edging the muddy flats which provided the citizens with their rock salt, a valuable item of trade. Make these fritters with the very small shrimps which are used in Britain for potted shrimps.

Serves 4

3 tablespoons bread or chickpea flour
1/2 teaspoon bicarbonate of soda
1/2 teaspoon salt
2 tablespoons olive oil
1/2 teaspoon pimentón (Spanish paprika)
1 tablespoon chopped parsley
1 tablespoon very finely chopped onion
110g (4oz) whole baby shrimps
Oil, for frying

Sift the flour, bicarbonate of soda and salt into a bowl, and gradually blend in 6 tablespoons water and the oil until you have a thin batter. Stir in the pimentón, parsley and onion. Fold in the shrimps.

Heat 2 fingers' depth of oil in a frying pan. When it is lightly hazed with blue, drop in the shrimp batter by the tablespoonful – not too many at a time or the oil temperature will drop. Fry until golden and crisp, turning once. Flatten the fritters with a draining spoon as they cook, to make sure the batter is well spread out and they are crisp all the way through. Serve piping hot straight from the pan, with a glass of chilled manzanilla to cool your tongue.

boquerones en abanico
anchovy fans

The cooks of Andalusia are admired by the smart folk of Madrid and Barcelona for their skill with the frying pan – not for anything else that's set on the table, apart from anchovy-stuffed olives and the dry, straw-pale wines of Jerez. An Andalusian cook, asked to explain the secret of her exquisite fried fish, will tell you it's the freshness of the catch, the quality of the flour, the flavour of the salt, the clarity and mildness of the oil. And then she will smile and say that all these things matter, but it's the sleight of hand which makes the difference. Fresh anchovies, along with sardines and *choquitos* (baby cuttlefish), are the cheapest and most plentiful of Andalusia's inshore harvest.

Serves 4

450g (1lb) fresh anchovies
4 tablespoons unbleached bread flour
1 teaspoon sea salt
Oil, for frying (a mixture of olive and sunflower is preferred)

Gut the little fish – you can do this just by running your finger down the soft belly and pulling out the contents, leaving the head in place. Rinse, drain and shake them dry – but not too dry or the coating won't stick.

Toss the flour with the salt on a plate. Pinch the tails of the fish together in fans of 3–5, depending on their size, and flip them through the flour, dampening your finger and thumb and pinching the tails together again to make sure they stick.

Heat a finger's depth of oil in a frying pan – Andalusian cooks rarely choose to deep-fry, and certainly not when cooking fish, since the leftover oil would be good for nothing else. When the surface is lightly hazed with blue, lay in the fish-fans head first, only 2 or 3 at a time, otherwise the temperature drops too fast. Fry until the coating crisps but has not yet gilded, turning them once. Transfer carefully to kitchen paper to drain. Serve piping hot with quartered lemons.

The same method can be applied to small sardines and also to fish which have no tails to pinch (to coat, just toss in flour in a sieve), such as baby squid, cuttlefish and *chunquetes* (tiny, transparent-bodied fry), though this is now an illegal crop.

holy week

To understand the andaluz temperament – the key to her domestic and every other habit – take yourself to the great city of Seville for Holy Week. You'll find few tourists in the streets since the weather has not yet turned to summer and the hotels and public eateries are only just beginning to ready themselves for the season. The bleak time between Jueves Santo and Viernes Madrugada – the vigil which links Holy Thursday with Black Friday – is the moment when the veil lifts to reveal the andaluz soul. The two rivals for the affections of Mother Church, the symbol of all mothers everywhere, are the Macarena and the Gran Poder – sorrowing Mother and all-powerful Son. That one protects the poor and the other the rich is accepted without question. Each has a place. 'I'm sure the Gran Poder wears silk,' says my neighbour, one of many black-clad widows in the crowd – impossible to tell if this is praise or blame.

Until an hour or two before they leave the cool interiors of their sanctuaries, the images may be visited and admired. Candles are lit in support of supplications – doubly sure of attention at this time. The most crowded tapas bar on the route serves food spiced with cinnamon, rich with sesame, sweetened with honey – *comida moro*, Moorish food, explains the lady on the barstool beside me.

As the sun drops over the delta and the sky turns red, sombre processions move out of the shadows on unseen shoulders, nothing visible beneath the draperies except the shuffling shoes. Inch by inch the tablas more forward, swaying like temple dancers, accompanied by double lines of masked penitents. All movement ceases every few paces while the float-bearers recover or are replaced by others, while their companions make an arch of candles. Excited children gather wax-balls for luck, holding them out to the candle-carriers. In Seville the penitents are known as *nazareños*, Nazarenes. They wear long black robes belted with rope, their shoulders and faces hidden under the tall pointed hoods familiar from movies featuring the Ku Klux Klan, an alarming

Nazareños demonstrate their wealth and piety during Semana Santa celebrations

association. The elaborate *pasos* – theatrical floats depicting the events of Holy Week – have more than an echo of carnival, though the burden is clearly very real. The more elaborate, the greater number of larger-than-life figures, the heavier the *paso*, the greater the forgiveness – or glory, since applause greets every manoeuvre. Each *hermandad* – brotherhood or guild – has its own suffering Christ and its own sorrowing Virgin. The richer the brotherhood, the more elaborate and numerous the supporting floats – for a carpenter-woodcarver, most respected of Spain's artisan-craftsmen, there's no greater honour than to be commissioned to carve scenes from the Passion.

pato a la sevillana
duck with olives and oranges

Wild duck was the pot-meat from the marshy delta of the Guadaquivir, the mighty river which once provided Seville's galleons with access to both the Mediterranean and the Atlantic. These days the delta – the royal hunting grounds of the Coto Doñana – is a vast nature reserve, and the bird on the tables of Seville is more likely to be tender and tame than tough and wild.

Serves 4

2 mallard (halved) or 4 teal (whole) or 1 domestic
    duck (jointed)
2 tablespoons olive oil
1–2 rosemary sprigs
1–2 thyme sprigs
2 bitter oranges, scrubbed, chopped into segments
    (remove the seeds) or 1 sweet orange and 1 lemon
1 tablespoon honey
2 garlic cloves, skinned and chopped
1 short cinnamon stick
1 teaspoon coriander seeds
2 tablespoons green olives
1 glass dry sherry or manzanilla

Wipe over the duck pieces and remove any stray feathers.

Heat the oil in a roomy casserole. Put in the duck pieces and fry until the skin takes a little colour. Add the rest of the ingredients and let it all bubble up. Add a glass of water, bring to the boil again, turn down the heat, put the lid on and leave to simmer gently for 30–40 minutes, until the duck is tender and the sauce thick and jammy. Taste and add salt if necessary – bearing in mind that the olives are already pretty salty. Serve with plain rice tossed with toasted almonds and orange segments. A salad of roughly sliced Cos lettuce with slivers of mild onion and tarragon is the proper Sevillan accompaniment.

mantecados finos
cinnamon almond cookies

Mantecados are a rich powdery shortbread made with lard rather than butter. Children love them and hope to find them in their shoes on the morning of the Three Kings' visit on 6 January – the day when all good Spanish children are rewarded with presents.

Makes 2 dozen

450g (1lb) pure soft pork lard
450g (1lb) caster sugar
4 egg yolks
Grated zest of 1 lemon
900g (2lb) plain flour
450g (1lb) ground almonds
1 teaspoon ground cinnamon

Soften the lard and whisk it until fluffy with the sugar, egg yolks and lemon zest. Sieve in enough flour mixed with the ground almonds and cinnamon to give a soft dough. Add a little lemon juice if necessary.

Preheat the oven to 200°C/400°F/gas mark 6.

Roll out the dough to the thickness of your thumb, and cut out rounds with a small wine glass. Transfer to a greased baking tray.

Bake for 15 minutes, and then turn the oven down to 180°C/350°F/gas mark 4 and bake for another 15–20 minutes until pale gold. Transfer the cookies carefully to a wire rack to cool – they are very crumbly.

When cool, wrap each cookie – a more appropriate word than biscuit, since these are neither crisp nor twice-cooked to make them so – in a square of tissue paper and store in an airtight tin until Christmas. A speciality of Seville, delicious with a little glass of the syrupy, black, liquorice-scented Pedro Ximenes from the bodegas of Jerez.

The Levante, the south-eastern corner of the mainland, takes its character from the long, mostly flat coastline which forms its eastern boundary, and its protection from the mountains to the west. In between lies a fertile plain of orchards which has earned it the title of the market-garden of Europe. Year-round sunshine – winter rains are torrential but brief – has attracted a huge population of winter sunseekers.

The alluvial plateau, irrigated by mountain water, supports a large population of farmers, both conventional and polytunnel. All kinds of fruit, vegetables and poultry now supplement the traditional diet of fish and rice. Fishing villages turned to tourism as soon as their livelihoods were threatened by dwindling fish stocks, but among the tourist high-rises the inshore fleets still land their catch daily. In Roman times, Alicante was called Lucentum, city of light, and with reason. Brilliant skies, even on cloudy days, illuminate the soft curve of the hills and the crested ridges which surround the bay. At the heart of the city is a seventeenth-century cathedral dedicated to St Nicholas, patron saint of ships, built on the site of a mosque. The broad esplanade which fronts the sea-wall – and serves as a promenade for the evening paseo and a place for children to play – is shaded by date-palms. Baby palms have their fronds tied up in bundles to help them withstand the levante, the hot wind from the east which unsettles everyone, man, woman and child.

In the post-Franco era, changes are most noticeable in the cities of the coast, including Valencia, the regional capital. Not least among these is that the citizens may now use their own language – indistin-guishable to the outside ear from the Catalan spoken in the Balearics or Barcelona. During the long years of the dictatorship, Valencia was forbidden to follow her own customs – with the exception of what went on the kitchen. Domestic skills were approved by the Generalissimo. The female wing of his Movimiento collected its members' recipes and published them as *Cocina Regional Española*, a

household manual issued to new members when I joined my local Association of Housewives – *amas de casa* – in Algeciras in the mid-1960s.

Many of Valencia's dishes are found throughout the Catalan-speaking regions, but some are peculiarly her own, and not simply because of the ingredients or the way they're cooked, but for the thought, the intellectual content behind the recipe. Take the paella valenciana, the rice dish which can be prepared nowhere else but in the open air, by men, preferably in the wetlands, among the orange and almond groves of the alluvial plain. If, as a foreigner and a female, you did any such thing – well, you might be forgiven for being a foreigner, but what you cooked could never be a true paella. It would be an *arroz*, a rice dish, and that would be the end of it.

Somewhat less contentious is the region's other gastronomic delight, the almond-and-honey turrón of Jijona (Xixona in the Catalan, Moorish at heart). A seasonal delicacy, prepared at the time of the autumn almond-harvest, it is in its proper form a smooth, slightly crunchy, compacted paste quite unlike marzipan or nougat, any other almond preparation known in Europe. The process is as ancient as the almond-groves the Moors planted to remind themselves of home, the gentle slopes of the Jordan valley. The nuts – previously skinned and given an all-over tan, much like the tourists on Benidorm beach – are mixed with honey and a little egg white which has been cooked until the sugar crystallises. Once the almonds are added, the mixture is traditionally ground with a stone rolling pin on a stone table, a crushing-anvil – in much the same way as the Aztecs prepared their drinking chocolate. There are other kinds of turrón made in the factories of Jijona – de yema (an egg-yolk marzipan), de Alicante (a nougat), torta imperial (a thin disc of almond-studded nougat enclosed in rice-paper wafers), one made with coconut and one in which chocolate features heavily. But the real turrón, the best and most delicious, is the honey-and-almond turrón de la piedra – stone-ground, each block flavoured with just a knife-tip of lemon zest and cinnamon, the way the ladies of the sultan's seraglio liked it.

The wetlands yield eels, frogs, snails and oyster mushrooms (parasitic on rotting ships' hulls as well as fallen stumps in woodland), all of which are ingredients for a rural paella. And in Murcia, among the various chorizos, longanizas and other pork products eaten with bread, you'll find a pâté-like preparation, morteruelo, a soft, mortar-pounded paste of pork with game – partridge, hare, rabbit – which also includes pine-kernels, a diagnostic ingredient, along with saffron, rice and oranges, of the cooking of the Levante.

The northernmost town of the region, the fortified citadel of Morella, is the centre, these days, of a thriving trade in black truffles gathered from the scrub-oak and cistus shrub of the surrounding mountainside. In the absence of much enthusiasm among the locals, who traditionally see the tubers as famine food, most of the crop is exported to the markets of the Périgord, where it fetches sky-high prices. The town's other speciality, *jamón de toro* – beef ham – appeared in the aftermath of the Reconquista, a way of avoiding the attentions of the Inquisition among a community whose members, though nominally Christian converts, were not prepared to risk their immortal souls.

Peñiscola, a rocky peninsula now half-buried in white-washed villas but once the last refuge of the medieval antipope, has a taste for strange sea creatures. In the market you'll find *datiles del mar*, sea dates, limpet-like creatures whose firm grip on their rock means their perch must be dragged ashore before their grip can be loosened. Others are limón del mar, sea lemon, a conch-like shellfish with a strong flavour of lemon zest; cajitas, delicious protuberance-covered sea snails, and enteritas, whole baby cuttlefish, grilled as soon as landed, an exquisite mouthful which includes the crunchy little cuttle as well as a tiny sac of jet-black ink which turns the teeth a royal purple. On the northern edge of the peninsula, in the seafood restaurants which line the harbour of the fishing-port of Denia – now a tourist destination – the speciality is the paella-like arroz abanda, rice apart, in which the rice, flavoured with the broth from the seafood which is the main ingredient, is presented as a separate dish.

Valencian Fisherwomen, 1915, by Joaquín Sorolla y Bastida

centolla con azafrán
crabmeat with saffron

The exquisitely flaky white meat of the spider crab – a round-bodied, clawless crustacean which looks exactly like a large spider, scarlet-carapaced when it comes out of the sea – is more highly prized than the meat of the large-clawed common crab. The Valencian dressing is a saffron-perfumed vinaigrette sharpened with bitter orange juice instead of vinegar. Langoustines and prawns are good prepared this way too.

Serves 4 as a starter

225g (8oz) crabmeat (plus empty carapaces, if available)
4 tablespoons olive oil
1 mild Spanish onion, cut vertically into half-moon slivers
1/2 teaspoon hot pimentón (Spanish paprika) or chilli powder
1/2 teaspoon saffron threads (lightly toasted in a dry pan) or saffron powder
2 tablespoons Spanish brandy
Juice and finely pared zest of 1 bitter orange, or 1/2 lemon and 1/2 sweet orange
2 hardboiled eggs, peeled and finely chopped
2 tablespoons chopped flat-leaf parsley

Pick over the crabmeat and remove any stray bits of shell.

Heat the oil in a small pan. Add the onion and cook gently for a few minutes until it softens. Add the pimentón, saffron and brandy. Let it bubble it up for a few minutes until you can no longer smell the alcohol. Remove from the heat and add the orange juice. Stir in the crabmeat, hardboiled eggs and parsley. Return the meat to the carapaces if you have them, or divide between small earthenware dishes. Finish with a few curls of orange zest.

escabeche de sardinas
hot pickled sardines

The fishermen's wives of Roquetas del Mar on the coast of Almeria gave the more perishable (and therefore less saleable) of the catch a vinegar-pickle to add a little shelf-life. Sardines – small, rich, oily fish which are good only when really fresh – benefit greatly from the treatment. Anchovies do too.

Serves 4 as a starter

900g (2lb) fresh sardines
2–3 garlic cloves, skinned and sliced
1–2 bay leaves, crumbled
Salt and pepper
150ml (1/4 pint) white wine vinegar or sherry vinegar
6 tablespoons olive oil
1 dried chilli, de-seeded and torn into small pieces

Rinse, de-scale and gut the sardines, then bone them by pulling the head downwards towards the tail. Layer the fish into a shallow casserole, sprinkling with garlic, crumbled bay leaf, salt and pepper as you go.

Preheat the oven to 170°C/325°F/gas mark 3.

Bring the vinegar to the boil with the same volume of water and pour it around the fish. Drizzle with the oil, sprinkle over the chilli and put on the lid, or cover with foil, shiny side down. Bake for 20–30 minutes, depending on the size of the fish. Leave to cool and serve at room temperature. This is good with a plain potato salad and a dish of fried green peppers (see p. 83).

Preparing the Dry Grapes, 1890, by Joaquín Sorolla y Bastida

valencia after dark

At the Nou Manolin, a restaurant in the centre of Alicante which may or may not still be there some ten years after my visit, I ate rosy slivers of salt-dried tuna, mojama, a delicacy which, as prices of salt-cod rose, replaced bacalao as the fish for the Friday fast. The belly is the most prized, the sweetest and juiciest, and the roes, when salted and dried and sealed under wax, are as good as all but the best botarga, the roe of the grey mullet, main ingredient in the Greek taramasalata, which fetches caviar prices. With it came fresh figs, slivers of serrano ham, baby onions pickled in red wine vinegar, and a round soft disk of coca topped with young leaves and pine-kernels. To finish, a square of leche frita - sweet custard croquette - and plate of turrón, the Moorish sweetmeat whose manufacture is close to the Arab halva, but which, being made with almonds and honey rather than sesame and sugar, is even more delicious.

In Valencia, much of the evening's amusements take place in and around the old red-light area tucked just behind the harbour, as it is in all ports where sailors take shore-leave, though its activities are more discreet these days. At six o'clock of a December evening not long after the change of regime which followed the death of Franco, beaded shades shed pools of light into bars where, instead of the usual dangling legs of serrano ham, the early shift of the ladies-of-the-night flashed six-inch heels and fish-net tights. Ever since she contributed the Borgia Popes to her old ally, the Vatican, Valencia has had a racy reputation. For the well-heeled man-about-town there's a rococo drinking club housed in a converted palace where pyramids of ripe fruit flank a statue of the Virgin lit by church candles; a pair of elderly lions doze in the courtyard and there are no prices on the drinks. No food is offered. Valencia never really took to the notion of tapas, though tourists expect them. Upright citizens, those who don't frequent gentlemen-only drinking clubs, are more for the communal pleasures of the paella pan, a Sunday outing for the family, and no one would think of eating a rice dish at any time other than midday.

menestra de verduras
artichoke and fava bean casserole

This is a gentle combination, simple but elegant. Both artichokes and beans come to Valencian markets in the first days of spring.

Serves 3–4 as a main course

About 150ml (¼ pint) olive oil
1 medium potato, peeled and diced
4–8 young artichokes, hearts only
700g (1½lb) shelled fava beans (frozen are fine)
1 large onion, finely chopped
2 tablespoons diced serrano ham or gammon
Salt
Hardboiled eggs, peeled and quartered

Gently heat the oil in a roomy frying pan and fry the diced potato until perfectly soft and lightly browned – don't let the oil overheat. Remove the potato with a draining spoon and transfer to a casserole. Pour out half the oil and reserve. Meanwhile, cut the artichoke hearts into pieces roughly the same size as the fava beans. Reheat the oil in the frying pan and add the artichoke hearts and beans. Cook gently until all the moisture has evaporated and tiny bubbles have formed around the vegetable pieces – too high a heat will harden the bean skins. Transfer to the casserole.

Reheat the reserved oil and fry the chopped onion – still gently – until soft and golden. Add the diced ham and let it feel the heat. Transfer the contents of the frying pan to the casserole, pour in enough water to cover and add salt sparingly – the ham is already salty. Let it bubble up until almost all the liquid has evaporated, leaving the vegetables bathed in a fragrant, oily sauce.

Finish with quartered hardboiled eggs and serve warm rather than piping hot, with a young red wine – the acidity cuts the richness of the juices – and bread. Sliced oranges with honey and toasted almonds are an appropriately Valencian conclusion.

alubias con trufas
white beans with black truffles

The black truffles traded in Morella – Spain's main black-truffle market – usually disappear into the satchels of the men from Périgord, to reappear, in all probability, at inflated prices in the company of foie gras in the delicatessens of Lyons and Paris. Until recent years, when the elegant little town discovered the value of the crop – *Tubor melanospermum* is gathered on the rocky hillsides in the cistus scrub – the truffle was poor folks' food, a meat substitute to add flavour to the bean-pot. Once eaten only in times of hardship, it's a reminder – at least for those old enough to remember – of the deprivations of the Civil War.

Serves 4

450g (1lb) large dried white beans
½ head of garlic
½ teaspoon black peppercorns
2–3 bay leaves

To finish
Olive oil
Rock salt
1–2 fine ripe truffles

Put the beans to soak overnight – or for at least 6 hours – in enough cold water to cover generously. Drain the beans and put them in a roomy pot with fresh water. Bring to the boil and skim off the foam. Meanwhile, hold the garlic in a flame, allowing the papery covering to blacken, then drop it in with the beans. Add the pepper and bay leaves and let it all bubble gently for an hour or two (depending on the beans' freshness and tenderness) until the beans are perfectly soft but still juicy. If you need to add water during the cooking, make sure it's boiling. Stir in about 4 tablespoons olive oil, add salt and leave to bubble up again for a few minutes to allow the oil to amalgamate with the juices.

Brush and rinse the truffles before cutting them into matchsticks or slivers and stirring them into the beans. Serve in deep soup plates, with more olive oil handed around separately.

paella valenciana
valencian paella

The basic raw materials for a paella are rice, oil, saffron, water and a shallow pan of a design which would have been familiar to the Romans. The rest of the ingredients are whatever comes to hand. According to season these can be: asparagus shoots, fennel fronds, the tender leaf-rosettes of the Spanish thistle (*Scolopax hispanicus*), summer savory, sorrel, wild garlic, snails or crayfish picked out from under the stones in the stream which provides the cooking broth. It's a midday dish, never served in the evening. Ask any Valencian paterfamilias for his personal recipe, and if he starts at dawn you'll still be there at sundown. A purpose-made paella pan – raw iron, double-handled, very shallow – is essential to its identity. If cooked in any other pan, even with exactly the same ingredients, it is merely *un arroz* – a rice-dish. Now you understand the principle, you may of course use any broad-based pan you consider suitable, always remembering that the heat source – charcoal or gas-ring – must be broad enough to allow even contact with the entire base of the pan.

Serves 7–8

110g (4oz) dried white haricot or butter beans (garrofón), soaked overnight
3–4 tablespoons olive oil
4–5 garlic cloves, skinned and crushed with a little salt
1 young wild rabbit or small chicken, jointed into bite-sized pieces
2–3 large ripe beef tomatoes, pulped (cut in half and grated)
About 12 saffron threads, soaked in a splash of boiling water
Handful ready-starved snails (failing that, a few sprigs of rosemary will do)
110g (4oz) shelled broad beans (fava)
1 teaspoon pimentón (Spanish paprika)
750g (1lb 10oz) round-grain or paella rice (risotto or pudding rice will do)
Handful thin green asparagus or green beans or chopped fresh fennel
Salt

Choose a paella pan of the right size for the company: paelleras are sold according to the participants, always an uneven number to allow for larger appetites or unexpected guests: 5, 7, 9 and so on. The pan must be large enough to accommodate the raw rice in a single layer.

Prepare a cooking fire – a barbecue or a built-in griddle on the cooker – and allow it to die down to white-hot circle of charcoal. Set the paella pan on the heat. As soon as the metal changes colour, add the oil. When it smokes a little, add the garlic and fry for a few minutes. Add the rabbit or chicken joints, salt lightly, and turn them until they are brown all over. Add the cooked white beans and their cooking water, bring back to the boil and add the tomatoes, saffron, snails (or rosemary), broad beans and pimentón. Leave to simmer gently for about 40 minutes, until the meat and beans are tender.

Sprinkle in the rice and enough water to submerge everything completely (in total you'll need roughly 2 measures of liquid to each measure of rice). Place the green vegetables – asparagus or beans or slivers of fennel – on the top to cook in the steam. Leave to cook without stirring for 12 minutes, adding more boiling water as the surface dries out. At the end the rice should still be juicy and the surface pitted with tiny craters. Remove from the heat, cover with a thick cloth and leave for 10 minutes for the rice to finish swelling.

Place an upturned plate in the middle of the rice: this serves to keep the extra portion warm for the unexpected guest. (You meet some funny types out in the campo.) Eat the paella straight from the pan, with bread or Cos lettuce leaves as scoops, tackling only the portion directly in front of you.

paella valenciana

Rice fields in the Ebro delta near Castellón, Levante

Lorenzo Millo Casas of the Spanish Gastronomic Academy published in 1987, as a somewhat tongue-in-cheek Christmas present to friends, a monograph on the serious matter of why the paella is never served at official banquets, even when these are held before vespers, the time which marks the division between what can be considered a meal in the middle of the day and one taken in the evening.

Roughly translated, the thrust is both practical and historical: 'First, one must remember the dish's essentially rural origins. Paella, as all the world knows, is no more than the Catalan or Valencian name for a frying pan. The paellera could only have been the lady who valiantly stirred the dish rather than the metal container in which the dish was prepared. The ingredients were whatever came to her hand – bacalao with a grain, assorted beans and vegetables, various meats, poultry and rabbits, game, or, from the Albufera, mallard and the silvery eel. It was many years before it occurred to the resourceful citizen-restaurateurs of Valencia to add seafood to the mix.

'Second, the paella is essentially an open-air festive dish, and, as such, falls within the masculine preserve. The paella is a pastoral dish, born under a shady tree. It is a man who must prepare it, a recognised paellero of good repute. It must be eaten out of the pan in which it is cooked, with the participants seated in a circle around it, each armed with his own wooden spoon.

'Third, there is no doubt that the enjoyment of any dish, or indeed any beverage, inspires a particular train of thought, which in turn leads to conversation of a particular kind – in the case of the paella, rural matters: the vicissitudes of the year's weather, the price of seed-corn, recent market-prices for agricultural products, with some diversion permitted into the subject of bullfighting or the Valencian game of pelota, which can, in some instances, lead to violent disagreements.

'In short, here we have a dish which, through diurnal habit, rural character and its provocation of verbal assault, is not in the least suited to a gathering of diplomats.

'But the real neglect of Valencia's favourite dish stems, I believe, from the singular dislike felt by the coleric Urban VIII for Philip IV's ambassador to Rome, Gaspar de Borgia y Velasco, Cardinal of Valencia. Don Gaspar had been entrusted with the delivery of an official protest at the celebration in the Vatican of a solemn thanksgiving "Te Deum" for the sacking of La Rochelle. Even though the matter concerned only a few God-forsaken Huguenots, it was felt by the Spanish Cortes that the Pope had failed to maintain his agreed neutrality in the matter of Spanish-French disagreement. The protest was couched in somewhat intemperate language. The Pope told the Ambassador to *taceas aut exit!* – shut up or get out. At this point the assembled prelates began to indulge in fisticuffs of a most unholy nature. Since that day, the golden rice of Valencia has never appeared on the papal dining table, or at any diplomatic gathering, for fear of reminding the incumbent Pope of that disastrous moment when the Cardinal of Valencia was responsible for reducing the Holy See to a brawling mob.'

arroz abanda
seafood with rice

This is the second and less well-known rice dish of Valencia, differing from the paella in that the fish and rice are served separately. First comes the fish, sometimes with potatoes if the fisherman's catch has been poor, and then the rice cooked in the fish broth – two courses for the price of one.

Serves 8

900g (2lb) round-grain rice (Calispera for choice, but any risotto or pudding rice will do)
900g (2lb) mixed fish steaks and fillets (a balance of firm fish such as monkfish, tuna, eel, squid; soft fish such as bream, plaice, lemon sole, mackerel; prawns and langoustines are optional extras)
6 garlic cloves
1 teaspoon salt
150ml (1/4 pint) olive oil
1 bay leaf, sprig 1 thyme, some dried fennel stalks
1 large mild onion, finely chopped
Handful parsley, finely chopped
1 tablespoon pimentón (Spanish paprika) or 1 ñora (dried red pepper), torn
12 saffron threads, soaked in a splash of boiling water
450g (1lb) tomatoes, skinned and chopped (or tinned)

To serve
Rough salt
Alioli (see method) or a garlicky mayonnaise

Pick over the rice and salt the fish steaks. If using squid, empty out their innards, discard the soft intestines and eyes, and slice the rest neatly into rings and tentacles. Skin the garlic and crush it with the salt with a knife point.

moros y cristianos
moors and christians

Heat 4 tablespoons of the oil in a shallow pan until lightly smoking. Put in the firm fish steaks. Add the crushed garlic and salt and fry for a few moments. Add a litre of cold water, the bay leaf, thyme and dried fennel stalks and bring to the boil. Turn down the heat and leave to simmer for 5–10 minutes, depending on the thickness of the steaks. Add the fillets of soft fish – bream, flatfish, mackerel – and the crustaceans (if including), bring back to the boil, turn down the heat and leave to simmer for minutes more. Lift out the fish with a draining spoon, pile it in a pretty dish and keep it warm, reserving the stock.

Heat the remaining oil in a wide frying pan or paellera. Add the onion and fry gently for at least 10 minutes until soft and golden (this is the soffrito), then stir in the chopped parsley, pimentón and saffron. Add the rice and turn the grains until they are well coated with aromatic oil. Add the tomatoes, followed by double the volume of fish stock to the volume of rice (you may need extra water). Bring to the boil and simmer for 15 minutes. Remove from the heat and leave to rest and swell, loosely covered, for 10 minutes.

Serve the fish first on a large plate, accompanied by rough salt and an alioli – 6 garlic cloves crushed with salt and blended with 300ml (1/2 pint) olive oil – or a well-garlicked mayonnaise. By the time the fish has all been eaten, the rice will be ready. A crisp cos-lettuce salad and a dish of sliced oranges or slivers of melon are all you need to complete the meal.

This dish commemorates the deliverance of Christian Spain from Muslim rule. The frontiers drifted back and forth over seven centuries, leaving a legacy of victories and defeats throughout the southern provinces. In the city of Valencia as well as in many of the towns and villages of the Levante, local victories are commemorated on the appropriate day by full-scale mock battles, fully costumed, in the narrow whitewashed streets. There's never a shortage of willing volunteers to act the parts of the glamorously bejewelled and turbaned losers, while the inevitable conclusion, a Christian victory, is celebrated with a dish of black beans or brown lentils and white rice.

Serves 4–6

The Moors
450g (1lb) black beans
1 bay leaf
2 tablespoons olive oil
1 onion, sliced
2–3 garlic cloves, skinned and crushed
1 large carrot, scraped and chopped
2 heaped tablespoons chopped parsley
1 tablespoon pimentón (Spanish paprika)
2–3 tomatoes, skinned and chopped
Salt and pepper

The Christians
600ml (1 pint) chicken stock or a mixture of water
    and white wine
225g (8oz) paella or risotto round-grain rice
1 garlic clove, finely chopped
1 onion, skinned and finely chopped
25 (1oz) lard or butter
1 teaspoon grated lemon zest
1/2 teaspoon freshly grated nutmeg
4 tablespoons grated sheep's cheese
1 egg, beaten with a fork

Put the beans to soak in cold water overnight. Drain them and bring them to the boil in enough water to cover them to a depth of 2 fingers. Add the bay leaf, turn down the heat, put the lid on and leave to bubble gently until the beans are soft: 1 1/2–2 hours. Add more boiling water as necessary, but not too much – you want the beans to end up cooked almost dry. Finish with the traditional Valencian soffrito: heat the oil in a small pan and add the onion, garlic, carrot, parsley and pimentón. Let it all fry gently for a few minutes, then turn up the heat and stir in the tomatoes. Let it bubble up into a rich little sauce, then stir it into the beans. Taste and add salt and pepper.

Meanwhile, 30 minutes before the beans are likely to be tender, bring the stock or water-and-wine to the boil and sprinkle in the rice, garlic and onion. Bring back to the boil, put the lid on loosely, turn down the heat and leave to cook until the rice is soft but still a little nutty at the heart, and the liquid is all absorbed – allow 18 minutes. Remove from the heat and beat in the lard or butter, lemon zest, nutmeg and grated cheese. Stir in the egg and salt and pepper to taste.

To assemble the dish, butter a ring mould, pack in the rice and set it to warm in a low oven for 10 minutes before turning it out onto a large round serving dish. If you prefer, you can mould the rice by hand, or pack it into little cocotte dishes and turn them out to make a ring around the edge of the plate. Fill the middle with black beans, either in neat little piles or heaped up. The battle is won: you have the Moors surrounded by the Christians. Serve with a fresh tomato sauce – battle grounds are always bloody.

ancas de rana en gabardina
frog's legs in raincoats

A recipe from the wetlands of Albufera, where the marshes have always yielded plentiful supplies of the raw materials. A jacket of egg and breadcrumbs provides the raincoat.

Serves 4–8 as a starter

8 pairs of frog's legs
4 tablespoons white wine
1 tablespoon olive oil
Juice of 1 lemon
2 garlic cloves, skinned and finely chopped
1 teaspoon thyme leaves (fresh or dried)
Salt and pepper

To finish
3–4 tablespoons seasoned flour
1 large or 2 small eggs or 1 large one
3–4 heaped tablespoons fresh breadcrumbs
2 tablespoons finely chopped parsley
Olive oil, for frying

To serve
Bitter oranges or lemons, quartered

Separate the pairs of frog's legs and set them to marinate for an hour or two at room temperature in the wine, olive oil, lemon juice, garlic, thyme, salt and freshly milled pepper.

Drain the frog's legs and pat them dry. Prepare the finishing ingredients. Spread the flour on one plate; combine the egg(s) with a tablespoon of the marinade on another; on a third, spread the breadcrumbs mixed with the parsley. Dredge the frog's legs through the flour, drop them in the egg and then press them firmly into the breadcrumbs and parsley mixture.

In a frying pan, heat enough oil just to submerge the little legs. As soon as a faint blue haze begins to rise, slip in the frog's legs – do them in batches – and fry gently, turning once, until the coating is crisp and golden. If the oil is too hot, the coating will brown before the frog's legs are cooked through. If it's too cool, the coating will fall off the meat.

Serve with quartered bitter oranges or lemons.

Olive groves in the Sierra de Alcaraz, Murcia

torta de naranjas
almond sponge with oranges

This is an upside-down cake from the orange groves of Valencia, fresh-flavoured and light as a feather. Serve as a special treat with well-iced *agu̶ de Valencia*: dry champagne and fresh orange juice

Serves 4–6

2 small oranges
4 eggs
175g (6oz) caster sugar
225g (8oz) ground almonds
1 small glass rum

Line the base of a shallow cake tin about 18cm (7in in diameter with baking parchment. Butter the side and sprinkle overall with a little sugar.

Rinse the oranges, scrubbing off any waxy coating used for preservation. Cut one of the oranges horizontally into very fine slices and place these in pretty pattern in the base of the cake tin. Grate the zest and squeeze the juice from the remaining orange and reserve. Preheat the oven to 190°C/375°F/gas mark 5.

Whisk the eggs, both whites and yolks together, unt frothy. Sprinkle in the sugar and beat until it is whit and stiff enough for the whisk to leave a trail. This easily done with an electric beater but it takes twice as long as you expect. Fold in the ground almonds and the orange zest. Don't be afraid to turn the mixture thoroughly to blend before spooning it into the tin and smoothing the top.

Bake for 45–50 minutes, until the cake is well browned and firm to the finger. Leave it to settle for 5 minutes and then tip it out onto a plate. Blend the rum with the orange juice and trickle it over the warm cake. If it's for children, leave out the alcohol and use a syrup made by dissolving 2 tablespoons honey in 4 tablespoons orange juice.

horchata
nut milkshake

Visitors to Spain may have noticed signs in juice bars or ice-cream parlours advertising horchata de chufas, and may have discovered it to be a refreshing milky drink which can also be bought in cartons in supermarkets and grocery stores. Although the commercial variety is made with tigernuts (*chufas*), this version is made with the more delicately flavoured and expensive almonds in the form in which it's widely available throughout the Middle East. You can make it in a liquidiser if you don't want to go to the trouble of grinding the nuts first.

Makes 1 litre

225g (8oz) freshly shelled almonds, scalded
and skinned
1.2 litres (2 pints) fresh spring water
2 tablespoons white cane sugar (or more)
1 cinnamon stick

Grind the almonds, stir into the water and leave to infuse overnight. Or drop the whole skinned almonds into the liquidiser with a ladleful of water and process very thoroughly, then dilute with the remaining water.

Next day, strain the milky liquid into a saucepan, stir in the sugar and add the cinnamon stick. Bring to the boil and leave to cool. Refrigerate, removing the cinnamon stick just before serving.

Serve iced in a long glass, with something sweet: a cinnamon cookie or one of the sticky cakes made for the feast of the Virgin. It's also a useful thirst-quenching chilli-tamer – good with anything billed as picante.

The traditional cooking of the Balearics – the islands of Majorca, Minorca and Ibiza – depends, as with all islands, on what can be grown, traded or otherwise acquired within one day's sailing of their shores. As nature dictates, it is based on bread, oil, vegetables and the fish with which the inshore waters are well supplied. Although the islands are no longer self-sufficient in olive oil, the ancient groves of Majorca's Tramuntana mountains produce good sweet oil milled from olives collected after the first frosts. The time-honoured meal taken to the groves is a block of dried figs pressed with aniseed and bread – *pa pages*, brown Majorcan bread, or *llonguet*, white bread roll – which can be eaten with the oil that runs from the ripe fruits when heaped together in the gathering baskets.

The secrets of oil-pressing, wine-making and the baking of *pa mallorqui*, white Majorcan bread, can be ascribed to the civilising presence of the Romans, who are also to be thanked for the *coca*, a flat-bread topped in similar fashion to the pizza: scholars suggest it is similar – or possibly identical – to the Roman *portada*, a round flat-bread with a savoury topping whose chief virtue, as with the *coca*, lay in portability.

While every smallholder on all three islands takes pride in the products of his own patch, Majorca is the most fertile, its gentle climate allowing, with adequate irrigation, the harvesting of three crops a year. The presence of lime in the soil and frequent shortages of rain have encouraged the development of strains of small, intensely fragrant tomatoes which, if left on the vine, can be hung on the rafters all winter. The pig is treated, much as it is on the mainland, as a means of stocking winter store-cupboards rather than as a source of fresh meat, with salting the main method of preserving.

La Calobra pass, Majorca

THE BALEARICS

The salt-flats of the islands have been in continuous use since Phoenician times. Majorcan bread is baked without salt, the better to appreciate the little grains of bay-salt which taste of minerals and crack between the teeth.

Minorca is famous for crustaceans, particularly the spiny lobsters, *Palinurus elephas*, which take refuge from the Mediterranean's winter storms in the deep waters of Cala Fornells, a cliff-ringed bay on the rocky north coast. Traditional recipes recommend cooking them in a caldereta, a shallow earthenware casserole, with tomato, olive oil and brandy. The local fisherman's soup is the burrida, a one-pot all-in rock-fish broth prepared to much the same recipe as the bourride of Marseilles.

The islands have a turbulent history – all of them harbour the remains of prehistoric peoples as well as Phoenicians, Greeks, Romans, even Vikings. Caught between a rock and a hard place, the Balearic islanders had no choice but to accept the occupation of whoever happened to be in the ascendancy in the Mediterranean at the time. They first came to the attention of the Roman world during the wars between Rome and Carthage. The Romans, always admiring of military prowess in others, recorded that a group of particularly effective marksmen recruited by the Carthaginians came from the Balearics, where children were taught the art of the sling-shot as soon as they could walk. Furthermore, they recorded, the parents trained their children in the importance of accuracy by placing a loaf of bread high in the branches of a tree and leaving their offspring to earn themselves their dinner.

Released from military duties, the islanders appear to have turned to piracy. There's a record of Roman intervention against their activities in the first century BC. The Visigoths were the next to take up residence, followed by the Moors, who planted almond trees and introduced the islanders to the cultivation of the fig – an indigenous tree whose fruit is unpalatable in the wild. Under Moorish protection, the islanders returned to the sea and piracy, mostly operating out of Palma. These activities were smartly suppressed by King James of Aragon in the thirteenth century, as part of the general stable-sweeping which took place after he reconquered much of his kingdom from the Moors. From then on, the islands have been more or less affiliated to the mainland.

At the time of the Moorish withdrawal, the island's indigenous herds of black pigs, the cerdo negro, whose meat had been prohibited under Muslim dietary laws and which had been permitted to roam free for the several centuries of Moorish rule, returned to favour in newly Christianised store-cupboards. And never mind if the island climate was unsuitable for preserving pork in the mainland manner, as hams and chorizos. The pigs were fattened on wild figs – a refinement peculiar to the islands, whose repertoire of pork products did not depend for its longevity on air-drying. Instead it relied on air-exclusion – potting and sealing under lard or oil, a method of preserving which suits the climate. The best known of these preparations is sobrassada, a raw-meat sausage-mixture traditionally chopped by hand and coloured and flavoured with pimentón milled from the island's round and fiery breed of capsicum, another post-Columban newcomer. The mixture is stuffed into a sausage-skin and cellared for at least three months – though modern manufacturers skip this step and dry it in special drying rooms. The result, whatever the method, is a spreading rather than a slicing sausage.

From the time of the Moors until the present, the islanders threw in their lot with their fellow Catalans, preferring absorption and adaptation to revolution. During the Civil War, cut off from contact with the mainland, the Balearics were occupied by Italian Fascists. Following the establishment of Franco's regime, Catalonia's regionality and language were suppressed from Madrid, only to re-emerge with the arrival of democracy at about the same time as mass-tourism. Although Ibiza acquired more than its fair share of the more exuberant elements, few corners of the islands are immune. This, naturally enough, has brought another wave of invaders to change the way the islanders live.

sobrassada
potted pork with pimentón

Sobrassada is a soft pork paste enclosed in a sausage skin, a way of conserving meat in a damp climate unsuitable for wind-drying. It can be treated like a spread and eaten with bread, or melted into the bean-pot, plain vegetable stew or a dish of snails for fortification and flavour. The inclusion of chorizo, while not strictly traditional, is an easy way to get the desired result if you're not killing your own pig.

Serves 6

450g (1lb) soft chorizo
225g (8oz) pure white rendered pork fat
2 tablespoons mild pimentón (Spanish paprika)
2 teaspoons dried marjoram or oregano
2 tablespoons sherry vinegar
2 teaspoons sea salt
1/2 teaspoon freshly ground pepper

Mash all the ingredients together thoroughly – use a food processor if you like. Store in the fridge and bring back to room temperature before using.

It's delicious as a spread in toasted sandwiches, or sliced as a topping for a coca: just pat a batch of once-risen bread dough out into a rectangle, dot with slices of the sobrassada and leave to rise again – the dough should be thick and billowy enough to soak up the rich juices. Or pat into balls and drop into muffin tins – they should not come more than half-way up the tin. Then bake in a preheated oven at 200°C/400°F/gas mark 6 for 25–30 minutes, until puffed and golden.

sopa de hinojo con queso tierno
fennel gratin with curd cheese

This bread gratin is flavoured with the feathery-leafed, slender-rooted fennel which grows wild on the verge of every road. The finishing touch is a blend of two island cheeses: a fresh, crumbly, white curd cheese, queso tierno, and the Minorcan hard cheese, *queso de Mahón*, a matured cow's milk cheese that bears comparison with Parmesan.

Serves 4

250g (9oz) wild green fennel (or 1 fennel bulb and its fronds)
8 slices of dense-textured country bread
4 tablespoons extra virgin olive oil
110g (4oz) fresh white cheese – ricotta or other curd cheese
1 tablespoon grated hard cheese
1 tablespoon dried oregano
Sea salt

Trim and slice the fennel (save the feathery fronds) and cook until tender in about 1 litre (1½ pints) lightly salted simmering water – allow 20 minutes. Drain, reserving both the fennel and the cooking broth.

Meanwhile, preheat the oven to 200°C/400°F/gas mark 6. Fry six of the bread slices in the olive oil until crisp and brown on both sides. Lay the fried bread in a gratin dish and spread with the white cheese and the cooked fennel. Crumble the remaining 2 slices of bread, toss with the grated hard cheese and the chopped fennel fronds, and sprinkle over the top. Finish with the oregano and sea salt. Drizzle with a little more oil and bake until brown and bubbling. Robust but good.

frít mallorquí
majorcan pork-fry

The islanders' fry-up, this fast food is quickly prepared to satisfy hunger when the business of the annual pig mantanza is under way, or to fortify the guests at a wedding banquet while the lamb is being roasted. Liver, kidneys and the like were traditionally available only at such times, though modern cooks can prepare the dish whenever they please. The vegetables vary with the season. The selection below is for summer – camp-fire cooking for a midsummer pilgrimage. It is particularly good when made with the little purple artichokes, which, starved of nutrients in the island's lime-rich soil, make up in intensity of flavour what they lack in size.

Serves 4

450g (1lb) small artichokes (purple, for choice)
¼ lemon
1 wine glass olive oil
450g (1lb) potatoes, peeled and cut into thin chips
2 garlic cloves, unskinned but flattened
2 large onions, finely sliced vertically
1 small fennel bulb, cut into slivers
1 red pepper, de-seeded and cut into matchsticks
450g (1lb) pig's or lamb's liver, cut into small cubes
1 tablespoon seasoned flour
Salt and pepper
1 teaspoon ground cinnamon

Trim the artichokes: slice off the stalks, scrape off any hard fibres and cut the tender interior into matchsticks; quarter the buds, nick out the furry little choke, then slice if large and leave as quarters if small. Transfer the prepared artichoke pieces to a bowl of cold water with a squeeze of lemon and reserve.

Heat half the oil in a frying pan and fry the potatoes gently with the garlic until soft and lightly caramelised. Remove to a sieve set over a bowl to catch the drippings. Reheat the oil and fry the onions gently until they soften and caramelise a little – a pinch of salt will help the process along. Remove and add to the potatoes in the sieve.

Add the potato drippings to the pan and reheat. Fry the slivers of fennel in the hot drippings until they have browned a little but remain crisp. Remove and add to the vegetables in the sieve. Add the remaining oil and let it heat up. Drain the artichokes and prepared stalks, pat dry, salt lightly and fry until the soft bits are tender and the leaves are crisp and bronzed. Remove and add to the vegetables in the sieve. Pour any extra sieve-drippings back into the pan and reheat. Fry the strips of red pepper until lightly caramelised and transfer to the sieve.

Dust the liver with the seasoned flour and toss over the heat for 3–4 minutes to brown the outside. Add a glass of water, let it bubble up, then turn down the heat and leave to cook gently for 10–15 minutes until the liver is perfectly tender and the juices have completely evaporated. Add the vegetables to the pan and turn everything gently over the heat for 5 minutes or so to blend the flavours.

Pile it all on a warm serving dish and finish with salt, pepper and a sprinkle of cinnamon.

langostinos amb mayonesa
langoustines with mayonnaise

The Minorcans have access to the king of Mediterranean crustaceans, the spiny lobster, *Palinurus elephas*, which makes its home in the deep waters of the island's rocky inlets. Since *Palinurus* and his brothers are in serious danger of being overfished, little lobster, or langoustine, will have to do. Confusion reigns as to what exactly this is. For the purpose of this recipe – as a vehicle for a sumptuous mayonnaise – the langoustine is a Dublin Bay prawn, a smallish, red and white, lobster-like creature with narrow claws and beady, black eyes, which is also known, somewhat confusingly, as scampi, Norway lobster and crayfish. Whatever the name, the langoustine is the most highly prized of the smaller crustaceans, commanding a price to match. Sweet-fleshed and succulent, it needs no other sauce but this mayonnaise, Minorca's contribution to world gastronomy – to give the inhabitants of Mahon, the island's harbour-capital, their due.

Serves 4 as a starter

2 dozen fresh raw langoustines or Dublin Bay prawns (scampi)

The mayonnaise
3 egg yolks
600ml (1 pint) olive oil (not too strong)
Juice of 1 lemon
Fine salt

To serve
Cracked ice (optional)
Quartered lemons
Rough salt

greixonera de caragols
braised snails with parsley and garlic

inse the langoustines in cold water. Bring a roomy
ot of generously salted water to the boil and drop
hem in. Wait until the water returns to the boil,
llow 1 minute, transfer to a colander and hold
hem briefly under the tap to stop the cooking
rocess and give them a shine.

Make the mayonnaise while the langoustines cool,
eing sure to start with all the ingredients at room
emperature. In a roomy bowl, use a fork to beat the
gg yolks with a little salt to blend. Using a wooden
poon, work in the oil with a circular motion, drop
y drop at first and more freely as the sauce
mulsifies and begins to thicken. Dilute with a
ablespoon of lemon juice after the addition of half
he oil. Continue to beat in the oil until you have a
hick, soft, buttery sauce which holds its shape on
he spoon. Stop now, or the sauce might curdle.
hould this happen – you can tell because the egg
uddenly seems to lose contact with the oil and it
urns into a runny, curdled-looking sauce – try
whisking a spoonful of boiling water into one
corner. If the corner regains its texture, carefully
work in the rest of sauce. If not, you will have to
tart again with another egg yolk, adding the
curdled mixture as if it were new oil. The usual
trictures about raw eggs apply.

Arrange the prawns on a dish of cracked ice – or
not, as you please. Hand round the mayonnaise,
quartered lemons and bowl of rough salt separately.
f you need to store the mayonnaise, keep it in the
ridge and don't stir it – just lift out what you need
with a spoon.

Snails are one of the wild crops which can be
gathered for free in the countryside. While all
snails are edible, two kinds are particularly
esteemed in Spain. In Andalusia they like the little
white and brown snails no bigger than a
thumbnail which aestivate on thistle-skeletons in
every meadow; in the Levante they prefer the
larger, meatier snails introduced by the Romans,
who kept them in captivity and fed them on wine
and aromatics to perfume the flesh. Majorcan
country people who gather their own snails
recommend that they be fattened up for a week or
two on coarse-ground wheat flour; after this
treatment they have to be soaked in lightly
vinegared water (several changes), well rinsed and
scrubbed with salt to get rid of their slithery foam.
Now they're ready to be simmered for 3–4 hours
with thyme, celery, cloves, garlic and bay leaves,
until perfectly tender; after this they can picked out
of the shell and the cloaca – the little curl of
intestine buried at the heart – pinched off and
discarded along with any undesirable debris. Wild
mushrooms available in season include *Lactarius
deliciosus*, the pine-mushroom or orange-tear, the
Catalan favourite.

Serves 4–6 as a tapa

48 snails, ready prepared

The sauce
6 tablespoons olive oil
2 large onions, finely sliced
2 garlic cloves, skinned and finely chopped
**110g (4oz) wild or cultivated mushrooms, trimmed
   and diced**
110g (4oz) sobrassada (or soft chorizo), sliced
450g (1lb) small sweet tomatoes, skinned and diced
300ml (1/2 pint) dry white wine
2 tablespoons brandy
Salt and pepper

Heat the oil in a shallow earthenware casserole or
heavy frying pan and gently fry the onions and
garlic until they soften – allow at least 15 minutes
and don't let them brown. Add the diced
mushrooms, sobrassada and tomatoes, and let it all
bubble up, stirring and mashing to soften the
tomatoes and thicken the sauce. Add the snails and
wine. Bring to the boil once more, then turn down
the heat and simmer for 20 minutes, until the sauce
and the snails are well married. Taste and season
with salt and pepper. Sprinkle with the brandy and
either light it with a match or let it bubble fiercely
for a few minutes to evaporate the alcohol.

To serve as tapas – the popular way to eat these
little morsels – transfer to individual earthenware
casseroles and serve with toothpicks to hook the
snails from their shells and plenty of bread to mop
up the rich scarlet juices.

Fields cover the hillsides of rural Majorca

calamars a la mallorquina
squid stuffed with raisins and pine-kernels

A simple stuffing for one of the Balearics' most plentiful catches – if the inshore boats run into a shoal of cephalopods, they catch enough for a feast.

Serves 4–6

900g (2lb) smallish squid or cuttlefish
1 large onion, finely chopped or grated
50g (2oz) pine-kernels, lightly toasted
50g (2oz) raisins
2 eggs, lightly beaten
About 110g (4oz) fresh breadcrumbs
Salt and pepper
1/2 teaspoon ground cinnamon
150ml (1/4 pint) olive oil
300ml (1/2 pint) white wine
1/2 teaspoon saffron threads, lightly toasted in a
  dry pan

Rinse the squid or cuttlefish to remove any vestiges of sand, take out the innards and the bone (squid have a long, thin, transparent bone; cuttlefish have an oval, white one) and reserve the caps. Cut the bundle of tentacles off just below the eyes and chop them up. Discard the soft innards. Make a stuffing by working together the chopped tentacles, finely chopped onion, pine-kernels, raisins, eggs and enough breadcrumbs to form a firmish paste.

Season with salt and pepper and a little cinnamon. Stuff the caps with the paste and lay neatly in a heavy frying pan or earthenware casserole. Add the oil, white wine and saffron, bring to the boil, turn down the heat and cook gently for about 20 minutes, rolling the caps over every now and then so they cook evenly. Serve with thick slabs of country bread.

coca d'espinacs
spinach pizzetas

The coca, a flatbread which may or may not be leavened with yeast and can be any shape you please – round, oval, rectangular or square – is distinguished from the Italian pizza at first glance by the absence of cheese. Traditionalists will tell you the true coca is simply a flour-and-water dough allowed to ferment in the sun, kneaded into a ball, patted out into a disc of a size suitable for a single portion, salted, drizzled with oil and baked in the embers of a goatherd's camp-fire. The traditional fuel being goat's droppings, you could expect to find little bits of burnt dung adhering to the base. This version is topped with spinach but you can play around with slices of sobrassada, fresh sardines and the small, fragrant vine-tomatoes – *tomátigues de ramellet* – which are hung in the rafters for storage long into the winter months. Fresh garlic can replace the onions and garlic clove.

Serves 2–4

The dough
110g (4oz) strong bread flour
Salt
1 hazelnut-sized piece fresh yeast (or equivalent
  dried)
About 4 tablespoons warm water
1 tablespoon olive oil or lard

The topping
250g (9oz) spinach leaves, rinsed, dried and
  shredded
2 large spring onions, trimmed and finely sliced
1 fine, fat garlic clove, skinned and cut into slivers
1 tablespoon pine-kernels
1 tablespoon raisins, plumped in a little
  wine (optional)
Olive oil, for drizzling

Sift the flour with a little salt into a warm bowl.

Dissolve the yeast in the warm water, then stir in the oil or lard. Sprinkle with a little flour and leave for about 15 minutes in a warm place until frothy. Make a well in the middle of the flour and pour in the yeast mixture. Knead well until the dough forms a ball which leaves the sides of the bowl clean – you may need more or less flour. Form the dough into a smooth ball, drop it back in the bowl, cover with a cloth or clingfilm and leave in a warm place until doubled in size – an hour or two, depending on the weather.

Preheat the oven to 230°C/450°F/gas mark 8. Knead the dough vigorously to distribute the air bubbles. Either cut in quarters and pat out each piece into a disc about the width of your hand, or stretch out the dough ball and pat it out to fill a baking tray – it shouldn't be more than 1cm (1/2in) thick. Spread with a generous layer of the shredded spinach, salt lightly and top with a layer of spring onions. Sprinkle with the chopped garlic, pine-kernels and optional raisins, drizzle with a little olive oil and leave for about 10 minutes to rise again.

Bake for 12–20 minutes, until the crust is puffy and blistered at the edges. Sprinkle with a little more oil before serving. This is good with a bowl of trempo, a refreshing salad of mild white onions and wickedly fragrant tomatoes, on the side.

pa amb oli

The good things of the Balearics would be nothing without bread and olive oil – *pa amb oli*. Musician Tomás Graves, son of poet and ethnologist Robert Graves, writing of his schooldays on Majorca in the 1960s, explains the mythology:

'The perfect pa amb oli has two secret ingredients: honesty and appetite. For centuries it was the pillar of the Balearic survival diet. It was the only thing left between hunger and starvation, feeding generation upon generation of islanders....The term pa amb oli means exactly that: bread and olive oil. It usually includes salt and scrubbed garlic, or sugar instead of salt for kids, if the oil is too strong or rancid.'

The tomato-rub considered essential on the mainland, he continues, is not recognised by the older generation of islanders, since, after all, the tomato is known to be a New World newcomer – only a few centuries old and not yet granted full citizenship.

Coastal cliffs near Deia, Majorca

granada de berenjena
aubergine and cinnamon egg cake

In the Balearics, where the Moorish influence remained strong long after the caliphates withdrew from the mainland, this light, delicately spiced, aubergine egg cake is called a granada, which might or might not be a reference to its provenance, the last stronghold of the Moors. The sauce, certainly, is as Arab as anyone might wish.

Serves 4

- tablespoons olive oil
- firm glossy aubergines, peeled and diced
- large onion, finely chopped
- teaspoon ground cinnamon
- eggs, beaten with a fork
- 150ml (1/4 pint) rich milk (goat's or cow's)
- Salt and pepper
- tablespoons finely crushed toasted breadcrumbs

The dipping sauce
- 110g (4oz) cooked chickpeas (tinned are fine)
- tablespoon sesame paste (tahini)
- tablespoon curd cheese
- tablespoon lemon juice
- 2–3 tablespoons olive oil

To finish:
- teaspoon crushed dried rosemary, blended with a little olive oil

Heat the oil in a roomy frying pan and gently fry the diced aubergines with the onion until soft and mushy – a little salt will help the juices run. Sprinkle in the cinnamon, remove from the heat and allow to cool a little. Mash thoroughly, or process in a food processor. Mix the eggs with the milk, season with salt and pepper, and beat the mixture into the aubergine purée, or add to the mixture in the food processor halfway through the blending.

Preheat the oven to 180°C/350°F/gas mark 4.

Lightly oil a *cazuela* – shallow earthenware baking dish – and sprinkle with the breadcrumbs. Tip in the egg and aubergine mixture and bake for 30–35 minutes, until just set. Turn it out of the mould onto a plate: loosen the edges, then tip it out all in one swift movement.

Meanwhile, make the sauce. Purée everything in a blender, with salt to taste, to make a soft, spoonable sauce – you may need a little water to dilute it – and tip it into a bowl. Swirl in the rosemary oil but don't mix it: the dark thread of oil should remain perfectly visible.

Serve the flan warm, with the sauce handed around separately.

arrebossat de conill
rabbit with cinnamon and almond-milk

Rabbit joints are simmered here with cloves and red wine, then bathed in an almond custard dusted with cinnamon – a Moorish recipe which survived the Reconquista.

Serves 4–6

- 2 wild rabbits or 1 domestic one, jointed
- 1 glass red wine
- 2 large onions, sliced
- 1–2 bay leaves, crumbled
- 2–3 cloves
- Salt and pepper
- 50g (2oz) blanched almonds
- 300ml (1/2 pint) creamy milk
- 3 egg yolks, mixed together
- 110g (4oz) brown sugar

To finish
- 6 slices of country bread
- 2 tablespoons pure pork lard or olive oil
- Ground cinnamon, for dusting

Rinse the rabbit joints and put them in a pot with the wine, onion, bay leaves, cloves, a few peppercorns, a pinch of salt and enough water to cover. Bring to the boil, turn down the heat, put the lid on tightly and leave to simmer gently for 40–60 minutes until the sauce is reduced to a couple of tablespoons and the joints are perfectly tender.

Meanwhile, process the almonds with the milk, yolks and sugar to make a runny cream. Transfer to a bowl, stir in the rabbit juices, set the bowl over a pan of simmering water and whisk over the heat until the custard thickens a little – remove before any bubbles break the surface.

Fry the bread in lard or oil until golden and crisp. Transfer to a serving dish and top with the rabbit joints. Serve with the savoury custard sauce.

ensaimadas amb canel
lardy cakes with cinnamon

Rich with lard and lightened with yeast, these sugary, snail-curled buns – though undeniably Majorcan in origin – are now popular as a breakfast bread all over Spain. The high proportion of oil and egg to flour slows the action of the yeast, so the dough takes a long time to rise – overnight is ideal.

Makes 4 buns

900g (2lb) strong bread flour
1 teaspoon salt
75g (3oz) fresh or 40g (1½oz) dried yeast
6 eggs, lightly beaten
225g (8oz) sugar
300ml (½ pint) mild olive oil
2 tablespoons pure white pork lard, softened
About 300ml (½ pint) warm water

Sift all but a handful of the flour with the salt into a warm bowl. Work the yeast with a little warm water – or follow the instructions on the packet if using dried or easy-blend. Mix the eggs with 175g (6oz) of the sugar, 150ml (¼ pint) of the oil and the softened lard. Work the yeast and the egg mixture into the flour until you have a soft, smooth dough. Drop it back into the bowl, cover with clingfilm or a damp cloth and leave it to rise in a warm, draught-free corner for an hour or two, until it has doubled in size.

Punch the dough down and work in the rest of the flour along with the remaining sugar, dissolved in a little warm water, and the remaining oil, and knead until perfectly smooth. Divide the dough into 4 pieces and roll each piece into a short fat rope. Coil into snail shapes and place on a greased bakery sheet. Cover with a clean cloth and set to rise for at least 8 hours – all night is best.

Preheat the oven to 180°C/350°F/gas mark 4. Bake the buns for 12–15 minutes, until well-risen and deliciously brown. Transfer to a rack to cool and dust liberally with sugar, or top with spiced pumpkin jam (see p. 209). Spread with a knifeful of sobrassada (see p. 42) or top with thin slivers of smoked bacon (*tocino ahumado*) or use as a dip for a bowl of milky breakfast coffee.

The jagged coastline of Formentera, Ibiza

robiols
apricot and orange turnovers

The turnover dough is mixed with orange juice and shortened with lard and olive oil. For cakes and pastries such as this, use a mild, rectified oil rather than a strong extra virgin. If virgin is all that's available, bring it up to boiling point and allow it to cool before incorporating it into the dough. I like an apricot filling, but any jam – *mermelada* – will do.

Makes a dozen

700g (1¹/₂lb) plain flour
¹/₂ teaspoon salt
110g (4oz) pure pork lard
3 tablespoons sugar
300ml (¹/₂ pint) light olive oil
3 egg yolks
Juice of 2 oranges – about 6 tablespoons – plus a
little thinly pared zest

To fill
450g (1lb) jam: apricot, strawberry, orange, plum,
apple or quince
110g (4oz) marzipan (optional)

Sift the flour and salt into a cool bowl and work in the lard with the tips of your fingers. Sprinkle in the sugar and work in the oil and egg yolks (saving a teaspoon of yolk for glazing). Add enough orange juice to give a softish dough. Form into a ball, cover with clingfilm and leave in a cool place to rest for 30 minutes or so.

Preheat the oven to 180°C/350°F/gas mark 4.

Roll out the pastry thinly, as for tartlets. With a pastry-cutter or a large, sharp-edged wine glass, cut saucer-sized rounds. Drop a sliver of the optional marzipan and a teaspoon of jam onto one side of each round, dampen the edges with a wet finger and fold over the other side to make a half-moon. Mark the edges with a fork to seal. Paint the tops with the reserved egg yolk beaten with its own volume of water, and finish with a curl or two of orange zest.

Bake for 20–25 minutes, until crisp and golden. Delicious with a chilled glass of cinnamon-flavoured horchata (see p.39) or a glass of *agua de Valencia* (cava cut fifty-fifty with fresh orange juice).

Catalonia's language, history and culinary traditions have much in common with those of the neighbouring regions of Provence and the Languedoc. A natural independence was reinforced by trade links with the merchants of Venice and through them with Istanbul, capital of the Ottoman Empire and the main route, after the withdrawal of the Moors from Andalusia, to the spices of the Orient. These ancient associations gave the Catalans an identity separate from that of the rest of Spain. An appetite for hard work makes the Catalans prosperous and eager to take advantage of opportunities – commercial and social – as soon as they present themselves. An adventurous turn of mind surfaces in a taste for cultural anarchy which often sets them at odds with mainstream Spain, particularly the Castilians, whose ability to resist change is all too evident in the literary hero most admired by every Castilian writer, Don Quixote, an anachronism even in Cervantes' time. The Catalans look elsewhere for their heroes, culinary as well as cultural. The first cookbook ever published in Spain – Barcelona, 1477 – is a manual of Italian court cuisine translated into Catalan. Perhaps because the Catalan spirit was so fiercely surpressed during the Franco years, there has lately been an astonishing flowering of its culture.

Regional cooking is still very much alive and kicking, particularly in the busy tapas bars and restaurants of Barcelona itself, but a new culinary style has developed alongside the old.

While traditional recipes are widely known and understood, a new wave of cerebral cooks disappears into the laboratory to seek innovative ways of exploiting man's most basic instinct, the satisfaction of appetite. The difference is in the philosophy. Although the cuisine is still dependent on the excellence of the ingredients – seasonality and regionality are sacrosanct – nothing must be taken for granted, all is permitted, everything changes. A substance which looks like sea-foam but tastes of truffle? Tobacco-flavoured ice cream? Chocolate with a scent of leather? Such things would be revolutionary elsewhere – in Catalonia, they're part of the architecture. There are links to be made between the artistic anarchy of Antonio Gaudí, the icon-tumbling surrealism of Salvador Dalí and the movement led by the world's most praised culinary alchemist, Ferran Adria.

Adria, rated among the three most influential chefs of our time, works his magic in the laboratory long before he migrates to the kitchen. His showcase is a tiny restaurant, El Bulli, in the little village of Rosas on the road between Barcelona and the French frontier. Over the past two decades, Adria has established what can be seen as an entirely new way of cooking but is, as is the nature of creative Catalans, a development of what was there already. To the informed eye of his local clientele, every dish on his menu – though no doubt there are exceptions – is a reference, a synthesis, an abstraction of what to any Catalan is a dish known and loved since childhood. It is

A shepherd leads his flock across a stubbly plain near Lérida.

this, an awareness of the past which informs but never dominates the present, which has made the Catalans who they are.

Within Spain, Catalonia's links are with Valencia and the Balearics rather than Castile and Aragon, the founding fathers of the nation and the rootstock of all things Spanish. Trade links with the eastern Mediterrean and the nations of Mahgreb brought a taste for eastern spices. Italian pasta, *fideu*, is cooked like a paella, though the dish has Moorish antecedents; desserts and the products of the pastry-maker's art are mainly of Arab inspiration – including, some say, puff pastry. Subtlety and invention come, in the main, with the four salsas of the Catalan kitchen: soffrito, picada, samfaina and alioli. The first two are used as flavouring additions before, during or after the cooking process; the other two are dipping sauces, served separately. A fifth, salsa romesco, is of more recent invention and is usually served with foods from the grill. These salsas, of varying complexity according to the cook's inclination and talent – the soffrito, in its simplest form, is no more than onions fried very gently in olive oil – are the key to Barcelona's sophisticated seafood dishes as well as the one-pot meals of the rural kitchen.

The staple foodstuffs of the region are bread and rice, with fideus treated in much the same way as rice. The boiling pot is for everyday: the traditional midday dish is *el bullit*, the boil-up, a vegetable stew which may or may not include eggs. Lamb, game, seafood, barnyard birds – particularly goose and duck – and distinctive pork products including cured sausage, *butifarra* – varieties are white or black, as with the French boudin – provide the pleasure. The *plancha*, an iron griddle which can be placed on the hearth or open-air cooking-fire, is used for grilling seafood and anything that tastes good if heat is applied to the point of carameli-sation. Among many candidates for the treatment, wild garlics, *calçots*, are the most celebrated; the sauce which accompanies them is salbitxada, a punchy little garlic and almond paste. In winter, the rural housewife cooks slow-simmered stews thickened with pulses and enriched, in the days before the intervention of northern bureaucrats, with her own *embutidos de cerdo* made with the meat of the household pig.

Antonio Gaudí's Batllo House, Barcelona

Catalan housewives were quick to appreciate the virtues of the American staples – not only store-cupboard beans (haricots – white, red, green or speckled), but also maize, a grain which thrives in the uplands where previous crops had struggled. Potatoes replaced the chestnut, already a vanishing crop at a time when the forests were felled, much as in the Brazilian forest today, to feed the need for timber – in those days ships which brought the treasure home.

As a result of the transatlantic trade, the Catalan vegetable patch acquired fiery little chillis, *Capsicum annuum* and *C. frutescens*, to replace imported peppercorns as the poor man's taste-tickler. Once the fieriness had been bred out to produce the mild, sweet salad-pepper which could be dried and milled, the capsicums took over from the costly saffron as a colouring tint – a ray of sunshine to please the eye as well as the palate. Modern recipes, gilding the lily, include both saffron and pimentón. Meanwhile the tomato received an even warmer welcome. Its sweetness, juiciness and glorious colour appealed so strongly to the Catalan palate that it was added to the national pick-me-up, *pa amb oli*, bread and oil, a preparation which – taken with the basic ingredients and the passion with which

pa amb tomàquet
bread and tomato

This is Italian bruschetta or the French tartine prepared and eaten with Spanish passion. The ingredients dictate the quality: you want dense-crumbed farmer's bread baked in a wood oven, the mildest, sweetest garlic, cold-pressed olive oil and tomatoes of an unusual strength of fragrance, flavour and viscosity. In Catalonia there are special rubbing-tomatoes grown for the purpose – *tomàquets de ramellet* (vine tomatoes). These are nothing much to look at, nor will you find them among the dazzling heaps of fruit and vegetables on the stalls which attract the queues of shoppers. As with all the best things – truffles, the first figs, wet walnuts – they're sold by the black-clad grannies who settle themselves outside the entrance, or at the far end of the line of stalls, and lay out their wares on a little collapsible table. Among the half-dozen brown eggs, little pyramids of lemons, small bunches of marjoram and parsley, you may notice, dangling from the edge of the table on a hanging string, a hank or two of greenish tomatoes, uneven in size and shape, tough-skinned, still on the branch. Once you become aware that these tomatoes are attracting attention, you might be tempted to enquire the price. The answer will be two or three times higher than the most perfect tomatoes in the marketplace. If curiosity tempts you to buy, you'll realise why. These are no ordinary tomatoes. They are tomatoes as they ought to taste, with chewy flesh, sweet, thick juice of a remarkable viscosity, and an astonishing fragrance. If you order pa am tomàquet in Catalonia – or if it appears on your restaurant table automatically – you may expect, if the place knows its business and hasn't been obliged to cater to ignorant tourists, that all five elements (bread, salt, tomatoes, garlic and oil) will arrive separately, allowing people to make their own combinations. Decisions involve the amount of garlic – to rub, sliver or chop? – the trickling-on of the oil – before or after the addition of the topping? – the amount of tomato and whether you merely use the juice of the tomato or top the bread with the pulped flesh as well.

Serves 4 (if you're hungry)

4–8 firm field-ripened tomatoes – size dictates quantity
Dense-crumbed country bread with plenty of texture, sliced as thick as your thumb – hunger dictates how many slices
4 new garlic cloves – firm and without the telltale green shoot that shows you they'll be bitter
Extra virgin olive oil – plenty

If you have managed to track down Catalan rubbing-tomatoes or other trustworthy fruits, there's no need for additional preparation. If your tomatoes are on the watery side, preheat the oven to 230°C/450°F/gas mark 8, cut the tomatoes in half, lay them on a baking tray, cut side down, and roast for 15–20 minutes, until perfectly soft. Slip them out of their skins and mash the pulp a little.

Meanwhile, toast the bread – best on a camping-grill set over a flame, so that it singes a little. Rub with the skinned garlic, trickle with the oil and spread thickly with the tomato pulp, pushing it well into the bread. If you're a true garlic lover, don't rub the bread with it, but chop it finely and sprinkle it over the top.

Serve as it is: no forks, no knives, just fingers.

rovellons amb longaniza
orange-tear mushrooms with chorizo

Longaniza, a slender chorizo coloured with pimentón, salted, smoked and wind-dried, is a speciality of the ancient Roman city of Lérida, now an industrial centre surrounded by irrigated market gardens. In this simple little dish it complements the earthy flavour of Catalonia's most popular wild fungus, though any firm-fleshed mushroom, wild or cultivated, can be substituted.

Serves 4

450g (1lb) orange-tear mushrooms (*Lactarius deliciosus*)
6 tablespoons olive oil
1 large onion, finely chopped
225g (8oz) longaniza or chorizo
3 garlic cloves, skinned and finely chopped
1 tablespoon toasted almonds, crushed
2 tablespoons fresh breadcrumbs
1 glass white wine
Salt and pepper

Brush the fungi and wipe carefully, trimming off any woody or wormy bits. Chop the stalks, slice the caps and reserve.

Heat the oil in a roomy frying pan and fry the onion gently until soft and golden. Remove the onion and reserve, then add the mushrooms. Fry over a low heat until the juices run, then turn up the heat and cook until the moisture has evaporated and they begin to fry again. Remove and add to the onion. Fry the slices of longaniza until they crisp a little, then remove and reserve. Add the garlic to the pan-drippings and fry for a moment before you stir in the almonds and breadcrumbs. As soon as the bread has taken up the juices and begun to brown, add the wine and bring to the boil briefly. Return the mushrooms and onions to the pan, and let them bubble up to amalgamate the flavours. Season to taste, heap in a serving dish and finish with the longaniza.

tortilla catalana
tortilla with black butifarra and beans

The rural housewife's quick standby, traditionally prepared to order when the workers return from the fields. Butifarra can be an all-meat, white boiling sausage; if made with blood, it becomes black pudding – *morcilla* – of which there are many variations throughout Iberia.

Serves 4

2 tablespoons olive oil or pure pork lard
8–12 slices butifarra negra (black pudding)
Pinch each marjoram, ground cumin and
  pimentón
3 tablespoons cooked haricot or butter beans,
  drained
4 eggs
Salt and pepper

Warm 1 tablespoon of the olive oil or lard in an omelette pan. Fry the sausage for a few minutes until the edges brown and the fat runs. Stir in the spices. Add the well-drained beans and warm them through.

Beat the eggs lightly with salt and pepper and stir in the sausage and bean mixture. Wipe the pan and heat the rest of the oil or lard. Tip in the egg mixture and cook very gently, like a thick pancake, neatening the sides as the egg sets and lifting up the middle to let the soft uncooked egg run underneath. Turn it once – hold the pan in one hand and flip the egg cake onto a plate, then slip it back into the pan to set the other side. Gently does it and don't overcook.

bolets amb patates
porcini mushrooms with potatoes

Porcini – known in Spain as setas, boletos and by several other regional names – are greatly appreciated in Catalonia, as is the snowy-fleshed, purple-topped *Russula cynoxantha* and the charcoal-burner (carbonera, also known as lloret), though the saffron milk cap (revellon) is the star. Cultivated button mushrooms, *champiñon de Paris*, will be nearly as good.

Serves 4 as a starter

450g (1lb) porcini mushrooms or other firm-
  fleshed fungi
450g (1lb) baby new potatoes, scrubbed but not
  peeled
Salt and pepper
4 tablespoons olive oil
2 heaped tablespoons fresh breadcrumbs
50g (2oz) hazelnuts, crushed or finely chopped
2 garlic cloves, skinned and finely chopped
2 heaped tablespoons chopped parsley
1 teaspoon dried oregano or chopped fresh
  marjoram
1/2 teaspoon crumbled dried thyme
1/2 teaspoon freshly grated nutmeg

Preheat the oven to 200°C/400°F/gas mark 6.

Wipe or brush the mushrooms (do not peel or wash them) and trim the stalks level with the caps, chopping the stalks finely and putting to one side. Meanwhile, cook the potatoes in boiling salted water until tender, then drain thoroughly.

Arrange the mushroom caps, stalk side upwards, in an earthenware cazuela or gratin dish which will just accommodate them. Trickle with all but 1 tablespoon of the oil and sprinkle with salt and freshly ground black pepper. Bake for 10 minutes, until the juices begin to run.

Meanwhile, in a small bowl, mix the finely chopped stalks with the breadcrumbs, nuts, garlic, herbs and nutmeg and season with salt and pepper. Add the juices from the mushrooms and spoon the mixture into the caps. Pop the potatoes into the gaps between the mushrooms, drizzle with the remaining tablespoon of oil and return the dish to the oven for another 10–15 minutes to crisp and gild the topping. Serve straight from the oven, still sizzling in the cooking dish.

The Benedictine monastery of Montserrat, in the hills outside Barcelona

rossejat de fideus a la marinera
seafood noodle paella

The Catalans cook noodles – an Arab introduction, though the jury's still out on whether the original inspiration was Italy – as if making a paella, in much the same way, that is, as the Italians cook risotto. A preliminary frying with flavourings – small pieces of meat or chicken, firm-fleshed seafood, onion or garlic – is followed by the addition of a cooking liquid, which can be water, wine or stock. A particularly Catalan refinement is the addition of a picada, a sophisticated finishing mix based on almonds and garlic, although this is omitted if you serve the dish with alioli. When served as a party dish the fideu features luxury ingredients such as prawns and squid. The cooking implement of choice – though any large frying-pan will do – is a paellera, a round, shallow, double-handled, raw-iron pan designed so that the food can be cooked in a single layer. You'll find the pans sold in sizes appropriate to an uneven number of people – three, five, seven and so on – to allow for the unexpected guest.

Serves 6–7

900g (2lb) mixed soup fish: rock-fish, eel and small crustaceans such as squill (mantis shrimp)
4 tablespoons olive oil
1 large onion, finely chopped
450g (1lb) ripe firm tomatoes, skinned and chopped
1 glass white wine
Salt
6 garlic cloves, unskinned but split with a single blow
450g (1lb) broken-up spaghetti, elbow-macaroni or any small soup pasta – children love the little rice-shaped pasta known as lluvia (rain)

The picada
2 tablespoons olive oil
2 tablespoons blanched almonds
2 garlic cloves, skinned and chopped
2 tablespoons chopped parsley
1 tablespoon pimentón (Spanish paprika)
1 teaspoon ground cinnamon
1/4 teaspoon saffron threads
1/2 teaspoon ground cloves
Juice and grated zest of 1 lemon

To finish (optional):
900g (2lb) mixed seafood: mussels, clams, squid, cuttlefish, prawns

Rinse the fish. Heat 1 tablespoon of the oil in a roomy stewpot and fry the onion. Add the tomatoes and let it all bubble up, mashing with a spoon to make a little sauce. Add the rinsed fish, wine and 1.5 litres (2½ pints) of fresh cold water. Bring to the boil, add salt and leave to simmer for 20–30 minutes, until the broth is well-flavoured. Push through a sieve and pour 2 litres (3½ pints) of the broth back into the pan, leaving it on the side of the stove to keep warm.

Meanwhile, prepare the picada. Heat the oil in a small frying pan. Fry the almonds and garlic until golden, then add the parsley and spices and let them fry for a moment. Tip the contents of the pan into a mortar and pound to a paste with the lemon juice and zest, or transfer everything to a food processor and give it a quick blitz. Reserve.

Heat a seven-person paella pan or a large frying pan, making sure the entire base of the pan is in contact with the heat. As soon as the metal changes colour (if using a paella pan), add the remaining olive oil, turn down the heat and add the cracked garlic cloves and noodles. Fry over a gentle heat, stirring constantly, until the noodles have turned a rich golden-brown. Add the reserved broth, bring to the boil, then turn down the heat and let it bubble gently for about 15 minutes until the broth has been absorbed. Taste and add more broth if the noodles are still a little chewy. Stir in the picada. Bring to the boil again, turn down the heat and leave to simmer gently for 5 minutes. Place the seafood (if using) on top, bring back to the boil, turn down the heat and cook until the shellfish have opened, the noodles are perfectly tender and the juices almost evaporated – another 5 minutes, or about 10 minutes in all.

Set the pan in the middle of the table for everyone to help themselves – as with paella, it is traditional to eat the portion immediately in front of you with wooden spoon, working neatly from the outside to the middle.

For dessert, serve the Catalan mel i mato – a slice of fresh white curd cheese drizzled with honey – which is even more delicious sprinkled with a few fresh walnuts.

rap a la brasa amb salsa romesco
grilled monkfish skewers with romesco sauce

Salsa romesco, a chilli and almond salsa without which no Catalan would touch grilled fish, goes with anything which works with tomato ketchup. It is the obligatory dipping-sauce for barbecued *calçots* (wild garlic) and is good with all grilled vegetables – asparagus, baby leeks, sliced aubergines and courgettes. The salsa is something of a cult in the city of Tarragona, its home territory, and fierce competitions are held annually to choose the best recipe. As for the fish, monkfish is one of the few white-fleshed ones robust enough to withstand the fierce heat of the barbecue. For extra elegance, add a handful of prawns to the line-up on the skewer.

Serves 4 as a starter

450g (1lb) filleted monkfish, cut into bite-sized cubes
2–3 tablespoons olive oil
Juice of 1 lemon
Salt and pepper
Pinch dried oregano

The salsa romesco
2 garlic cloves, skinned and crushed
2 tablespoons fresh breadcrumbs, fried crisp in a little olive oil
2 tablespoons toasted almonds
2 roasted or fried red peppers, de-seeded
2 large tomatoes, skinned, de-seeded and roughly chopped
1 fresh red chilli, de-seeded and chopped
4 tablespoons red wine vinegar
150ml (1/4 pint) olive oil

Thread the monkfish cubes on skewers and sprinkle with the oil, lemon juice, salt and pepper. Leave to marinate while you make the salsa.

Drop the garlic, 1 teaspoon salt, the breadcrumbs and almonds into a food processor and grind to a paste. Add the peppers, tomatoes, chilli and vinegar and process some more. Pour in the oil in a thin trickle, as for a mayonnaise, until the sauce is thick and shiny.

Preheat the grill or light the barbecue – let it get really hot. Drain the monkfish, then sprinkle with a little more oil and the oregano. Grill for 4–5 minutes no more, turning so the heat reaches all sides, until the monkfish is opaque with lightly caramelised edges.

Serve with the sauce on the side.

Parc Guell, designed by Gaudí, in Barcelona

el bullit
vegetable hot-pot

bullit – boil-up – is the thick vegetable stew that
serves as the midday meal in a traditional Catalan
household. Some will tell you it's really a vehicle
for the gloriously garlicky sauce, the alioli which
invariably accompanies it. In summer serve the
alioli with raw vegetables and bread – no sense in
making life hard for yourself.

Serves 4

00g (2lb) carrots, scrubbed or scraped and cut
  into short lengths
00g (2lb) potatoes, peeled and chunked if mature,
  whole if young and new
00g (2lb) small turnips, peeled and cubed
  small cabbage, sliced through the equator,
  or 1 large broccoli head, divided into florets
Handful green beans, topped and tailed
Salt

The sauce
5 garlic cloves
About 150ml (1/4 pint) olive oil

In a roomy pan, bring to the boil enough salted
water to cover the vegetables. If you have a good
homemade stock – maybe from boiled beef, bacon
or chicken – use that instead. Add the vegetables to
the boiling liquid in the order given, bringing the
broth back to the boil each time. The whole
operation will take about 20 minutes. Drain
everything in a colander as soon as the vegetables
are tender – reserving the broth – and pass them
under cold water to halt the cooking process.

Meanwhile, settle down with a pestle and mortar
to make the alioli – a tranquil task which can't be
hurried. Skin the garlic, chop it roughly and crush
it in the mortar with 1/4 teaspoon salt. When it's
pounded to a paste, start adding the oil in a thin
stream. Keep pounding with the pestle and

trickling in the oil until the mixture is good and
thick. Those uncertain of acceptable results can
include an egg yolk, as if making mayonnaise,
which gives a richer but less piquant sauce. A drop
of lemon juice sharpens the flavour. If you're in a
hurry, make the alioli in a liquidiser: just drop all
the ingredients in the goblet along with a slice of
boiled potato or a crust of bread, soaked and
squeezed dry, to stabilise the mix. Leave it in the

mortar – or transfer to a bowl – and hand it round
as a dip for the vegetables.

Serve the broth with slices of bread in each bowl, or
hand the bread around separately, as you please.
Alternatively, don't drain the vegetables but serve
them in their broth, with the alioli handed round for
people to stir in as much as they please.

oca ambs peres
roast goose with pears

One of the great dishes of the Catalan kitchen, this is eaten by the inhabitants of the village of Sali in the province of Gerona on the feast day that celebrates the winter solstice. This version requires a tender young goose, though a well-fattened duck can take its place. Of all domesticated creatures, the goose is the most efficient converter of feed to meat. It is also obdurately seasonal, refusing to breed except in its allotted cycle. This year's bird at Michaelmas will be young and tender. By the time Christmas comes around, it is altogether larger and tougher.

Serves 6–8

The bird
1 young goose or 1 large duck, about 2.7kg (6lb)
2 tablespoons fresh pork lard or goose dripping
3 garlic cloves, skinned
1 bay leaf

The pears
6–8 small firm pears
2 tablespoons fresh pork lard or goose dripping
1 large mild onion, skinned and finely chopped
1–2 garlic cloves, skinned and chopped
1 tablespoon pine-kernels
1 tablespoon raisins
1 tablespoon finely chopped parsley
1 teaspoon ground cinnamon
2 large tomatoes, scalded, skinned and chopped
1 small glass anis-flavoured white brandy
 (or Kummel)

To finish
4 tablespoons sugar

pavo con almendras y azafrán
turkey with almonds and saffron

ipe the bird and prick the skin all over without
ping through to the meat. Choose a casserole large
nough to accommodate the whole bird. Warm the
rd or goose dripping, put in the bird and turn it
ver until it gilds a little and the fat begins to run.
dd the garlic and bay leaf. Cover and leave to cook
ently in its own juices for about 1½ hours, turning
gularly, until it is perfectly cooked through. Or
ast the bird in a preheated oven at
30°C/350°F/gas mark 4 for about 1½ hours.
Naturally, the bird would be easier to handle and
ore quickly cooked if it was jointed, but the effect
ould not be nearly as festive.)

eanwhile, peel the pears, leaving the stalk in
ace. In a roomy pan, melt the lard or dripping and
y the onion, garlic, pine-kernels, raisins, chopped
arsley and cinnamon. When all is shiny and soft,
dd the tomatoes and simmer until it collapses into
thick sauce. Add a glass of water and the anis and
t it bubble up again. Place the peeled pears in the
auce, stalk end up, bring back to the boil, turn the
eat down, cover and leave to simmer for about
0 minutes. Remove the pears carefully with a
raining spoon and reserve. Pour the sauce round
he goose and let everything simmer together for
nother 20 minutes or so. Turn the heat up if the
auce is not thick enough.

rrange the goose on a warm serving dish, put the
ears around it, stalk upwards, and keep the sauce
varm. Call everyone to the table. Now finish the
ish: melt the sugar gently in 1 tablespoon water in
small pan, stirring until all the crystals have
issolved, then increase the heat and let it
aramelise and turn a rich walnut-brown. Remove
he pan from the heat immediately and pour a little
f the caramel over each pear – it will harden
traight away, but not for long. Carve the goose
vithout delay and serve each portion with its own
ear. Hand the sauce around separately.

The Spanish turkey – lean, muscular and no bigger
than a chicken when in its native habitat, the
forests of Central America – was first imported by
the Jesuits, who declared it a festive bird and
managed for more than a century to keep a
profitable monopoly on breeding it for the table,
earning the bird its irreverent nickname, *el jesuito*.
If all you can find is one of those hormone-heavy
monsters that have taken its place, guinea fowl, a
flighty African native, makes an excellent
replacement.

Serves 6

1.8kg (4lb) turkey joints, on the bone, or 2 guinea
   fowl, jointed
6 tablespoons fresh white pork lard or olive oil
1 thick slice of day-old bread
6 garlic cloves, unskinned but flattened
2 tablespoons blanched almonds, crushed or
   finely chopped
1 small bunch of parsley, chopped
½ teaspoon ground cloves
1 teaspoon ground cinnamon
6 saffron threads soaked in 1 tablespoon boiling
   water
Juice and grated zest of 1 lemon
1 glass white wine
1 onion, finely chopped

Chop the bird joints into bite-sized pieces – a heavy
knife tapped through the bone with a hammer does
the trick.

Heat 2 tablespoons of the lard or oil in a heavy
frying pan. Fry the bread and garlic until both are
golden. Stir in the crushed almonds and let them
roast for a minute. Add the parsley, stir once and
remove from the heat. Transfer the contents of the
pan to a food processor or tip into a mortar. Process
or pound to a thick paste with the spices, saffron
and its soaking water, lemon juice and zest. Dilute
with the wine and reserve.

Reheat the pan, melt the rest of the lard or oil and
fry the turkey pieces and the onion. When the
meat is a little browned and the onions are soft –
after 15 minutes or so – stir in the flavouring paste.
Bring to the boil, cover and turn down the heat.
Simmer gently until the turkey is cooked right
through – 20–30 minutes should suffice. Add a little
more water as the sauce dries out. Serve with
freshly baked coca or bolillos: very dense-crumbed
white rolls, oval in shape, with pointed ends.

llebre amb xocolata
hare with almonds and chocolate

This is a speciality of Ampurias, an island fort in the days of the Romans, now joined to the mainland at a particularly wild and rocky part of the Costa Brava. One of the most famous dishes of the Catalan kitchen, this rich, dark stew is thickened in the Italian manner, with dark chocolate, preferably unsweetened – an ingredient once imported from the New World, which was used first as an enhancement to the blood which thickened the sauces traditionally served with wild meat and then replaced it all together. The recipe works well with all game: partridge, pigeon, rabbit, venison and wild boar. It's good on the first day, even better on the second, and it freezes well.

Serves 4–6

1 hare (about 12 pieces) or 2 rabbits,
2 tablespoons seasoned flour
110g (4oz) tocino or fatty bacon, diced

The summer drought parches the fields near Clariana de Cardener, Catalonia

4 tablespoons olive oil
12 shallots or pickling onions, skinned
1 glass red wine
2 tablespoons crushed, toasted almonds
2 tablespoons crushed, toasted pine-kernels
2 squares or 25g (1oz) black chocolate (at least 70 per cent cocoa solids) or 2 tablespoons unsweetened cocoa powder
Salt and chilli (flakes or a crumbled, de-seeded, dried chilli)

To serve (optional)
Plain-cooked chestnuts

Remove the whitish membrane which covers the hare's saddle and hind legs: use a sharp knife and slip it between the membrane and the flesh. If this is not done, the hare will be tough. Joint it into 12–16 pieces. Rinse, pat dry and dust with the seasoned flour.

In a heavy casserole, melt the tocino or bacon until the fat runs. Add the oil and onions and let them fry gently until they soften and gild. Push them aside, add the pieces of hare and turn them in the hot fat until they seize and brown a little. Pour in the wine and enough water to submerge the joints, bring to the boil, turn down the heat, cover and simmer gently for 30–40 minutes, until the meat is tender and the juices reduced to a cupful. Stir in the nuts and the chocolate or cocoa and cook gently for another 10 minutes, until the sauce is rich and thick. Taste and season with salt and chilli flakes.

This is good with a dish of plain-cooked chestnuts, whole or puréed. Leftovers can be encased in two rounds of coca dough: knead 450g (1lb) flour and a pinch of salt with 2 egg yolks, 2 tablespoons olive oil and enough water to make a soft workable dough, and bake for 40 minutes in a preheated oven at 180°C/350°F/gas mark 4.

leche frita
custard cream fritters

'Fried milk' – more accurately described as custard fritters – is a lovely and unusual dessert popular throughout Spain (though I first tasted it in Barcelona). It is made by egg-and-breadcrumbing a very thick custard. The basic cream can be flavoured with vanilla – use perfumed sugar, vanilla essence or a scraping of vanilla seeds from the pod – or with a curl of lemon or orange zest and a squeeze of the juice. For grownups, a drop of fruit brandy is a good addition: pacharán or whatever you have in the cupboard.

Serves 4–6

600ml (1 pint) milk
25g (1oz) softened butter
50g (2oz) cornflour
1 teaspoon flour
4 tablespoons sugar
1 egg and 4 yolks
Light olive oil, for frying

To coat
2 large eggs
1 tablespoon milk
About 110g (4oz) fine breadcrumbs

To finish
Sugar and ground cinnamon

ut the milk, butter, cornflour, flour, sugar, egg and olks in a liquidiser and process thoroughly or hisk everything thoroughly together by hand. The utter will make the mix seem somewhat lumpy: no atter, it melts down.

eat the mixture gently in a saucepan over a low eat or in a bowl set over gently boiling water. Keep hisking and stirring to prevent it sticking to the ottom. Just before it comes to the boil, turn down e heat and simmer, whisking constantly, until it is ick enough to set when you drop a blob on a cold aucer. If it needs extra thickening, whisk in another vel tablespoon of cornflour slaked in cold milk.

ine a shallow baking tin with clingfilm, or oil ghtly, and pour in a layer of custard as thick as our thumb. Let it cool, then transfer to the fridge to rm (you can pop it in the freezer, if you're in a urry).

hirty minutes before you're ready to fry, cut the ustard into 5cm (2in) squares and prepare the oatings: beat the eggs with the milk in a shallow oup plate and spread the breadcrumbs on another late. Dip the squares in the egg-and-milk to coat hem, then press them gently into the breadcrumbs, naking sure all sides are covered. Check there are o gaps – if there are, repair them with a dab of egg nd a sprinkling of crumbs. Return the coated quares to the fridge to set the jackets.

n a heavy frying pan, heat enough oil to submerge he squares. When it is lightly hazed with blue, arefully fry the squares straight from the fridge, a ew at a time, turning then once. Drain on kitchen aper. Arrange them on a warm plate, sprinkle with ugar and cinnamon and serve immediately. They re delicious with sliced oranges or peaches dressed vith honey.

Still Life with Game Fowl c.1600, by Juan Sánchez Cotán

the catalan tradition

Many have written knowledgeably of the Catalan kitchen, foreigners as well as native-born. Only a Catalan would risk writing a book in his own language with the intention of teaching his grandmother how to cook. But in the wake of the Franco years, Catalan housewives were hard-pressed to remember how granny had actually done it. The gap was filled in 1992 by Josep Lladonosa i Giro with the truly monumental *El gran llibre de la cuina catalana*: although he includes nearly a thousand recipes, the author finds it advisable to apologise for his lack of comprehensivity.

Chef by profession, historian by choice, Lladonosa, mindful of his knowledgeable audience, takes care to edit his recipes into a form which is recognisably Catalan, taking, as he puts it, account of the region's historical evolution, identifying which ingredients can be considered native and which have earned their place more recently, and under what circumstances. In the course of his introduction, he highlights the salsas as the distinguishing factor which separates the cooking of Catalonia from all others. Nor – on the grounds that Catalan cooking has always been open to innovation – does he confine himself to historical recipes. His soffregit includes tomato, and he lists chocolate and dried pimentos (ñoras) as possible inclusions in a picada, a medieval mix which calls for toasted nuts (almonds, hazelnuts, pine kernels are all more or less indigenous) to be pounded with garlic, parsley and olive oil. The picada and the soffregit, he explains, serve as seasonings or flavourings in much the same way as salt and pepper; they can only come with practice: you must cook them again and again, never looking to left or right, till they become second nature, as natural as the crushing of peppercorns or the milling of salt. The other two salsas, samfaina and alioli, he identifies as mixtures which enhance the main ingredients but cannot be counted as flavourings. Samfaina, a pisto-like mix of vegetables, is a sauce in which the main ingredient is finished rather than an integral part of the dish: as in salt-cod with samfaina, frog's legs with samfaina, chicken with samfaina and so on. And although the alioli – an emulsion of raw garlic and olive oil – is sometimes stirred into a stew instead of the picada, it too is basically a dipping sauce, served separately from the main ingredient, as an enhancement. Confused? It comes with the territory.

the basque country

The people of the Pays Vasco, the Basque Country – Euskadi, in the language of its inhabitants – are proud to be who they are, a pride which extends to all aspects of their culture, including what goes on in the kitchen. Geography, too, has made them who they are. This is a region of mountain peaks and inhospitable wildernesses as well as soft green hills with orchards and pastures, which drew its prosperity from the inhabitants' willingness to put to sea in fragile ships. A sea-faring people – a nation which gave its name to the dangerous waters of the Bay of Biscay – filled its cooking pot by tilling the soil, but earned its living from the harvest of the deep. The fishing harbours of Guipuzcoa and Vizcaya – on whose white beaches I spent lazy summers as a child – are dwarfed, in modern times, by one of Spain's great industrial centres, the port and hinterland of Bilbao.

San Sebastian was the summer centre of government in Franco's time, and my family, on diplomatic posting in Madrid in the early 1950s, moved to the seaside town of Zarauz throughout the holidays. My brother and I netted the shallows of the bay for tiny shrimp, *quisquillas*, and searched the tide-pools for greeny-blue swimmer crabs, *necoras*, which have exquisite little lacy-edged flippers. Our mother's cook taught us to eat everything we found, shell and all, salty and crunchy, still warm from the boiling pot. In the evening, exhausted from the day's adventures, we ate spoonfuls of golden apple-jam, *mermelada de manzana*, with *pan perdido*, eggy bread fried in butter and dusted with cinnamon. Soothed by mugs of hot milk sweetened with honey to which the cook, unknown to our mother, had added a few drops of *orujo*, apple brandy, we slept soundly every night.

Houses back onto a river near San Sebastian

Drawing a line between one regional cuisine and another is always a delicate task, and never more so than when a fair part of the population finds itself on a different side of a political border. Some Basques are French, some are Spanish: nevertheless, their ethnic identity is most clearly defined in Spain, where the three Basque provinces of Viscaya, Guipuzco and Alava have achieved regional autonomy, although the capital, Vitoria or Gasteiz, is a city of the plain, surrounded by vast wheatfields which seem to belong more naturally to the plains of Castile. Emotionally and culturally – leaving politics aside – the neighbouring province of Navarra and its capital Pamplona, as well as the regions which form the foothills of the Pyrenees, can be included among the Basques.

The origins of the people remain as mysterious as their language. Comparisons have been drawn between the Euskera, Hungarian and Finnish, though this view has lately been abandoned. Romance aside, all that is known is that a tribe which spoke the language of the Basques settled in and around the Pyrenees *circa* 200BC, and have kept themselves to themselves ever since.

Unlike the rest of Spain, the people of these rocky ramparts (and those of Asturias and Galicia) were never under the Moorish thumb, so there was never a prohibition on the eating of pork. Basque sty-pigs are originally of the Celtic breed brought from Britain, rather than the semi-wild pigs of the Iberian plateau.

In the green hills of the lowlands are to be found cider orchards, lush pastures and vegetable gardens, though an appreciation of greens is of rather more recent date than the traditional taste for root vegetables. While the Basque likes his wine – the whites are drunk young and pétillant (chacolí) and the light Riojas are preferred to the heavier red wines of the south – cider is the national drink. It's bottled up for drinking soon after Christmas, preferably when the moon is on the wane – a time of diminished activity in the barrel as well as all other things affected by the pull of the tide. Those used to the drier, flatter ciders of Asturias and Galicia will find the Basque version sweetish and very fizzy. You can sample it in the cidrerías, along with a chance to taste the juicy pork products characteristic of apple country.

There is a taste for beef, as always in dairy country. Eating-places off the beaten track are the caserios, farmhouses converted into rustic restaurants, serving hearty dishes such as estofado de rabo de buey, oxtail stew; and huge steaks on the bone, chuletón de buey – meat which traditionally came from the oxen which worked the fields and were at the end of their useful life. And every town has its asadores, restaurants specialising in grilled meat. The haricot beans of the New World were widely accepted as soon as they arrived, replacing the fava and chestnuts of the pre-Columban diet. Rojas, the red kidney beans of Tolosa, go into soups enriched with pork belly and flavoured with white leeks. Pochas, tender white haricot beans picked before they are completely ripe, are cooked with woodland game such as pigeons and partridges. The Basques take their wild foods – particularly mushrooms – very seriously indeed. Around thirty separate edible species of fungi are gathered, many of them avoided elsewhere. Basque cooks use four times as much parsley as those of any other Spanish region: you'll see big

The church bell-tower dominates the village of Otxandio

bunches of it on sale on the market, often prettily tied with ribbon. Much of it goes to make salsa verde, a delicate emulsion of olive oil and garlic coloured and flavoured with parsley, served with fish and shellfish all along the coast. Desserts are homely farmhouse fare, nothing flighty or Moorish: rice puddings, custard tarts, mamia – fresh curd cheese eaten with honey.

'The Basques are different,' explained food writer Samuel Chamberlain from a French perspective in 1952. 'They play pelota from childhood. They write romantic poems and indulge in vivacious native dances...Nearly everyone in the Basque country is a gourmet according to his means, and the farmer in the hillside chalet is just as particular about his fare as is the chatelain in Pau. This tradition springs from rich resources: the good earth and sea are kind.'

piperrada
peppers and tomatoes with eggs

A juicy combination of eggs and sunny summer vegetables, one of the world's classic dishes. The vegetables can be prepared ahead, reheated, and the eggs stirred in at the last minute. Aubergines and courgettes are sometimes included among the vegetables.

Serves 4 as a tapa, 1 as a main dish

4 tablespoons olive oil
2 garlic cloves, skinned and finely sliced
1 mild Spanish onion, diced
1 green pepper, de-seeded and finely sliced
1 red pepper, de-seeded and finely sliced
1 tablespoon chopped serrano ham (optional)
2 large ripe tomatoes, scalded, skinned and diced
Salt and pepper
3–4 free-range eggs

Heat the oil in a tortilla or omelette pan. Turn the garlic, onion and peppers in the hot oil until they soften – but don't let them take colour. Add the ham, if using, and the tomatoes and let it all bubble up to make a thick sauce. Season with salt and pepper. Mix the eggs with a fork – don't overmix – and stir them into the vegetables. Don't stir again. Remove from the heat as soon as the eggs are softly set.

gambas al ajillo
prawns in garlic and oil

One of the greatest pleasures of the tapa table, this mouthwateringly simple dish is stimulating to the eye as well as to the palate, and worth preparing only if the prawns are perfectly fresh and raw. It's also known as gambas pilpil, possibly for the little popping noise the oil makes as it heats up the fish. The trick is not to overheat the oil or overcook the prawns. Tapa bars which specialise in the preparation serve it in shallow earthenware with small wooden forks so that customers do not burn their tongues. Crab is also excellent prepared in this way, though it needs an extra splash of sherry or brandy to keep it moist.

Serves 4 as a tapa

225g (8oz) perfectly fresh small prawns
2–3 tablespoons olive oil
1 garlic clove, skinned and sliced
2–3 small dried red chilli peppers, de-seeded and left whole
Salt

Peel the prawns, removing the heads but leaving on the tails (or not, as you please).

Heat the oil in a small shallow casserole, either on top of the stove or in the oven. When the oil is warm but has not yet reached frying temperature, add the garlic, prawns and chilli peppers and heat until the prawns turn opaque. Serve as soon as the oil is bubbling, in their cooking dish, with enough bread to mop up all the delicious oil.

navajas con salsa verde
razor-shells with green sauce

A vinaigrette coloured and flavoured with parsley is the automatic accompaniment for fish throughout the region. Here, as I remember it from childhood holidays in what was at the time the little fishing village of Zarauz, it's served with razor-shells opened on the grill. The recipe works just as well for any species of bivalve: scallops, mussels, clams.

Serves 2–4 (depending on appetites)

12 razor-shells

The sauce
2–3 tablespoons chopped flat-leaf parsley
2–3 spring onions or young leeks, finely chopped
1 garlic clove, skinned and finely chopped
1 tablespoon vinegar or lemon juice
4 tablespoons olive oil
1 green chilli, finely chopped (optional)
Salt

Soak the razor-shells in cold water for an hour or two so that they spit out any sand – this should be done whichever bivalve you use. If your choice is mussels, don't scrape off the little hank of beard until just before you're ready to cook.

Mix the sauce ingredients and set aside for an hour or two to blend the flavours.

Heat a griddle or heavy iron frying pan until very hot. Place the shellfish on the hot surface and wait until they open in their own steam. Remove them immediately from the heat. Serve with the sauce.

caballa en escabeche
vinegar-pickled mackerel

When a fishing fleet finds a shoal of mackerel, it catches them by the boatful – presenting, in pre-refrigeration days, a storage problem. Pickle-baths were a way not only to conserve the catch for a few extra days, but also to add variety to the diet.

Serves 6 as a tapa

900g (2lb) mackerel (or sardines, anchovies or small bream)
3 heaped tablespoons flour
1 tablespoon pimentón (Spanish paprika)
1 teaspoon sea salt
3 tablespoons olive oil
1/2 mild Spanish onion, finely sliced
2 garlic cloves, skinned and cut in slivers
1 carrot, scraped and sliced
2 tablespoons chopped flat-leaf parsley
1 teaspoon dried oregano
1 bay leaf, crumbled
1/2 teaspoon crushed peppercorns
5 tablespoons vinegar

Gut, dehead and rinse the fish and chop straight through the bone to give 3–4 thick cutlets per fish. Sift the flour with the pimentón and salt onto a plate. Flip the cutlets through the flour.

Meanwhile, heat the oil in a large frying pan. When a faint blue haze rises, add the fish and fry until golden, turning to make sure all sides feel the heat. Don't overcook: the fish should still be firm. Transfer the cutlets to a shallow dish. Fry the onion and garlic gently in the oil that remains in the pan (add a little more if you need it). When they soften and gild a little, add the carrot, chopped parsley, oregano, bay, pepper, vinegar and 3 tablespoons water and let bubble up for 3–4 minutes, scraping to mix in all the bits that have stuck to the pan. Pour over the fish. Cover loosely and leave overnight in a cool place. It's ready to eat in a day, and even better in three.

txangurro al horno
crab with leeks and parsley baked in the oven

The Basques are less enthusiastic about the common crab than they are about the spider crab (*txangurro*), a crustacean caught in large numbers off the coast of Guipuzcoa as well as all round the coasts of Europe. Spider crabs, as their name suggests, are spiky-bodied, long-legged creatures which lack well-developed claws, making them unappealing to those who don't know how good they taste. The white meat – there's no brown – takes patience to pick, being hidden in the body and the long legs. Naturally, the dish can be made with the meat of the clawed or common crab, ready prepared or still in the shell. Allow one medium-sized crustacean per person, ready boiled, as the meat needs to cool and set before it can be extracted. Pick the meat out yourself – you'll need the carapaces.

Serves 4

4 whole ready-cooked crabs
8 tablespoons olive oil
4 tablespoons butter
2 medium onions, finely chopped
2 medium leeks, white only, finely chopped
450g (1lb) tomatoes (fresh or canned)
2 tablespoons brandy
1 tablespoon chopped tarragon (optional)
Salt and pepper
2 tablespoons fresh breadcrumbs
2 tablespoons chopped parsley

Pick all the meat out of the crabs – from the legs and carapaces – and save any liquor from the shells.

Heat the oil with half the butter in a frying pan. Add the onions and leeks and cook gently until soft and golden. Add the tomatoes (if using fresh, scald, skin and chop them first) and simmer until well reduced and thickened. Stir in the crabmeat and any juice and turn everything together over the heat. When it's bubbling, pour on the brandy, set a match to it and stand well back – the flames will burn off the alcohol and caramelise the crabmeat a little. Stir in the tarragon, then taste and add salt and pepper.

Pack the mixture into the crab shells, sprinkle with breadcrumbs mixed with parsley, dot with the remaining butter and bake in a hot oven for 15–20 minutes, until brown and merrily bubbling.

Boats moored in the harbour at San Sebastián

marmita-kua
tunafish and potato casserole

This fisherman's one-pot stew – one of those dishes which takes its name from the container in which it's cooked – is so much a part of Basque culture that the *sociedades gastronomicas*, men-only cooking clubs, organise annual competitions to find the best recipe. Innovation is acceptable, provided the basic rules are followed. Garlic is sometimes added, as are green peppers, and some people favour placing a slice of bread in the plate before ladling in the fish and potatoes.

Serves 4 as a main dish

900g (2lb) tunafish (bonito, for preference), cut
  into bite-sized pieces
Salt
1 wine glass olive oil
2 mild red onions, finely sliced
2–3 large, ripe tomatoes, scalded, skinned and
  chopped
1 tablespoon pimentón (Spanish paprika)
900g (2lb) yellow-fleshed potatoes, peeled and cut
  into bite-sized chunks

To finish
4 thick slices of country bread

Salt the tuna and set aside.

Heat the oil in a cooking pot and add the onions. Let them sizzle gently until they soften and gild but don't let them burn. Add the tomatoes and pimentón and let them bubble up. Add the potatoes, turn them in the oily juices, and add just enough cold water to submerge everything. Bring slowly to the boil and cook, loosely covered, until the potatoes are tender but hold their shape – about 20 minutes. Add the tuna, bring to the boil and then turn down the heat. Lid loosely and cook for a further 5–6 minutes – no more or the fish will toughen. Serve in shallow soup plates, with bread.

chipirones en su tinta
cuttlefish in their own ink

In this classic dish of the Pays Vasco, the two smaller cephalopods – cuttlefish and squid (the octopus is also a member of the cephalopod family) – are cooked with their own ink. You can buy the creatures ready prepared with their ink saved in a little plastic bag. The squid has a pointed, cone-like body supported by a transparent bone which looks like clear plastic, while the cuttlefish is rounder-bodied and darker in colour, with a porous white bone, nature's toothpowder, much appreciated by canaries. Cuttle ink is splendidly black – a kind of oceanic soot which dyes everything it touches and is used to make Chinese black ink. It has a delicate flavour, a little like violets, not particularly fishy, which makes the effort of collecting it worthwhile.

Serves 4 as a main dish, 8 as a tapa

900g (2lb) small cuttlefish or squid, with their ink
8 tablespoons olive oil
2 onions, chopped
2 cloves garlic, skinned and chopped
450g (1lb) tomatoes, scalded, skinned and chopped
  – canned are fine
2 tablespoons fresh breadcrumbs
2 tablespoons chopped parsley
Salt and pepper

To prepare the cuttlefish yourself, wash them thoroughly – cephalopods are sandy creatures. Pull the tentacles and innards, including the flat piece of bone-like cuttle, away from the body. Look for the silvery ink-sacs among the innards. Break the sacs into a small sieve placed over a bowl and reserve the inky liquid. It doesn't matter if you can't find all the sacs: 1 or 2 are quite enough to turn the dish midnight black.

Discard all but the bodies and tentacles. Chop the tentacles into small pieces and use them to stuff the hollowed out bodies.

Heat the oil in a heavy sauté pan. Add the onions and garlic and fry gently until they soften. Add the tomatoes. Let the mixture bubble up and cook to a thick sauce. Place the stuffed cuttlefish in the sauce, cover and poach gently until the cuttlefish are soft, adding a little water as necessary so that the juices do not dry out. This will take 20–30 minutes. Remove the cuttlefish to a warm plate while you finish the sauce.

Mash up the ink with the breadcrumbs and parsley. Off the heat stir the ink mixture into the tomato sauce – some people push the sauce through a sieve first – or put all the sauce ingredients into a liquidiser and process to a smooth black purée before returning the sauce to the pan. Lay in the cuttlefish. Reheat gently, allowing one big 'belch'. Taste and add salt and pepper.

fishermen of the basque country

The Basques are traditionally a sea-going people, providing many of the sailors on Columbus's ships. There's good evidence to suggest that their whaling ships and those following the cod migrations made landfall in the New World long before Castilian galleons were launched into the setting sun. The whalers as well as the merchantmen were provisioned with salt cod, *bacalao*, a foodstuff which, in spite of the introduction of refrigeration as a more convenient means of preservation, remains firmly on the Basque menu. Of the many hundreds of salt-cod dishes, the most characteristic is bacalao a la viscaina, a dish which, by combining salt cod with salt bacon, leeks and parsley, delivers all the flavours of traditional Basque cuisine. As the cod stocks diminished, Basque fishermen turned their attentions to hake which, when caught in the cold waters of the Bay of Biscay, is small and firm-fleshed, and provides one of the most characteristic Basque dishes, kokotxas. These are the fatty flaps under the fish's chin, a rare treat when cooked *al pil-pil* – in an earthenware dish set over a high flame, shaken vigorously so that the little morsels produce their own creamy sauce.

All the larger towns have restaurants which specialise in salt-cod dishes, delivering an atmosphere in which, to put it delicately, the sailor is home from the sea. The sea-faring theme is highlighted in the annual competitions the men-only cooking clubs, *sociedades gastronómicas*, organise to find the best marmita-kua, a fisherman's stew of very ancient provenance indeed, for all that it now contains the New World's potatoes.

Though of recent years many have of the sociedades have chosen to open their doors to women, the men traditionally gathered together to cook for each other. These fraternal gatherings, while stimulating innovation, provide a forum for teaching the old ways, a pattern common among sea-going communities who seek to recreate the camaraderie of shipboard by preparing the dishes the sailors cooked for themselves. While some will tell you they joined the sociedad

because their women wouldn't let them cook in their own kitchens, the culinary ethos is competitive, much as in a restaurant kitchen. The Basques' reputation for good food is rivalled only by their reputation as stupendous trenchermen, a happy combination which has resulted in more starred restaurants (and famous chefs) than in any other region.

Fishing boats, San Sebastián

bacalao a la viscaina
salt-cod with salt-pork, leeks and parsley

The traditional flavours of the Basque kitchen all in one pot. If salt-cod is hard to obtain – or, more likely, prohibitively expensive – use any fresh white fish, filleted and skinned, and add a shake of anchovy sauce or a couple of canned anchovies to bring up the flavour.

Serves 4

450g (1lb) salt-cod (dried weight), soaked in several changes of water for 48 hours
4 tablespoons olive oil
4 leeks, finely sliced
4 garlic cloves, skinned and sliced
4 large potatoes, peeled and diced
1/4–1/2 teaspoon roughly crushed peppercorns
1 bay leaf

The viscaina sauce

110g (4oz) salt-pork belly or unsmoked streaky bacon, diced
2 large Spanish onions or 2 leeks, finely sliced
4 tablespoons olive oil
4 dried red peppers, de-seeded and torn, or 4 tablespoons pimentón (Spanish paprika)
4 tablespoons chopped parsley
Yolks of 2 hardboiled eggs, mashed

Put the soaked salt-cod in a large saucepan with enough water to cover generously, bring to the boil, skim, turn down the heat and simmer gently for 10 minutes. With a draining spoon, transfer the fish to a sieve and reserve the broth. Carefully skin and bone the fish, leaving the pieces as whole as possible.

Heat the oil in the pan and gently fry the leeks and garlic for 10 minutes – don't let them take colour. Pour in the fish broth, bring to the boil and add the potatoes, peppercorns and bay leaf. Bring back to the boil, turn down the heat and simmer for 15–20 minutes, until the potatoes are tender.

Meanwhile, make the sauce. Put the pork or bacon, onions or leeks, oil and peppers or pimentón in a small pan with a ladleful of the fish stock and leave to cook very gently for 40–50 minutes, until the onions are perfectly soft and the water has evaporated. Stir in the parsley and mashed egg yolk.

Return the salt-cod to the pan with the potatoes and allow to reheat in the steam. Serve in deep soup plates, with the sauce handed around separately – or add it to the stew, as you please.

codornices a la bilbaina
quails with parsley and garlic

Farmed quail are a succulent, ecologically acceptable replacement for chimbos – little songbirds of every kind – which were once the main ingredient in this recipe from Bilbao. Quails being relatively large (more than a single mouthful), they cook more evenly and quickly when spatchcocked: split right down the back and flattened. The Basques like the taste of butter in their cooking. When it is used for frying, as here, the inclusion of oil allows a higher temperature without danger of burning.

Serves 4 as a main course, 8 as a tapa

4 tablespoons butter
4 tablespoons oil
8 quail, spatchcocked (split in half right down the back)
8 tablespoons fresh breadcrumbs
2 garlic cloves, skinned and chopped
8 tablespoons chopped parsley (lots)

Heat the butter and oil in a sauté pan or heavy frying pan. Lay in the spatchcocked birds – spread out like flattened frogs – and fry them gently, turning once, until they are golden brown all over and cooked right through: 10–15 minutes. They're done when the juices run clear – a skewer pushed through the thigh will tell you all you need to know.

Take out the birds and transfer to a warm serving plate. Reheat the drippings in the pan and stir in the breadcrumbs, garlic and parsley. Allow them to fry and crisp a little – a couple of minutes, stirring with a spoon – but take care they don't burn. Top the birds with the crisp breadcrumbs. Eat with your fingers.

mermelada de manzanas con canela
apple marmalade with cinnamon

A thick, soft apple purée, whose sweetness comes from a handful of raisins or sultanas without the need for additional sugar – perfect for babies and children. To store, seal the marmalade in a well-rinsed jar and sterilise for about 30 minutes in a bain-marie in a medium oven – 170°C/325°F/gas mark 3 – until you can see bubbles forming. Or freeze. Pan perdido (see right) makes an excellent tart filling.

Serves 4

900g (2lb) eating apples, peeled, cored and cut
  into chunks
2 tablespoons raisins or sultanas
1 small cinnamon stick
3–4 cloves

Bring the fruit to the boil in a saucepan with a splash of water and the cinnamon and cloves (tie the spices in a scrap of muslin). Turn down the heat and let it bubble gently for about 30 minutes, until thick and jammy. Remove the spices. You can pot it up in clean jars rinsed out with apple brandy to sterilise, or serve it warm from the pan.

pan perdido con canela
eggy bread with cinnamon

Bread fingers are dunked in beaten egg and fried crisp. Particularly good with thick drinking chocolate for breakfast.

Serves 4

1 egg
2–3 tablespoons milk
1 teaspoon sugar
4–8 slices day-old bread (with or without crusts)
25g (1oz) butter
1 tablespoon oil

To finish
Ground cinnamon
Sugar

Mix the egg with the milk and sugar and soak the bread fingers for 10 minutes or so. Heat the butter and oil in a small frying pan. Fry the fingers, turning once, until crisp. Sprinkle with cinnamon and extra sugar for the pleasure of the crunch.

pastel vasco con guinda
cream cake with sour cherries

A sophisticated layering of buttery shortcake and creamy custard all baked together to make a soft-hearted dessert. The optional flavouring of pacharán, the Basque version of sloe gin (see p.97) underlines the flavour of the equally optional guindas: wild cherries, little scarlet fruits much loved by birds, which are an indigenous crop free for the gathering in early summer. Fresh red cherries, pitted, can substitute.

Serves 6–8

The shortcake
Handful wild cherries, pitted and soaked in 1
  tablespoon pacharán
Beaten egg, for brushing
350g (12 oz) plain flour
1/2 teaspoon salt
1 whole egg and 2 yolks
200g (7oz) caster sugar
200g (7oz) butter, chopped small
Juice and finely grated zest of 1 lemon

The custard
225 ml (8fl oz) creamy milk
Seeds from a short vanilla pod
2 egg yolks
2 tablespoons castor sugar
1 tablespoon plain flour

To finish
Icing sugar

First make the custard – it needs time to cool. Put all the ingredients in a liquidiser and process until well blended, or whisk everything together until smooth. Heat gently in a heavy pan, whisking steadily. As soon as it comes to the boil, remove, and allow to cool. Fold in the cherries and pacharán.

Preheat the oven to 180°C/350°F/gas mark 4.

Sift the flour with the salt. Make a well in the middle and drop in the rest of the shortcake ingredients. Work it all together with your hand – the warmth will melt the butter and assist the blending – or drop everything in a processor and mix to a soft, smooth dough. Cover and leave to rest in a cool place for 30 minutes.

Butter a 20cm (8in) cake tin and line it with baking parchment.

Press two thirds of the dough into the base of the tin. Spread the custard over the dough, leaving an edge as broad as your thumb. Pat out the rest of the dough to make a lid and place it over the filling. Brush with a little beaten egg and bake for 50–60 minutes, until nicely browned. Dust with icing sugar. .

galicia, asturias & cantabria

Geography and latitude – 'the last wind-beaten ridges of the Pyrenees sinking gently along a deeply digitated coast', as one traveller described the landscape – dictate the

domestic habit of Spain's northwesterly provinces. The harvest of the sea is supplemented with excellent beef, veal, dairy products and vegetables from the lush, rain-sodden interior.

The traditional grain foods, barley and rye, suitable for porridges and griddlecakes though not for yeast-raised breads, were replaced as winter fodder for man and beast by the New World's maize. This, along with potatoes – a miracle crop which required very little land and even less labour – was ideal for the *minifundios*, the region's independent smallholding peasantry. The northern bean-pot includes red beans and green flageolets as well as particularly succulent varieties of the white beans popular in the rest of Spain. Pasties and pies – large empanadas and fist-sized empanadillas – reflect the traditional Celtic skill with a rolling-pin.

A common larder, shared landscape and similar climate ensure that the same raw materials – fish, dairy, upland grains, pulses combined with pork products – are prepared to more or less the same recipes throughout the region. There is nevertheless an awareness of where the dishes were originally conceived: pulpo a la gallega – octopus with pimentón – is firmly identified as a Galician dish, though it's equally enjoyed in Cantabria and Asturias. Empanadas de atún – double-crusted rectangular tunafish pies – though Asturian, are nonetheless to be found in Galicia and Cantabria.

Galicia has always been a place apart. While the inhabitants of Cantabria and Asturias would count themselves as Latins, the Galicians, culturally and emotionally, as their name indicates, know

themselves to be Celts, even though their language is of Roman origin. Nevertheless, political ties with Asturias are strong: Galicia was integrated into the principality of Asturias at a time when the rest of Spain was under the Moors and the region served as the last redoubt of Christianity south of the Pyrenees. Her precipitous coastline curves from the Bay of Biscay round to the Atlantic, with Vigo as the main port and the headland of Finisterre marking what was, for many centuries, the end of the known world. Inland is cattle-country with lush pastures, forest and mountain sheltering isolated communities with a tradition of hospitality to travellers – though only if they come unarmed.

Three major ports serve the population of this most remote corner of the peninsula as a window on the wider world: Santander, though well-known to visitors from Britain as a ferry terminal, serves as a container port handling much of the trade with Europe; La Coruña grew prosperous on the New World interchange; Vigo remains Spain's most important deep-sea fishing harbour and serves the sardine-canning industry. When traveller Mrs. Gascoigne Hartley paid a visit to a sardine cannery in the early 1900s, she found the female workers remarkably well provided-for: 'I was glad to learn that both the women and men are well-paid and that there is no separation between the tasks allotted to the two sexes, capacity alone dictating the kind of work done. What I chiefly remember was the fine appearance of the women. Many of them are mothers, and there is an admirable crèche in connection with the sardine factories where their children are cared for. The workrooms open directly onto the bay; here the boats come, the fish are landed and the silver heaps are washed. The airy rooms were scarcely redolent even of fish; and the most scrupulous cleanliness was evident.'

Throughout the northern territories, the sense of self-worth which led to such a surprisingly modern approach to employment comes partly from a tradition of self-sufficiency, partly from an outward-poking culture developed and refined over the centuries through contact with the outside world. Though the links can partly be explained by proximity – fishermen who trawl the same fishing grounds, farmers who take their produce to the same markets – an even stronger thread joins one community to its neighbour, the well-worn pilgrim route to Santiago de Compostela which, for more than a thousand years, has ranked with Jerusalem and Rome as one of the three holiest places in Christendom. The towns and villages along the route – and there are many – discharge their obligations to God and His pilgrims by offering hospitality. This, usually modest and often church-sponsored, gave many an opportunity to exchange news from elsewhere, a precious commodity in the days when all information came as word-of-mouth. The pilgrims' routes are well defined: ancient pathways easily recognisable from the sign of the scallop, the pilgrim shell, which appears on buildings as well as on marker-stones and road signs along the way.

The Pilgrimage to the Basque Country, twentieth century, by José Arrué

The heartland of Asturias – a title of enough political importance to serve the heir to the Spanish throne – is the mountainous wilderness known as the Picos de Europa. It was from here that the armies of the Reconquista were launched. Sparsely inhabited, with lush green valleys watered by soft white mists, the foothills of the Picos tumble into the sea, leaving a narrow coastal strip along which fishing communities (and tourists) huddle round a few picturesque manmade harbours.

Around Eastertime, the land is a patchwork of black earth and emerald pastures in which contented brown cows suckle their curly-headed calves. Round the sprawling stone-build farmhouses, apple trees are bowed with blossom, humming with bees. Each farmhouse has a huerta – kitchen garden – protected by a low wall of unmortared stone in which the leeks and cabbages of winter give way to the beans, peppers and tomatoes of high summer. Further up the valleys, broad swathes of pine and chestnut forest provide cover for game. Towering above are the peaks themselves, snow-capped throughout the year.

The inhabitants, mostly subsistence farmers, earn a modest income from the dairy industry, but still grow their own vegetables, crop

their own orchards and keep a household pig for the winter store-cupboard. Little wine is produced, but the region's apple-orchards provide excellent cider which is given its sparkle in the way it's poured: from a great height into straight-sided tumblers made of remarkably delicate glass.

Some still make cheese – particularly Cabrales, Spain's most famous blue – for sale in the village stores. But most, defeated by regulations or simply unable to spend the time, send the milk directly to the central creamery for bottling and butter-making. In Franco's time this was exclusively under the name of La Asturiana, forever associating the dairy industry with the region.

To the east of Asturias lies the autonomous region of Cantabria. Here the surviving inshore fishing fleets land a rich haul from the cold waters of the Bay of Biscay: hake, tuna, cuttlefish, flat-fish, squid. Behind the coast, the land is well watered and fertile, with pastures for dairy and beef cattle, stretches of forested hills to shelter game, numerous rivers and streams where salmon and trout can be caught – though these, as everywhere, are much depleted. The rivers and their wetlands are also the source of Cantabria's main claim to culinary distinction, *angulas* – elvers, baby eels no longer than a darning-needle, the caviar of the tapa table.

caldereta gallega
galician fish soup

The caldereta is an all-in fisherman's soup which takes the name of the pot in which it cooks. This is the way they like to cook it in Galicia. The fish varies according to the catch: candidates for inclusion are those which have little commercial value – too small, too bony, too fiddly to prepare, too few in number to be worth marketing. Among these are baby *salmonete* (red mullet), *nécoras*, *chopos* and *santiaguinos* (local varieties of crab), *cigalas* (crayfish), *camarones* (shrimp), *rape* (monkfish), *merluza* (hake), *calamar* and *sepia* (squid, cuttlefish), *mariscos* (shellfish), *centolla* (spider crab), *mero* (black grouper) and *lenguado* (sole).

Serves 4

1.35kg (3lb) whole small fish, shellfish (shucked, meat only), crustaceans, cephalopods
Salt
4 tablespoons olive oil
2 large onions, finely sliced
1 tablespoon chopped parsley
1 tablespoon pimentón (Spanish paprika)
1/2 teaspoon crushed peppercorns

To finish
1 glass white wine
Freshly grated nutmeg
1 dried chilli, de-seeded and torn

Rinse the fish, slice any which are larger than bite-size – most can go in whole – salt lightly and transfer to a roomy pot with the rest of the ingredients. Leave everything to marinate for an hour.

Add enough water to submerge everything to a depth of one finger's width. Bring gently to the boil, allow one big 'belch', then add the finishing wine, a pinch of nutmeg and the chilli. Cover, and simmer gently for 20 minutes. Taste and correct the seasoning.

You can serve the soup as it is and allow your guests to negotiate the bones. Or you can tip the contents of the pan into a large sieve set over a bowl to catch the broth and return the visible pieces of fish, shellfish and crustacean meat to the broth, discarding the bones. Press the debris in the sieve to extract the remaining broth. Reheat to just below boiling and serve poured over slices of dry bread. Or cook a few slices of potato in the strained broth before you return the solids.

~ieras de vigo
grilled scallops

~r this simple little dish, buy your scallops live
~d in the shell. Failing scallops, oysters will do.

~rves 6 as a tapa, 2 as a starter

~ medium scallops
~ tablespoon chopped parsley
~ garlic clove, skinned and finely chopped
~lt and pepper
~ tablespoons fresh breadcrumbs
~ nugget of butter
~ pinch of clove (the little buds crumble quite
~ easily)

~reheat the grill. Open the scallops – shove a
~ort, strong knife between the two shells and
~ver them open – trim off the frill (the creature's
~yes) and slip the knife between the muscle and
~e shell, taking care not to break the bright
~range roe. Remove the little sandy digestive sac
~nd dice the rest, leaving the roe whole. Fold the
~callop meat and roe with the parsley and garlic,
~eason with salt and pepper and divide the
~ixture between the deeper of the shells. Finish
~ith a sprinkling of breadcrumbs, a dot of butter
~nd the merest hint of clove – crumble the little
~ud at the tip, reserving the nail for another
~ecipe.

~op under the grill until the breadcrumbs crisp.
~lternatively bake in a preheated oven at
~80˚C/350˚F/gas mark 4.

almejas en vino
clams cooked in wine

Dozens of different bivalves – scallops, oysters and
mussels, as well as the full complement of clams –
are found on Iberian shores. While the larger ones
are either eaten raw or opened briefly on the grill,
the smaller varieties are usually opened in a
loosely covered frying pan with a splash of wine
and enough olive oil to make a little sauce. The
most prized of these smaller shellfish (with a price
to match) are the creamy, orange-fleshed *conchas
finas* – also known as *almendras de mar*, sea-
almonds, for their shape and for the porcelain-
smoothness of the purple-tinged shell. The oddest
are the deliciously sea-juiced but weird-looking
razor-shells, sold in bundles in the markets,
spilling tubular protuberances of a startlingly
gynaecological colour and shape.

Serves 4

900g (2lb) clams, cockles, or mussels (live in shells)
2 tablespoons olive oil
2 garlic cloves, skinned and finely chopped
1 glass white wine
a handful of parsley, finely chopped

Wash the shellfish in plenty of cold water, checking
over and discarding any broken or filled with sand.

Put the oil to heat in a well-tempered, shallow,
earthenware casserole or roomy frying pan. When
lightly hazed with blue, sprinkle in the garlic and
allow it to soften a little. Add the wine and parsley
and let it boil for a couple of minutes to evaporate
the alcohol. Add the shellfish, cover with a lid and
turn up the heat, shaking or stirring to redistribute
the shells so that all have a chance to cook. If you
have no lid, keep them moving with a spoon. It will
take 3–4 minutes for all the shells to pop open.

When all are ready, remove from the heat and serve
immediately. Don't overcook or the scraps of flesh
will toughen. Don't reheat – they're just as good cold.

sepia con pochas
cuttlefish with white beans

The Cantabrian combination of cuttlefish with white beans is unusual but delicious; you'll find a similar dish in Cadiz in southern Andalusia, where it's usually made with fava rather than white beans. The combination works equally well with squid. You can tell the difference between cuttlefish and squid quite easily on the slab: cuttlefish are round-bodied and their 'bone' is a chalky wedge of softish material much appreciated by caged birds; the squid has a longer, cone-shaped body and its 'bone' looks as if it's made of clear plastic and is pretty indestructable. Generically, the cuttlefish is a smaller creature – though you can have large examples of one and small of the other.

Serves 4

450g (1lb) cuttlefish (or squid)
2 tablespoons olive oil
2 garlic cloves, skinned and sliced
225g (8oz) large plump dried haricot or butter
  beans, soaked overnight
1 wine glass white wine
1 teaspoon crumbled dried oregano or marjoram
Salt and pepper

Rinse the cuttlefish, taking out the chalky cuttle and soft innards and separating the tentacles and body. If the cuttlefish are large, you'll need to scrape the spiky little toenails off the tentacles. Discard the innards and the eyes and chop up the rest, including the body. Squid should be treated in the same way.

Put a shallow heat-proof earthenware casserole or a heavy frying pan on to heat gently with the oil. Add the garlic and let it soften. Slip in the cuttlefish and leave to cook gently in the oil until it yields up its own juices – about 10 minutes.

Add the beans (drain them first), the wine and the same volume of water and let it all bubble up. Sprinkle in the oregano or marjoram, season, put the lid on and leave to cook gently for 20 minutes or so, until the cuttlefish is tender. Remove the lid, turn up the heat and let it bubble fiercely for a moment or two, until the juices and the oil emulsify and form a pale, creamy sauce – miraculous, really.

pulpo gallego
octopus with olive oil and pimentón

The best and simplest way to prepare octopus, served from bubbling cauldrons at every public celebration from Finesterre to Santander, but most particularly a speciality of the fishing communities of Galicia. Dried octopus – sold as a leathery tangle of suckered arms which needs soaking in several changes of fresh water for at least 48 hours – is prepared in the same way. You need a whole octopus. A larger one will do if that's what happens to be available, but remember to allow proportionately longer cooking.

Serves 6–8 as a tapa

1 small octopus, about 900g (2lb)

The sauce:
2–3 garlic cloves, skinned and finely sliced
1 teaspoon salt
6 tablespoons olive oil

To finish
Pimentón (Spanish paprika), for sprinkling

Pop your octopus in the freezer for 48 hours to tenderise – a lot easier on the biceps than beating it on the rocks, a task which any self-respecting octopus fisherman takes great pride in performing, as well as describing, for the passing tourist.

Once your octopus has been suitably tenderised, bring a pan of unsalted water to the boil. Dip the creature in the boiling water three times, removing it and bringing the water back to the boil each time (as tradition requires). Bring the water back to the boil, pop in the octopus, put the lid on loosely, turn down the heat and simmer until tender. Small octopus takes about 2 hours to soften – the only state in which an octopus can be pleasurably consumed – large ones up to 4 hours.

pulpo gallego

In the early 1950s, at a time when few tourists had discovered the joys of sunshine and Spanish beaches, traveller Nina Epton appreciated the octopus as served to the horse-traders at the festival of St James at Compostela during the last week of July:

'The horse fair is a traditional part of St James' fiesta, and the pulpo, or hot squid, is the traditional adjunct of every fiesta in Galicia. Let the fastidious make all the grimaces they will! If you have not yet tasted purple, pustular, leathery pulpo under the sweet-scented pine-trees, accompanied by an earthenware bowl of rough red wine, then you have missed one of the good things of life in summertime Galicia. You should not be deterred by the velvety black exterior of the dented petrol tins steaming away like witches' cauldrons under the crackling wood fires, the pliant tentacles of the squids as they curl delicately inwards, or by the stern looks of the tough peasant women who stir the bubbling pan with a knobbly twig. Have patience. Sit down if you like on that bench by the long trestle table beside those cunning dealers who have just been putting the horses through their paces. Your pulpo will be served cut up into tiny pieces (the flesh is blue-white like lobster's under a delicate violet skin) upon a large white plate. Here is a toothpick to eat it with, and your bowl of wine…'

Meanwhile, make the sauce by blending all the ingredients in a mortar or food processor.

Drain the octopus and turn it inside out, removing the innards and the sharp beak-like mouth. Don't skin it – the soft purple veil that protects the creamy flesh is a sign the octopus was fresh when it went into the pot – just slice into bite-sized pieces. Arrange the slices on a wooden board or plate – the porous surface absorbs residual moisture – and dress with the sauce and the pimentón, handing round a dish of salt separately.

Serve at room temperature, never chilled or straight from the pot. Octopus meat is dense and rich: if it's served too cold the flavour's ruined, too hot and your digestion will suffer. Once dressed with oil (save the pimentón for finishing or the colour will leach), it keeps for a week under wraps in the fridge – convenient if your octopus was on the large side.

tortos de maíz con huevos y chorizo
cornmeal crispbreads with eggs and chorizo

Everything on the table is produced in house, says Aurina, chef-proprietor of the Bar Xich in the little village of Mestas de Ardisana in the foothills of the Picos de Europa, who serves her famous tortos with eggs and chorizo. The family has enough land to grow maize as well as to pasture a few cows – milk is the family's cash crop, as is usual in the Picos. The whey left over from the butter and cheese-making goes to feed the household porker; the hams are salt-cured for winter; the rest of the meat is used to make her own excellent chorizos, which are hung in the chimney to take the smoke; and the plentiful lard goes to enrich a maize-meal sausage, which she serves with tender green haricot beans – *habas verdes* – a catch-crop between the maize stalks. There are apples and beehives in the orchard, vegetables in the garden and trout in the stream. Leftover tortos go to the chickens, which lay double-yolked eggs of an astonishingly vibrant gold. Neat? Of course. Cabrales, the cheese, is wrapped in leaves – chestnut or maple – and aged in much the same way as Stilton. Brussels has decreed it must be wrapped in tinfoil, for reasons of health and safety, when sold commercially – a decision that comes as something of a surprise to those who've been wrapping it in leaves for at least five hundred years.

Makes 6–8 tortos (depending on your skill)

250g (9oz) medium-ground cornmeal (polenta)
1 teaspoon salt
About 125ml (4fl oz) cold water
Olive oil, for frying

To serve
4–8 small soft frying-chorizos (picante or mild, as you please)
4–8 fresh eggs

Sift the cornmeal into a roomy bowl or tip it directly on the table in a heap, and mix in a little salt. Work in enough cold water to make a dough – not too soft and not too hard, just right for kneading. Work it until smooth, press it into a ball and leave it aside for an hour wrapped in clingfilm or under a damp cloth.

Break off a piece of dough about the size of a small egg and put it in the corner of a clean cloth or sandwich it between 2 sheets of clingfilm. Pressing firmly, flatten it with your hand – it should not be too thick or it will be tough, and not too thin or it will break.

Heat a finger's width of oil in a frying pan, enough to submerge the torto, and slip it in. Fry it on both sides until it's crisp and golden. Transfer to kitchen paper to drain. Continue until all are ready. Serve immediately – a torto is fit only for the chickens when it's cold.

Meanwhile, fry the chorizos in a little olive oil (you won't need much) and remove to a serving dish to keep warm while you fry the eggs in the pan drippings – you may need a little more oil so that the edges frill and crisp. Alternatively, serve your tortos with honey and butter, or jam and curd cheese, or with a cream made with Cabrales, the local blue cheese (see right).

crema de cabrales
potted blue cheese with cream

Cabrales is a pungent, blue-veined cheese made from cow's milk, dense, rich and dusted throughout with greeny-blue mould, rivalling Roquefort and Stilton in depth of flavour. In the spring after overwintering, when the cheese is too strong for most people's tastes, it's blended with its own volume of fresh curd cheese and eaten with a cornmeal torto (see left) hot from the pan. Good for breakfast on a chilly morning in the Picos, or spooned into boat-shaped chicory leaves and eaten with a sparkling tumblerful of Asturian cider.

Serves 4

250g (9oz) mature Cabrales (or any other blue cheese)
250g (9oz) fresh curd cheese (queso fresco, though ricotta is fine)
4 tablespoons cream

Put all three ingredients in a liquidiser and process to a thick purée, or mash together by hand – the traditional way. If it's a little stiff for the liquidiser blades, moisten with a dash of apple brandy or cider.

In the general store in Cabrales, the village which has given its name to the region's most famous product, I noticed an open sack of cornmeal set conveniently beside the door, scoop and hand-held scales at the ready. Experience told me this must be the raw material for the torto, a griddle-bread I had already sampled in one of the little farmhouse restaurants which offer hospitality to those prepared to risk the mountain roads. The proprietors of the store, mother and daughter, explained the torto's history: 'The land's too poor for wheat, so we grow what we call Indian corn – maize. When it was brought here from the Indies many centuries ago, the people found it easier to grow than the old grains, barley and rye, which anyway were no good for baking. No one had ever baked bread with yeast – the torto was what we ate, and that could just as easily be made with Indian corn. In the old days, when the butter went to the landlord and no-one had the money to buy oil from elsewhere, you baked the tortos between leaves – chestnut or maple – the ones they used to wrap the Cabrales cheese. You waited till the leaves were dry before you stored them; when you needed them you had to soak them, then you patted out the torto between the leaves, using as many as were needed to cover both sides. Then you could cook it just like that, first one side, then the other, without oil or lard or butter. And then it was already wrapped for you to take to the fields.'

Mountain village near Potes, Cantabria

pimientos de Padrón
fried baby green peppers

The most esteemed of all frying peppers are the little grass-green peppers of Padrón. Small (bite-sized, actually), triangular in shape, fragrant, with the added pleasure that though most are mild, a few are fiery, they miraculously retain their brilliant colour and crispness after frying. Padrón is a modest little fishing village at the head of the Arousa estuary on the pilgrim route to Compostela, whose non-gastronomic claim to fame – not easily substantiated – is that it was here, on this very quayside, that Santiago, the Apostle James – politically incorrectly known as Matamoro, Moor-slayer – made first landfall after his flight from the Holy Land.

Serves 4–6 as a tapa

450g (1lb) bite-sized green peppers (a few hot, mostly mild)
Olive oil, for deep-frying
Sea salt

Wipe the peppers, but leave them whole.

Heat the oil in a frying pan until a faint blue haze rises. Throw in the peppers. Cook them fiercely but briefly, turning until all sides take a little colour. Turn the heat right down and put the lid on. Cook over a gentle heat until the peppers are soft. Take out the peppers with a draining spoon, sprinkle with salt and serve immediately, providing plenty of bread for mopping fingers.

empanada de atún
tuna and red pepper pie

Food for the pocket, easily packed for a picnic or for a fisherman to take on a day's outing. Look out for it in the grocery stores of Llanes, where it's sold in abundance, baked fresh every day. Recipes vary – some people include tomatoes, others parsley, and some leave out the garlic. In Cantabria the tuna might well be replaced with salmon.

Serves 6–8

450g (1lb) fresh tunafish steaks, skinned and de-boned
6 tablespoons olive oil
1–2 garlic cloves
1 large onion, finely sliced
2 large red peppers, de-seeded and diced
2 large potatoes, peeled and cut into cubes
1 teaspoon dried thyme
Salt and crumbled dried chilli
1 glass white wine
1 hardboiled egg, sliced

The pastry
275g (10oz) strong bread flour
1/2 teaspoon salt
25g (1oz) fresh yeast (half this if dried)
2 tablespoons white wine
50g (2oz) fresh pork lard or olive oil
150ml (1/4 pint) milk or water
1 egg yolk, mixed with a little milk, for glazing

Dice the tuna, salt lightly and set aside.

Now make the pastry. Sift the flour with the salt into a warm bowl and use the tips of your fingers to rub in the yeast – if using dried, just mix it in. Put the wine, lard or oil, and milk or water into a small pan and heat it to blood temperature. Pour the warm liquid into the flour. Knead everything together until you have a smooth elastic dough.

Drop the doughball back into the bowl, cover with clingfilm and leave to rise in a warm place for an hour or two, until doubled in size.

Meanwhile, make the filling. Heat the oil gently in a frying pan and fry the garlic, onion, peppers and potatoes, season with thyme, salt and a pinch of chilli and cook, loosely covered, over a low heat until soft and golden – don't let anything brown. Add the wine, let it bubble up until the alcohol evaporates, then remove the pan from the heat and leave to cool. Fold in the diced tuna.

Cut the dough into two pieces, one a little larger than the other. Using a well-floured fist or rolling pin, pat or roll out the dough into two large rectangles (one slightly bigger than the other) about as thick as your little finger. Grease a baking tray and line it with the larger rectangle of dough.

Spread half the filling over the dough, leaving a margin round the edge, cover with the sliced hardboiled egg and top with the rest of the filling. Dampen the edges and place the remaining dough sheet on top. Curl the edges over each other to enclose, mark with a fork to seal, prick the top, brush with a little of the egg yolk and milk mixture, and leave to rise again for another 30 minutes.

Preheat the oven to 180°C/350°F/gas mark 4.

Bake the pie for 40–60 minutes, until well puffed and golden. Serve at room temperature, cut into neat squares.

empanada gallega
galician game pie

Nina Epton, travelling through Galicia in the 1950s, appreciated local hospitality: 'Señor Carrera, the local grandee of Scots descent, was an excellent host...Seating us under the welcome shade of a vine-covered trellis, he unpacked a parcel as large as a suitcase, from which he produced the plat du jour. This was an empanada, a Galician pie, of such vast proportions, such an original shape and with such appetising contents (chicken, meat, fried onions and red peppers oozed out from their pastry prison as soon as Señor Carrera cut the pie open with his pocket-knife)...The top of this aristocratic pie was a faithful reproduction in golden crust of Señor Carrera's escutcheon.'

There are no rules about what goes into the stuffing: chicken, pork, lamb, beef, veal, vegetables, fish – it's a matter of attitude.

Serves 6

The filling
2 tablespoons fresh pork lard
1 onion, finely chopped
1 garlic clove, skinned and crushed
2 red peppers, de-seeded and diced
110g (4oz) salt-cured ham or lean bacon, diced
1 small smoked chorizo, diced
450g (1lb) game meat (rabbit, partridge, venison),
  in small cubes
Salt and pepper
Dried chilli flakes
1 glass red or white wine
3–4 saffron threads, soaked in 1 tablespoon
  boiling water
1 teaspoon dried thyme

Galicia at its greenest

The pastry
275g (10oz) self-raising flour
1/2 teaspoon salt
50g (2oz) fresh pork lard or olive oil
2 tablespoons white wine
150ml (1/4 pint) milk or water
Milk, for brushing

To make the filling, melt the lard in a frying pan and gently fry the onion, garlic and peppers. When the vegetables are soft, push them to one side and add the ham or bacon and chorizo and fry together for a few minutes – just long enough to melt the fat. Remove and reserve.

Reheat the drippings and fry the meat until everything takes a little colour. Season with salt and a little chilli. Return the reserved vegetables, add the wine, the saffron with its water, and the thyme. Let it bubble up, then put the lid on and simmer until the liquid has evaporated and the meat is tender. Taste and add salt and freshly milled pepper. Leave aside to cool while you preheat the oven to 200°C/400°F/gas mark 6 and mix the pastry.

Make a well in the flour and sprinkle in the salt. Put the lard or oil, wine and milk or water into a small pan and heat to blood temperature. Pour the warm liquid into the flour and work the dry and wet ingredients together until you have a smooth elastic dough. You may need more liquid or more flour. On a well-floured board with a floured rolling pin, using short firm strokes, roll out the dough into two rectangles, one about 25cm (10in) long by 20cm (8in) wide and the other slightly smaller. Cut a 1cm (1/2in) ribbon off the long side of the smaller piece and reserve. Transfer the larger piece of pastry to a greased baking tray. Spread the filling into a neat rectangle in the middle, leaving a narrow margin at each side. Tuck the pastry up each side of the filling and place the remaining pastry sheet over the top to enclose. Dampen the edges and press them together between your finger and a fork. Prick the lid, brush it with milk, and decorate with diamond-shaped leaves made with the reserved ribbon of pastry.

Bake for 30 minutes, until the pastry is golden and set. Turn the heat down to 180°C/350°F/gas mark 4 and cook for another 30 minutes, until the filling is cooked and the pastry nicely browned. Serve at hand warmth – the best temperature for a pasty.

fabada asturiana
haricot beans with salt-pork and black pudding

The beauty of the dish lies in the quality of Asturia's plump, buttery white beans: pochas. Originally the dish was made with dried broad beans (fava), the native bean of Europe, but they were replaced with the New World's more delicate haricots. The fabada is as variable as any of the other beans-and-bones one-pot stews of Spain and Portugal – and elsewhere, for that matter. Asturians claim that France's famous cassoulet is no more than a fabada asturiana which has found itself on the wrong side of the Pyrenees. The basic recipe is somewhere in between.

Serves 6–8

700g (1½lb) large dried haricot beans
1–2 short lengths serrano ham bone
  (or a bacon knuckle)
225g (8oz) salt-pork belly or unsmoked streaky
  bacon (in one piece)
salted pig's trotters, ears and tail
  (optional, but good)
1 whole head of garlic
6 peppercorns, roughly crushed
1 dried red pepper, de-seeded and crumbled
  (or 1 tablespoon pimentón)
½ teaspoon saffron threads
225g (8oz) – 2 links – morcilla asturiana
  (black pudding)
salt

To finish
Chopped parsley

To serve
2 eggs or 2 tablespoons soup noodles (fideos)

Soak the beans overnight. Drain them, put them in a roomy boiling pot with the rest of the ingredients except the morcilla, but don't add any salt yet. Add enough fresh water to cover everything, then add half as much water again.

Bring to the boil, turn down the heat, put the lid on loosely and leave to simmer gently for 1½–3 hours (depending on the age of the beans) without stirring until both meat and beans are perfectly soft and tender. If you need to add more water during the cooking, make sure it's boiling. Add the morcilla and simmer for another 10 minutes. Taste and add salt – you may not need any if the bacon was on the salty side.

Transfer the beans to a deep dish and top with the meats, neatly sliced, and a ladleful of the broth stirred with a handful of chopped parsley. Serve the rest of the broth as a first course, fortified either with beaten egg (it sets and forms threads as soon as it hits the boiling broth) or a handful of soup noodles.

caldo gallego
galician beans and greens

A soup, a stew, or something in between. This version of Galicia's one-pot dinner is from the Roman-founded city of Orense, close to the Portuguese border. It's good with a dish of pimientos de Padrón (see p. 83) on the side.

Serves 6

275g (10oz) dried white beans (haricot or butter),
  soaked overnight
450g (1lb) stewing veal or beef (in 1 piece)
1 short length serrano ham bone or unsmoked
  bacon hock
225g (8oz) salt-pork belly
2–3 soft boiling chorizos or morcilla
450g (1lb) boiling-fowl joints
2 pig's trotters or ½ pig's head, blanched (optional)
900g (2lb) potatoes, peeled and quartered
450g (1lb) young turnips, with their tops
1 medium green (Savoy) cabbage, thickly sliced

Drain the beans, wipe over the meats and put them in a large stewpot with plenty of cold fresh water – add enough water to cover everything and then add as much again. Bring to the boil. Turn down the heat to a simmer, put the lid on and leave it all to bubble gently for 2–2½ hours.

After 2 hours, ladle half the broth into another saucepan and leave the original to carry on cooking – if you need to add more water, make sure it's boiling. In the second pan, cook the potatoes and the turnips, scrubbed and quartered (reserve and shred their greens), for 15 minutes or so, until nearly soft. Add the shredded turnip-greens and cabbage, bring back to the boil, cover and cook for another 6–10 minutes, until all is tender. Serve the broth with the cabbage, turnips and potatoes in a deep dish, the beans and sausages on another, and the meats, neatly sliced, on a third. Provide each participant with a deep soup plate, a spoon and plenty of bread and red wine.

flan
caramel custard

While a baked egg custard is a popular dessert throughout Spain, the main ingredient, milk, places it firmly in dairy country. Regional variations replace the milk with apple juice – tart and rather delicious.

Serves 4

The caramel
4 heaped tablespoons granulated sugar
2 tablespoons water (optional)

The custard
600ml (1 pint) creamy milk
3 eggs and 2 yolks
1 drop vanilla essence
2 tablespoons sugar or honey

Make the caramel in a small pan. Gently melt the sugar, stirring all the time with a wooden spoon over a steady heat until the sugar caramelises to a rich chestnut brown. This will take only a moment or two. Add the water off the heat – be careful as it will splutter. Stir over a low flame until you have a thick dark syrup. Pour this caramel into the soufflé dish or individual moulds you will use for the custard. Tip to coat the base. Once you've had a little practice – speed is vital – you'll be able to do without the water. To get hardened caramel off the pan, fill it with water and bring to the boil again.

Preheat the oven to 170°C/325°F/gas mark 3.

Mix the milk, eggs, egg yolks, vanilla essence and sugar or honey together to blend – don't whisk – and pour into the mould(s). Arrange them in a bain-marie – a roasting tin – and pour in enough boiling water to come halfway up the sides. Transfer to the oven and bake for 45–50 minutes (if large) or 25–30 minutes (if small) until the custard is just set. Or cook the custards in a bath of simmering water on top of the stove. Remove and allow to cool.

Run a knife round the rim and turn out the custards when you are ready to serve them. They will make their own delicious caramel sauce. If the custard is full of tiny holes, turn down the heat a little next time.

pastel de santiago
almond cake

Almonds, sugar, whisked eggs and lemon zest: light and delicious, this is a breakfast worthy of a pilgrim on the road to Santiago. Well, anyone can dream.

Makes 1 cake

350g (12oz) whole unskinned almonds
4 eggs
175g (6oz) caster sugar
Grated zest of 1 lemon
Butter, for greasing

Pound or process the almonds to a coarse powder – stop before they turn to oil.

Preheat the oven to 190°C/375°F/gas mark 5.

Whisk the eggs together until frothy. Gradually whisk in the sugar and continue to beat until they are white and stiff enough for the whisk to leave a trail. This is easiest with an electric beater – it takes twice as long as you expect. Fold in the powdered almonds and the lemon zest, turning the mixture with a metal spoon until there are no more dry pockets.

Line an 18cm (7in) round cake tin with greaseproof paper and butter thoroughly. Tip the mixture into the tin.

Bake for 45–50 minutes, until the cake is well-browned and firm to the finger. Let it to settle for 5 minutes and then tip it out onto a rack and leave to cool. It will shrink a little as it cools.

A farmer ploughs his fields along the Galician coast

Navarra, the territory which stretches from the Pyrenees in the north to the banks of the River Ebro in the south, was first settled by the ancestors of Basques, sharing that nation's conviction that freedom to choose how he lives is a right for which a man must be prepared to fight. While her culture and domestic habit were formed by a mutually profitable association with her neighbours on both sides of the border, Navarra has always managed to claim an unusual degree of autonomy. Freedom of speech was enshrined in law as early as the year 850, under Iñigo Arista, her first king.

Domestically she is equally eclectic. Dishes reflect the influence of all three of her neighbours – the Basques, the Aragonese and the French – with a fair sprinkling of fraternisation with the Moors of the Levante. While her northern territory is shaped by the Pyrenees the great pass of Roncevalles is within her boundaries – she shares with her smaller neighbour Rioja the benefits of the red-earthed vineyards which, protected by rolling hills, stretch on either side of the banks of the Ebro and its tributary, the Oja.

In the valleys and mountains of the Pyrenean region, Navarra is shepherding country, a land of independent pastoralists who live in slate-roofed villages – self-governing when this was an option – rather than isolated farmhouses. Here historical and cultural links are particularly strong with the Basques, with whom many would identify. In the southern regions, however – a land of forest and plai – the inhabitants look to the one-time kingdom of Aragon, founding

Terraced fields near Ujue, Navarra

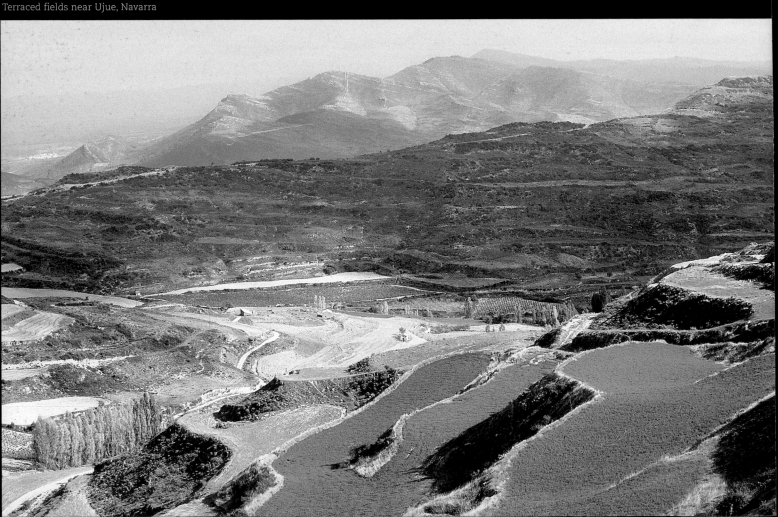

father of the Spanish nation. Rioja, tucked between Navarra and the central plateau of Castile, would have little claim to an identity of her own were it not for the wealth of her vineyards.

The culinary reputation of both regions is for hearty cooking for big people with big appetites. Rioja has vintners' stews, many including the game which takes shelter in the vineyards. The bean dish of Navarra is the garbure navarense, a one-pot stew which, though as variable as the French dish of the same name, is based on the ingredients the land favours: fava beans, cabbage, pork and potatoes, all of which are used to good effect in other dishes. Regional specialities include the chorizos and bull-meat dishes of Pamplona as well as vegetable stews – meat an optional extra – in which the cooking broth is wine and magnificent scarlet peppers and tomatoes provide the flavours of the sun.

Local treats include particularly succulent vineyard snails prepared in the simplest way by popping them in the embers of a campfire to roast like chestnuts, when they need no sauce but a drop of vinegar. Land not needed for the vineyards (as in wine-growing regions everywhere, wine can be made only from grapes grown in the territories which have earned their denomination of origin) is turned over to the market gardens which supply the great cities of the plain – Burgos, Madrid, Salamanca – with early vegetables and fruit. Pimentón peppers are grown and processed here: dried and milled for adding colour and fragrance to stews, or carefully prepared and bottled or jarred as piquillo peppers.

The medicinal tipple of Navarra is pacharan, sweetened white brandy – in the old days, home-distilled – to which sloes have imparted their colour, a magnificent royal purple, as well as an excitingly mouth-puckering sourness. When used as an anti-scorbutic – scurvy-preventer – the preparation provided enough Vitamin C to see many a rural household through the winter months.

Both regions lack direct access to the sea, a geographical limitation which kept fresh sea fish off the menu until the appearance, no more than fifty years ago, of refrigerated transport. In medieval times a lack of fresh fish was a very real deprivation since devout Catholics – including those who wished for any kind of social or political advancement – were obliged to follow the rules of fast. Meatless days decreed by Rome included Wednesdays as well as Fridays and the eves of all major saints' days as well as the forty days of Lent and the twelve days preceding Christmas, leaving more than half the year in which meat-eating was prohibited. As necessity dictated, housewives developed a repertoire of meatless stews and bean dishes which obeyed the rules of fast – enlivened, if money was available, with a little bacalao or salt-cured anchovies. Although river fish and trout from the clear waters of the mountains might perhaps be available, these were seen as a treat, to be savoured with good things such as wine and ham.

Sweetmeats were also prohibited on fast days, making them doubly popular on feast days, not least because their origins were a little suspect, being, in the main, Arab. In Rioja desserts are known by their Moorish name of golmajerias. Pastries are airy confections of *milojas*, thousand-leaves, a descendent of Arabia's filo doughs and Morocco's pastry, *ouaka* – dough leaves skilfully produced not by rolling or stretching the dough, but by dabbing a ball of uncooked flour-and-water on a griddle. The marzipan which comes easily in lands where almond trees flourish is particularly appreciated in places where the almond is an imported luxury. In the chilly uplands of the Serranía de Cameros the Christmas sweetmeat, mazapanes de Soto, is made with powdered almonds bulked with cooked potato, a thrifty solution to a problem of both scarcity and expense, since the New World tuber arrived shortly after the Moors withdrew, thriving in areas where other staples struggle.

Regional cheeses include an unpasteurised fresh goat's milk cheese, Camerano, a curd cheese, refreshingly sharp, which, like southern Italy's ricotta, is eaten with honey as a dessert.

cardo gratinado
gratin of cardoons

A close relative of the artichoke, the cardoon is popular in winter when there's nothing else around. The simplest way to serve it is plain-boiled and dressed with olive oil, vinegar and salt, with or without the added refinement of chopped hardboiled egg, a crushed anchovy and a handful of parsley. When preparing cardoon for the pot, remember it's very bitter unless properly trimmed of all its leaves. Cardoon recipes also work well with celery or chard-stalks (save the leaves to shred and stir into the bean-pot). The enrichment for the white sauce is curd cheese: the Riojans are proud of their Camerano cheese, which is made with unpasteurised goat's milk and has a deliciously sharp flavour.

Serves 4 as a side dish, 2 as the main event

1 cardoon head
1 tablespoon lemon juice or vinegar
2 tablespoons olive oil
2 tablespoons plain flour
1 tablespoon white wine or dry sherry
350ml (12fl oz) chicken stock or broth from the bean-pot
110g (4oz) fresh white curd cheese (cottage rather than cream)
1–2 salt-cured anchovies (from the barrel or canned in oil)
Salt and pepper

To finish
1 tablespoon each mild pimentón (Spanish paprika), chopped parsley, finely chopped garlic and fresh breadcrumbs crisped in a little olive oil

Use only the tender inner stalks of the cardoon – as you would expect from a member of the artichoke family, the upper part is tougher than the base. De-string them as you would tough stalks of celery, and trim off the little fringe of leaf which edges the stalks. Cut into bite-sized lengths.

Bring a pan of salted water to the boil. Add the lemon juice or vinegar and the chopped stalks. Bring back to the boil, put the lid on and cook for 20 minutes, until perfectly tender. Drain well, and arrange in a shallow gratin dish.

Meanwhile make a béchamel, as a white sauce is known in Spain. Heat the oil in a small, heavy-based saucepan, stir in the flour and cook gently until the mixture looks sandy – 2–3 minutes. Don't let it brown. Add the wine, let it bubble up and whisk over the heat until it thickens. Add the stock gradually, whisking to avoid lumps, and simmer until the sauce is thick enough to coat the back of a wooden spoon. Beat in the curd cheese and the anchovies (brush off the salt, de-whisker and soak in milk for an hour if they're from the barrel).

Reheat briefly (if the sauce splits, use a whisk or processor to bring it back to smoothness), taste and add salt and pepper. Pour the sauce over and around the chopped cardoons.

Sprinkle with the finishing ingredients and slide the dish under the grill to brown and bubble.

lomo en adobo
pimentón-pickled pork fillet

Grilled over vineyard clippings and popped into a crisp-crusted, dense-crumbed white roll, this is the fast food of Rioja. Make it in larger quantities for freezing after it has been marinated and is ready for slicing and grilling – since it's to be cut thin, there's no need for lengthy de-frosting.

Serves 4–6 as a tapa

350g (12oz) pork fillet
2 tablespoons mild pimentón (Spanish paprika)
1/2 teaspoon oregano
1/2 teaspoon thyme
1 bay leaf
1 garlic clove, skinned and crushed with 1 teaspoon salt
1 tablespoon olive oil

Dry the pork fillet. Mix the pimentón, oregano, thyme, bay leaf, garlic and salt with the oil and rub it into the meat, coating it on all sides. Wrap the meat in foil or clingfilm and put it in the fridge to take the flavours overnight – you can leave it there for a week, improving daily.

When you are ready to cook, cut the fillet on the diagonal into 8–10 thin medallions.

Heat a barbecue or griddle until smoking hot. Wipe with an oiled scrap of cloth, and smack on the medallions. Allow no more than 3–4 minutes to seal and caramelise the exterior, turning the medallions once. As a tapa, serve each medallion on a round of bread of the same size; as a snack, slip into a crisp-crusted bread roll. Provide quartered lemons for squeezing, to cut the richness.

coliflor refrito con ajos
refried cauliflower with garlic cloves

I have a great fondness for this dish: the technique works just as well with broccoli and improves any member of the cabbage family.

Serves 4 as a tapa

1 medium caulifower, divided into
  bite-sized florets
4 tablespoons olive oil
6 garlic cloves, unskinned but crushed
1 tablespoon pimentón (Spanish paprika)
2 tablespoons chopped parsley
1 tablespoon wine vinegar
Salt and pepper

Cook the cauliflower florets in boiling salted water until tender but not squishy – about 15 minutes. Drain thoroughly.

Heat the oil in a roomy frying pan. Turn the garlic in the hot oil until it softens and takes a little colour. Add the cauliflower florets. Fry gently for as long as it takes to brown them slightly. Turn them with the pimentón, parsley and vinegar, salt and freshly milled pepper. That's all.

tortilla de pimientos piquillos y habas
red pepper and fava omelette

A robust tortilla which combines the earthiness of the fava bean with the gaiety and sweetness of the piquillo pepper (for its preparation, see the recipe for Roasted Red Peppers with Anchovies, p. 93).

Serves 4 as a starter

2 handfuls fava beans – 450g (1lb) unshelled
2 tablespoons olive oil
1 small glass white wine
225g (8oz) prepared piquillo peppers
4 large eggs
Salt and pepper

First prepare the beans. At the beginning of the season when the beans are scarcely formed, use the pods whole (they have a delicate asparagus-like flavour), and string and chop, following the curve of the beans. Mid-season, shell the beans but don't skin them. Later in the season, shell and skin them. If they are ready-shelled, you'll need only 225g (8oz).

Warm 1 tablespoon of the olive oil in a raw-iron tortilla pan, or whatever you use to cook an omelette.

Turn the beans in the hot oil for a moment and the pour in the wine. Put the lid on the pan and leave t simmer gently for 10–15 minutes, until they're soft Let the beans bubble up at the end to evaporate all the moisture, then stir in the prepared peppers.

Beat the eggs lightly with salt and pepper and add the beans and peppers. Heat the rest of the oil in th pan. Tip in the egg mixture and cook gently, lifting up the middle to let the uncooked egg run underneath. Keep the heat low or the base will toughen before the middle is set – covering the pan loosely will help. As soon as the edges begin to set - the middle must remain moist – turn it so the other side can feel the heat. Be brave. Place a plate on the top, hold it firmly against the metal rim, and revers the whole thing so that the tortilla lands upside down on the plate. Slip it back into the pan to cook the other side (you may need a little more oil), usin a spatula to neaten the sides. Slip it out onto a plate Don't overcook it – it'll set more as it cools and a tortilla should always be soft-hearted. Serve warm or at room temperature, never chilled.

Vineyard near La Guardia, wine-making capital of La Rioja

pimientos del piquillo con anchoas
roasted red peppers with anchovies

piquillo peppers are triangular, crimson, bitter-sweet descendants of Peru's chile de arbol, known as the bush-chilli to distinguish it from its cousin, the lantern-shaped vine-chilli, a Mexican native. The two species, both fiery by nature, are the ancestors of all our modern capsicums, both hot and mild. The piquillos – early arrivals from the New World and closer to their roots than most of their tribe – are bitter and unpalatable raw, which, since they belong to the nightshade family, is no surprise. They only become truly delicious after roasting and skinning, a task which needs both patience and skill, so buy them ready-prepared: they come in jars and tins.

Since the blistering method greatly improves even the dullest of greenhouse peppers, it's worth practising on red (ripe) salad peppers. They won't have the same depth of flavour as piquillos – but no matter, the salty little anchovies help to make up for their shortcomings.

serves 4

1000g (2lb) ripe red capsicum peppers – piquillos for preference
1 small can anchovies in oil
slivers of garlic (optional)

Roast the whole peppers on the barbecue or over a gas flame or under the grill until the skin is black and blistered. Beware the steam, though: it has more than a touch of toxicity.

Drop the peppers in a plastic bag – brown paper works just as well – and leave for 10 minutes for the steam to loosen the skin. Then hull and de-seed the peppers and carefully scrape off all vestiges of skin, blistered or not. Cut the flesh into triangular segments if the peppers' natural shape permits. Otherwise, cut into broad ribbons.

Arrange the prepared peppers on a flat dish. Finish with a trickle of olive oil and the anchovies separated into fillets (you can include the pickling oil, if it's olive oil). There's no need for salt. The contrast between the salty little fish and the sweet scarlet flesh is irresistible.

truchas con setas en vino de Rioja
trout with ham and ceps in red wine

This reward for the fisherman's patience, cooked at the end of the day over a small brush fire, uses only his own gatherings and the wine and ham which have come with him in his satchel. Line-caught fish, fungi, slivers of rosy mountain ham and herbs from the hillside – what could be better?

Serves 2–4, as hunger dictates

4 fine fat trout, cleaned and gutted
Salt and pepper
A few thyme sprigs
4 long slices of serrano ham (with plenty of the sweet golden fat)
110g (4oz) ceps or any other wild fungi, cleaned and sliced
300ml (½ pint) red wine

Wipe the cavity of each fish and salt lightly. Pop in a sprig of thyme and a sprinkling of pepper. Wrap each fish in a jacket of ham, making sure the fat is on the outside.

Heat a frying pan and lay in the fish. Fry gently, allowing 5 minutes per side – press the middle with your finger to make sure the flesh is firm. Remove and reserve.

Fry the fungi in the fatty juices in the pan, salting them lightly. You may need a little extra butter or lard. As soon as the fungi have yielded up their water and begun to fry again, add the wine and let it bubble up until it no longer smells of alcohol and has concentrated and thickened. Sauce the trout with the juices from the pan. Perfection.

perdizes con col
partridges with cabbage

This countryman's winter dish is suitable for older birds past their first spring which are too tough to roast. The flexibility of the beak and claws will tell you if the bird is young or old. If the bird is in feather when it comes to you, you can always skin rather than pluck it and save yourself a deal of trouble. The recipe is also suitable for pheasant or poussin (baby chicken), neither of which has much character of its own.

Serves 4

4 partridges (elderly ones are fine)
1 mild red onion, finely chopped
4 garlic cloves, skinned and crushed
1 glass light red wine
Salt and pepper
Handful sweet green grapes or soaked raisins
1 large green cabbage
4 tablespoons olive oil
1 tablespoon flour
450g (1lb) ripe firm tomatoes, scalded, skinned and chopped
1 short cinammon stick
2–3 cloves
1 bay leaf and 1 thyme sprig

Wipe the partridges and remove any stray feathers. Put the birds in a bowl with the onion, garlic, wine, salt and pepper and leave them to take the flavour for an hour or two. Remove the birds from the marinade, pat dry, pop a few grapes or raisins inside the cavity of each and put to one side. Reserve the marinade.

Next prepare the cabbage. Select eight of the most perfect outer leaves as wrappers for the birds, nick out the hard white stalk at the base so that the lea can be easily rolled and reserve. Slice the rest of th cabbage vertically, including a bit of the central stalk to hold the slices together. Transfer to a panfu of boiling salted water, bring back to the boil and drain immediately. Reserve.

Heat the oil in a roomy casserole – you will need enough room for the cabbage slices as well as the birds. Put in the birds and turn them carefully in th hot oil until they are browned on all sides. Remove and wrap each bird in a jacket of cabbage leaves, securing it with toothpicks – the universal serving-tool in tapa bars – or colourless string. Dust the cabbage slices lightly with flour and fry briefly in the oily juices until they take a little colour, then remove and reserve.

Add the chopped tomatoes to the juices in the pan and let them bubble up for a moment. Add the marinade, cinnamon stick, cloves, bay leaf, thyme and a glass of water and bring it all back to the boil. Return the jacketed birds to the casserole, tuck in the cabbage slices, put the lid on loosely and leave to bubble gently for 20–30 minutes, until the birds are perfectly tender.

adereta de cordero
braised lamb with serrano ham

ountain lambs, born later in the year than valley
mbs and of smaller build, are allowed to fatten
n spring herbs, making their meat firmer and
ore richly flavoured than that of milk-fed
nimals. A gentle braising with wine and serrano
am makes the most of their virtues.

erves 4

small leg or shoulder of lamb, boned and
butterflied
/2 teaspoon crushed peppercorns
tablespoon pimentón (Spanish paprika)
teaspoon dried thyme
–2 thick slices of serrano ham
small glass olive oil
glasses dry white wine
bay leaves

prinkle the cut side of the meat with pepper,
imentón and thyme and cover with the ham.
here's no need for salt, since the ham is already
uite salty enough. Roll the meat up and tie it into a
eat little bolster.

reheat the oven to 180°C/350°F/gas mark 4.
ransfer the meat to a casserole which will just
ccommodate it, pouring in a little oil before you
ettle it in. Drizzle with the rest of the oil and
he wine and tuck in the bay leaves. Cover loosely
vith foil and bake, basting intermittently, for about
1/2 hours, until the meat is tender and well
rowned. You may need to add a little water from
ime to time to stop the dish from drying out and
t's best to lower the heat a notch halfway through
he cooking. Allow to rest for 10 minutes before you
lice it. Serve with its own juices, with plain white
ice tossed with toasted almonds and raisins.

estofado de rabo de toro
spiced braised oxtail

This is a bull-running dish from Pamplona,
fortified capital of the ancient kingdom of Navarra.
The city has always served as a marketplace for
the trans-Pyrenean trade: the bull-running
tradition, while embellished over the centuries
with folklore and fantasy, is simply a result of
what happened naturally when beef-cattle, frisky
from grazing on rich summer pastures, were
brought to market. Every day during the Festival of
San Fermin (the festival of the running of the
bulls) bull meat goes on sale cheaply to a
population which in the past ate meat at no other
time. Dishes made with bull meat are slow-
simmered since the meat, being very fresh and
coming from mature animals, is likely to be tough.

Serves 6

2–3 oxtails (depending on size), chopped into their
   natural sections
4 tablespoons olive oil
110g (4oz) serrano ham or gammon, diced (or a
   length of serrano ham bone)
1 large onion, sliced
2 cloves garlic, skinned and crushed with 1
   teaspoon salt
1 stick celery, chopped
1 carrot, scrubbed and chopped
900g (2lb) tomatoes, scalded, skinned and chopped
1 tablespoon pimentón (Spanish paprika) or
   1 dried red pepper, de-seeded and torn
2–3 dried chillies
1–2 short cinnamon sticks or 1 teaspoon
   ground cinnamon
1/2 teaspoon crushed peppercorns
3–4 cloves
1–2 bay leaves
1 bottle red wine
Salt and pepper

Wipe and trim the excess fat off the oxtails, then
rinse and pat dry. Heat the oil in a casserole which
will comfortably accommodate all the oxtail pieces,
and turn them in the hot oil until they take colour.
Remove and reserve. Fry the serrano ham or
gammon, onion, garlic, celery and carrot gently
until the vegetables soften and caramelise a little –
don't let them brown. Add the tomatoes, spices, bay
leaves and wine and let it all bubble up until the
tomato flesh has collapsed.

Return the oxtail to the pot. Add enough water to
submerge everything and bring back to the boil.
Season, turn down the heat, put the lid on tightly
and leave to cook on a very low heat – or in a
preheated oven at 150°C/300°F/gas mark 2 – for
3–4 hours, until the meat is falling off the bones.
Check from time to time, and add a little boiling
water if necessary.

Serve with bread, for Pamplona is a prosperous city
and only country folk eat potatoes at festival time.
Good today, even better tomorrow, this stew freezes
brilliantly.

Bullfighting in Pamplona

pollo en salsa de clavijo
chicken with spiced parsley sauce

This dish is a speciality of Clavijo, near Logroño, the battlefield on which the first miraculous appearance of the Apostle James – Santiago de Campostella – rallied the Christian armies against the Moors. At the time of the battle, AD 844, the armies of the Prophet seemed set to march unhindered across the length and breadth of Christian Europe.

Serves 4

1 free-range chicken, with giblets
4 tablespoons olive oil
1 glass white wine
2–3 garlic cloves, skinned and crushed
1 thyme sprig
2 bay leaves
Peppercorns
1 onion, quartered

The sauce
2 tablespoons olive oil
1 tablespoon plain flour
1/2 teaspoon ground cloves
1 teaspoon ground cinnamon
1 tablespoon chopped parsley
Salt and pepper

Joint the chicken into about a dozen meaty pieces (setting aside whatever you reject) and put the joints in a bowl with the oil, wine, garlic, thyme, 1 of the bay leaves and a little salt, turning to coat. Cover and leave to marinate for a couple of hours at room temperature, or overnight in the fridge.

Meanwhile bring the giblets and uninteresting bony bits – back and wing-tips – to the boil in 600ml (1 pint) water, with the remaining bay leaf, a few peppercorns and the onion. Turn down the heat and leave to simmer until reduced to about 300ml (1/2 pint) well-flavoured broth. Strain out the solids and reserve the broth.

Preheat the oven to maximum: 230°C/450°F/gas mark 8.

Drain the chicken joints, reserving the marinade, and pat dry. Transfer the joints to a roasting tray and roast for 5 minutes at the high heat. Turn the oven down to 180°C/350°F/gas mark 4 and roast for another 45–50 minutes, basting every now and then with the reserved marinade, until the joints are cooked right through – don't let them dry out. Transfer to a warm serving dish, reserving the juices from the roasting tin.

Meanwhile make the sauce. Heat the oil in a small saucepan. Sprinkle in the flour and fry gently until sandy: 2–3 minutes. Don't let it brown. Sprinkle in the spices and add the reserved broth. Bring to the boil and let it bubble gently, whisking, until it thickens. Stir in the parsley and the roasting juices (a nugget of cold butter will make it even more delicious). Taste and add salt and pepper. Spoon half the sauce over the chicken and hand the rest around separately.

conejo ajo-arriero
mule-driver's rabbit with garlic

Mule-drivers were the travelling-salesmen of unmotorised Spain, moving all over the country selling the good wines of Rioja and Navarra. Anything described as *ajo-arriero* (garlic-tailed) can be expected to be well garlicked and include a dash of vinegar. This is best made with a couple of plump young rabbits caught red-handed in the vineyards, though a free-range chicken can replace the farmed rabbit.

Serves 4

2 wild rabbits or 1 farmed one, jointed
6 garlic cloves, unskinned but crushed
4 tablespoons olive oil
Salt and pepper
1 tablespoon wine vinegar
2 tablespoons flour
2 tablespoons chopped parsley
1 generous glass red wine

Chop the rabbit joints into smaller, bite-sized pieces by tapping a knife neatly through the bones. Put the pieces in a bowl with the garlic, 1 tablespoon of the oil, salt, pepper and vinegar. Leave them to marinate for an hour or two – overnight is best.

Drain off the marinade, reserving the garlic, and dust the joints with flour – drop everything in a plastic bag and give it a shake.

Heat the remaining oil in a casserole or frying pan. Put in the rabbit joints and fry gently, turning until well browned. Add the reserved garlic and the parsley and continue to fry until the garlic softens. Add the wine and let it bubble up, then turn down the heat, put the lid on loosely and leave to cook on a low heat for 20–30 minutes, until the meat is cooked through but still moist and tender and the juices have practically evaporated, leaving a deliciously garlicky little slick of sauce.

melocotones en vino
peaches in red wine

Here, peaches – ideally the large, firm, yellow-fleshed ones which arrive mid-season – are poached in a wine syrup flavoured with cinnamon. To prepare white-fleshed peaches, use white wine and flavour them with a vanilla pod.

Serves 4

4 large yellow-fleshed peaches
1 bottle dry red wine
110g (4oz) caster sugar
1 short cinnamon stick

Scald the peaches – put them in a colander and drench with boiling water – and slip off the skins, reserving the water. In a roomy saucepan large enough to accommodate the fruit, bring the wine to the boil with the sugar and cinnamon, stirring until the crystals are completely dissolved. Lower the peaches into the syrup, add enough of the reserved peach-water to cover the fruits, return to the boil, turn down the heat and simmer gently for 20 minutes, basting regularly, until the fruit is tender and the spice has developed its full flavour. Remove from the heat and allow the peaches to cool in the syrup. This is delicious with a spoonful of fresh white curd cheese – choose one sharp enough to balance the sweetness – or crème fraîche. In Rioja the automatic choice would be Camerano, a local goat's-milk cheese with an exquisitely piquant flavour.

pacharán
sloe brandy

Basic white brandy can no longer be home-distilled – heaven forbid the taxman should not receive his dues – so shop-bought will have to do. When gathering sloes, wait until after the first frost has softened the skins or give them 48 hours in the freezer. You can, if you wish, use sweet anis brandy (anís dulce), widely available in Spain, as the base, in which case omit the sugar.

Makes 1 litre (1¾ pints)

450g (1lb) sloes
Caster sugar
1 litre (1¾ pints) white fruit brandy (eau de vie)
1 teaspoon aniseeds

Prick the sloes all over with a needle, then roll them in sugar and pop them in a bottle with the white brandy. Seal and leave on a sunny windowsill for a month (3 is even better), turning the bottle when you remember. Strain, rebottle and cork. Store in a cool place away from the light. Possible additional flavourings are cinnamon, a vanilla pod or coffee beans.

aragon

Shepherding country, wild and sparsely inhabited in its forested heartland – last refuge of wolves and bears and now a magnificent national park – the territories of the kingdom of Aragon stretched, in medieval times, from the ramparts of the Pyrenees to the floodplain of Valencia, the northern limit of the caliphates. Historically Aragon's identity comes less from a notion of nationhood than from one of strife – long centuries of confrontation with the Moors. A kingdom with little in the way of natural resources nevertheless managed to parley itself into a position of strength as the rampart against Muslim invasion, the ever-present threat for seven centuries.

Political alliances with the regional powers of Italy and France and union with Catalonia – the kingdom of Aragon once included Roussillon, the Balearics, Naples and Sicily – influenced her domestic as well as cultural habits. Judicious royal marriages and the commercial acumen of her ruling family, the counts of Barcelona, consolidated her position, though the marriage of Catherine of Aragon with Henry VIII of England was a notable exception. Most successful of all was the union of Ferdinand of Aragon with Isabella of Castile, the combined might of whose armies led to the defeat of the Moors at Granada in 1492. In the aftermath of the last battle of the Reconquista, the two sovereign powers became joint founding fathers of the Spanish nation – an event commemorated to this day in the royal title, Reyes de los Españas, Kings of the Spains.

A garrison nation, obliged constantly to take up arms, has no time till the soil, still less to gather harvest. No doubt because of this the traditional Aragonese diet relies heavily on meat. The main meat

View of Zaragoza, early sixteenth century, by Diego de Velázquez

nimals are sheep, providing both mutton and lamb, supplemented
y the hunter's bag – game from the forest. The bean dish includes
ame; lamb is cooked with tomatoes and garlic; stews of mutton or
alt-cod are brightened with red peppers. As the Christmas treat, the
ams of Teruel, a product of forest-foraging pigs, are deservedly
amous – the bones go to flavour the bean-pot and the scraps are
sed for croquetas. There is an understanding, too, of more modest
vild-gatherings – snails, fungi and leaves such as borage, a foodstuff
vhich is elsewhere used to feed domestic animals. Spinach-like
eaves listed by Gerald Brenan in the 1950s as consumed by the
illagers of Yegen in the Alpujarras – last refuge of the Moors in
pain – are *colleja*, bladder-campion, *Silene inflata*; *cerraja*, the young
eaves of the common sowthistle; *vinagretta*, sorrel; and chicory. Two
arieties of thistle are also eaten as young bud-rosettes: the golden
histle, *Scolymus hispanicus*, commonly known as *tagarina*; and the
nilk thistle, *Silybum marianum*, eaten in large quantities in Andalusia
luring the famine following the Civil War.

Opportunist meals aside, Aragon's central plateau, in those parts
nade fertile by the waters of the Ebro, supplies the region with
excellent vegetables and fruit. Terraced orchards yield apples,
peaches and cherries for candying. The oils of Teruel are pressed
rom the fruits of olive trees planted by the Romans and milled, until
hydraulic presses imported from France replaced them, between
millstones crafted by the Moors. There are vineyards too, producing
robust red wines for home consumption as they have for two
housand years. These wines – considered too rough for export
unless for blending – have recently been joined by some admirable
modern wines, including a cava.

The old ways are valuable only as long as they are useful, a lesson
the Aragonese learned early in their history. For the first century of
the kingdom's existence, the capital was Jaca, a fortified citadel in
the mountains; as soon as the caliphs had been persuaded, by force
of arms, to relinquish their grip, the seat of power was moved to
the gentler regions of Zaragoza. The Moors left behind a tradition
of craftsmanship which reappeared under Christian patronage as
he multi-patterned Mudejar style of architecture, and, somewhat

Still Life with Golden Bream, 1808–12, by Francisco de Goya

These treats aside, Aragon, as befits a warrior kingdom, has a
reputation for plain food honestly prepared. Her lack of natural
attributes – the arid southern highlands have been described as an
African desert, while the northern peaks are snow-covered
throughout the year – has, in the past, delivered times of famine to
add to the deprivations which are the inevitable price of constant
warfare. Armies empty store-cupboards just as readily as nature. At
the time of the Peninsular Wars, soldiers of both sides, always
hungry, were known to the country people as *bisoños*, those who
need, although this time the invaders, Napoleon's imperialist
armies, came from the north.

The terrible consequences of those wars and the famines which
followed were recorded by Francisco Goya, court portraitist to the
Bourbon dynasty, who might, had he not been a true son of Aragon,
have turned his back on the consequences of their decisions and
continued to earn a soft living from the great and the greedy.
Despairing of his masters, he channelled his genius into recording
the plight of those who pay their price: images so dreadful, so clear-
sighted, so much more terrible than any imaginings, that no-one
who has seen them can ever forget. All the more poignant that,
born and bred in the gentle farmlands of Zaragoza, he had, in
earlier life, painted delicious portraits of the homely dishes of his
childhood.

caracoles en salsa picante
snails in hot tomato sauce

Vineyard snails, fattened on vine leaves (a method which guarantees the creatures will not have ingested anything unpleasant), need no lengthy period of starvation but can simply be scrubbed in several changes of water and salt, then popped on the grill to roast. When ready – a matter of 10–20 minutes – they can either be eaten straight from the shell with a drop of vinegar, or reheated, as here, in a thick tomato and red pepper sauce enlivened with chilli.

Serves 6 as a tapa

3 dozen large snails, ready prepared

The sauce
12 ripe tomatoes, scalded, skinned and chopped
8 garlic cloves, skinned and roughly chopped
2 tablespoons toasted hazelnuts or almonds, crushed
4 red peppers, roasted, de-seeded and skinned
2 dried chillies, de-seeded and crumbled
  or 1 teaspoon hot pimentón (Spanish paprika)
  or powdered chilli
200ml (7fl oz) olive oil
3 tablespoons wine vinegar
1 teaspoon salt
Pinch sugar

Remove the snails from their shells and pinch off the little black intestine you'll find at the end, then pop them back in their shells – this is not necessary if the snails have been commercially prepared.

Put all the sauce ingredients in a blender and purée, or work everything together by hand. Bring to the boil in a roomy saucepan and simmer gently for 10–15 minutes to blend the flavours and evaporate the excess moisture. Stir in the snails, bring back to the boil and serve in small earthenware casseroles, with toothpicks for picking and bread for mopping your fingers as well as the juices.

migas del pastor con espinacas
spinach with shepherd's breadcrumbs

The idea is simple: edible greens, wilted in their own juices, are eaten with shepherd's migas. Migas are cubes of stale bread, soaked and fried in aromatic pork dripping, another of Spain's many stale-bread dishes. The spices are not essential, but they taste good. Any spinach-like greens, wild or tame, will do. If using chard, save the stalks for another dish.

Serves 4

The migas
225g (8oz) stale sourdough bread (at least 3 days old)
4 tablespoons pork lard or olive oil
4 garlic cloves, skinned
2 tablespoons diced serrano ham scraps or chorizo
1 tablespoon pimentón (Spanish paprika)
1 teaspoon dried oregano, crumbled
1 teaspoon ground cumin
Salt

The greens
450g (1lb) leaf-spinach or chard (leaves only – save the stalks for the cardoon recipe on p. 90)
4 tablespoons olive oil
1 teaspoon wine vinegar

Prepare the migas first. Dice the bread and put it in a bowl. Sprinkle with lightly salted water – don't soak it, but use just enough to revive the crumb. Leave for a few hours or overnight.

Prepare the spinach. Rinse, pick over, shred and cook the fresh leaves in a covered pan with a little salt and the minimum of water. This will take about 5 minutes. Drain it well, toss it over the heat with the oil and finish with a sprinkling of vinegar.

Meanwhile, heat the lard or oil in a frying pan and add the garlic and ham or chorizo. Let the garlic soften and gild, then stir in the bread, pimentón, oregano and cumin. Fry, stirring with a wooden spoon, until crisp and golden. Serve in individual bowls with the greens – together or separately, as you please. You could also add a fried egg per person or a handful of white grapes stirred into the migas just before you take the pan off the heat.

lenguas de cordero en salsa de tomate
lamb's tongues in tomato sauce

truchas en salsa de almendras
trout in almond sauce

The lamb's tongues can be prepared in advance and reheated in the sauce when you are ready to serve. Ox tongue can be treated in the same way, though you'll have to treble the cooking time.

Serves 4

4 lamb's tongues, trimmed
1 carrot, scraped and chopped
1 onion, quartered
2–3 outer sticks green celery, chopped
1 bay leaf
6 peppercorns
Salt

Sos del Rey Católico, near Zaragoza

The sauce
4 tablespoons olive oil
1 tablespoon chopped serrano ham or gammon
1 large onion, finely chopped
2–3 garlic cloves, skinned and chopped
450g (1lb) tomatoes, scalded, skinned and chopped (canned is fine)
150ml (1/4 pint) red wine
1–2 thyme sprigs
Salt and pepper

To finish
Toasted pine-kernels

Rinse the tongues and put them in a saucepan with enough water to cover. Bring to the boil, skim and add the aromatics: carrot, onion, celery, bay, peppercorns and a little salt. Bring back to the boil, turn down the heat, cover and leave to simmer for 1–1 1/2 hours, until tender. Remove with a draining spoon and strain and reserve a ladleful of the broth. As soon as the tongues are cool enough to handle, peel off the thick skin – it should slip off quite easily – and remove any little bones. Cut the meat into thick slices on the diagonal.

Meanwhile, make the sauce. Heat the oil in an earthenware olla or frying pan and add the ham, onion and garlic. Let everything soften and take colour. Add the tomatoes and fry until they melt to a mush. Add the wine and thyme and let it bubble up to evaporate the alcohol. Cook over a gentle heat until you have a thick sauce. Dilute with the reserved broth and bring back to the boil. Taste and add salt and pepper if necessary.

Lay the sliced meat in the sauce and reheat gently. Transfer to a warm serving dish and finish with a sprinkle of toasted pine-kernels. A dish of fried green peppers (p. 83) makes a good accompaniment.

Crispy pan-fried trout – rainbow and brown are both to be found in the streams of upper Aragon – are served here with an almond sauce. Classic combination, unusual delivery.

Serves 4

4 fine fat trout, each weighing about 350g (12oz)
2 tablespoons seasoned flour
2 tablespoons olive oil
1 tablespoon breadcrumbs
1 garlic clove, skinned and cut into fine slivers
1 tablespoon blanched almonds
1 tablespoon wine vinegar
1 tablespoon chopped parsley
1/4 teaspoon saffron threads, soaked in a splash o[f] water, or 1 tablespoon pimentón (Spanish paprik[a])
Salt and pepper

To finish:
1 tablespoon blanched almonds, dry-fried and chopped

Rinse the trout, but don't wipe them: they need the s[...] veil that covers their flanks for the coating to stick. F[...] them through the seasoned flour. Heat half the oil in [...] frying pan. Fry the breadcrumbs, garlic and almonds until lightly golden. Pound the contents of the pan w[ith] the vinegar, parsley and saffron or pimentón – or tip [...] into a food processor – until they form a thick paste.

Heat the remaining oil in the pan and lay in the tro[ut.] Fry gently, turning the fish once, for 5–6 minutes in [...] all, until firm and cooked through – test with your thumb. Transfer to a warm serving dish.

Reheat the pan, add a glass of water and bring to th[e] boil while you scrape in all the sticky brown bits. Ti[p] in the almond paste and let it bubble up, stirring to blend, until it thickens. Taste and season. Pour the sauce over the trout and finish with the almonds.

pollo chilindrón
spiced chicken with peppers

A speciality of Zaragoza in Aragon, the aromatic scarlet sauce turns the dish into a festive one and makes the most ordinary chicken taste great. To serve as finger food, joint the chicken into bite-sized pieces: chop the back in two, cut the breast into 6 pieces, divide the drumsticks at the joint and chop the thigh in half. This is easiest if you tap a knife through the bone with a hammer. It is good made a day ahead and served at room temperature.

Serves 4–6

1 small free-range chicken, jointed
4 tablespoons olive oil
4 tablespoons diced serrano ham (or lean bacon)
1 large onion, vertically sliced
3–4 cloves garlic, skinned and sliced
3 red peppers, de-seeded and cut into strips
450g (1lb) tomatoes, scalded, skinned and chopped
(or canned plum tomatoes)
1–2 bay leaves
2–3 cloves
1 small cinnamon stick
2–3 dried chillies, de-seeded and chopped
salt

Wipe over the chicken joints and pat dry (particularly important if they were frozen). Heat the oil in a heavy iron casserole over a medium heat, lay in the chicken joints and fry gently until they brown a little – about 5 minutes. Push the chicken to one side (or remove and reserve, if the casserole is too small) and add the chopped ham, onion, garlic and peppers. Fry gently, stirring regularly, until the vegetables soften and caramelise a little – about 10 minutes.

Add the tomatoes, bay leaves, cloves, cinnamon stick and chilli, let it bubble up, return the chicken pieces (if removed) to the pot, turn down the heat, put the lid on loosely and leave to cook gently, until

the sauce is jammy and thick – 50–60 minutes cooking time in all.

Serve at room temperature, with chunks of soft-crumbed bread for mopping up the juices.

croquetas de jamón serrano
serrano ham croquettes

The art of the croqueta is a birthright – a skill learned at your mother's knee. Every Spanish cook knows exactly how their mother did it but few would attempt to explain it. All I can tell you is that, in the hands of a skilled croqueta-artist, this crisp little mouthful – a crunchy jacket enclosing an exquisitely melting heart – is one of the most delicious things you'll ever taste. There's no secret to the recipe. Success lies in that least obvious of all culinary skill, sleight of hand, for the trick, if such there is, is in the frying. The basic panada – a thick béchamel – is made with whatever broth is available, enhanced with whatever scraps come to hand: serrano ham, a joint of chicken from the boiling pot, shredded salt-cod, a handful of prawns or freshly picked crab, grated cheese or fungi from the woods (useful if the haul's been a little meagre). If nothing else is available, a ladleful of broth from the puchero with a handful of freshly chopped parsley or a grating of nutmeg will do. Once the panada has cooled and firmed, it's formed into roly-poly little bolsters, coated with egg and breadcrumbs, fried crisp and eaten hot. Simple. Careful housewives dry their leftover bread to make breadcrumbs for the coating; everyone else buys ready-made from the baker. Here the suggested flavouring is the mountain ham of Teruel. Ideally the frying oil would come from the Roman-planted olive groves of Baja Aragon, which produce the much-admired, delicate, golden oils of Alcañiz.

Serves 8 as a tapa, 4 as a starter

The panada
5 tablespoons olive oil
8 level tablespoons plain flour
600ml (1 pint) ham or chicken broth (or the broth from the puchero)
2 tablespoons finely chopped serrano ham scraps
1/2 teaspoon freshly grated nutmeg
Sea salt and freshly ground pepper

The coating
4 tablespoons seasoned flour
2 eggs, mixed with 2 tablespoons water
6 heaped tablespoons fine dried breadcrumbs

Oil, for frying

First make the panada. Heat the oil gently in a heavy-bottomed pan. Using a wooden spoon, stir in the flour and let it froth up for a moment. Beat in the broth gradually (it's easier if you use a whisk at this point), bring to the boil, turn down the heat and whisk over a gentle heat until you have a very thick, soft, shiny sauce which promises a firm set. This is the beginner's version. The more skilful you become, the thinner you can make the sauce, and the more delicate the croquettes will be. Until you're sure of your skill, you need something you can handle. Stir in the chopped ham and nutmeg.

Taste and add salt and freshly milled pepper. Spread the panada in a thick layer on a cold plate. Leave to cool a little, then place an inverted plate on top, or cover with clingfilm. Leave to firm up in the fridge for at least 4 hours, preferably overnight.

When you are ready to cook, spread the flour on one plate, the egg on a second and the breadcrumbs on a third.

With a knife, mark the panada into 20–25 short, stubby fingers. Roll each finger first in flour, then in the egg mixture and finally press firmly into the breadcrumbs. All surfaces should be well coated or the croquette will burst into the oil. Continue until the panada is all used up and return the croquettes to the fridge for another hour or two to set the coating. Mend any little tears visible to the eye. At this point, you can freeze the croquettes for later: if you make them no larger than your thumb, they won't need de-frosting but can be dropped straight into the hot oil.

Heat two fingers' depth of oil in a frying pan – you need enough to submerge the croquetas completely. When the surface is lightly hazed with blue, test with a cube of bread: bubbles should form immediately and the crumb should brown within a minute. If the bread burns, the oil is too hot and the croquetas will burst as soon as they hit the oil; if the oil is too cool and fails to brown the bread, the croquetas will be soggy and collapse in the pan. When the oil is just right, slip in the croquetas a few at a time – not too many or the oil temperature will drop. Fry, rolling them over once, until crisp and golden brown. Transfer to kitchen paper to drain. Continue until all are done.

Serve immediately, piping hot, with good red Aragonese wine to cool your blistered tongue.

olleta de cordero con jamón
braised lamb with ham and wine

The gentle braising tenderises the meat of a well-grown mountain lamb, allowing the flavours to melt into each other and form a rich, sticky, little sauce. Perfect with a dish of plain-cooked chickpeas or haricot beans flavoured with a couple of cloves and a few peppercorns – add no salt until the beans are soft.

Serves 4

1 thick slice of serrano ham
About 125ml (4fl oz) olive oil
900g (2lb) boned shoulder or leg of lamb
1/2 bottle robust red wine
2 bay leaves
1 short cinnamon stick
A whole head of garlic, broken into cloves

To serve (optional):
Plain-cooked chickpeas or haricot beans

Preheat the oven to 170°C/325°F/gas mark 3. Lay the ham on the de-boned side of the meat. Roll the lamb up and tie it into a neat little bolster. Transfer to a well-fitting casserole into which you have poured a little of the oil. Add no extra salt – there is plenty in the ham. Drizzle with the rest of the oil and the wine. Tuck in the bay leaves, cinnamon and garlic cloves. Cover loosely with foil and transfer to the oven, basting from time to time, for about 1½ hours, until the meat is tender and well browned – you may need to add a little water from time to time to stop it drying out. After an hour, remove the foil.

Allow the meat to settle for 10 minutes or so before slicing. Lay the slices on a heap of plain cooked chickpeas or haricot beans (*pochas*) – if you choose chickpeas, stir in a handful of diced potato 20 minutes before the end. Sauce with the garlicky juices.

torta imperial
the emperor's almond cake

The emperor in whose honour this confection was created – be it Charlemagne or Napoleon or the Bourbon prince who held, and forfeited, the Pyrenean passes – was fortunate indeed. There can be no question of its excellence: Spanish ingredients prepared with Moorish skill with a touch of French sophistication – it can only be good.

Serves 8–10

The meringue layers
5 tablespoons ground almonds (or hazelnuts)
2 tablespoons cornflour
275g (10oz) caster sugar
6 egg whites

The praline
150g (6oz) almonds or hazelnuts (whole and unskinned)
150g (6oz) caster sugar

The caramel cream
5 tablespoons sugar
9 tablespoons water
6 egg yolks
350g (12oz) unsalted butter, softened

First make the meringue layers. Preheat the oven to 130°C/250°F/gas mark ½ – meringues need a very low, dry heat, the temperature of sunshine on a summer day in the mountains. Fold together the ground almonds, cornflour and all but 6 tablespoons of the sugar and set aside. In a very clean bowl, whisk the egg whites until stiff. Sprinkle in the remaining sugar and continue beating until the mixture is glossy and holds a peak when you lift the whisk. Fold in the almond mixture.

Line three shallow, round 20cm (8in) baking tins or Swiss-roll tins with baking parchment. Spread in the meringue mixture – use a spatula dipped in boiling water. Bake until crisp and dry, 40–45 minutes. Transfer the rounds carefully to a wire rack to cool.

Meanwhile, make the praline. Put the sugar and the nuts in a small heavy-bottomed saucepan and heat gently, stirring until the crystals have completely dissolved. Continue to cook until the sugar is caramelised to a deep golden brown and the nuts p a little to show they are toasted –170°C/338°F on th sugar thermometer. This is the praline. Spread it on an oiled tray or board to cool and harden. Sandwich the praline between 2 layers of clingfilm and crush with a rolling pin, or break it up and give it a quick blitz in a food processor – briefly, or it will turn into paste.

Now make the cream. In a small saucepan, heat the sugar with the water until dissolved, then boil steadily until the syrup reaches the soft ball stage: a clear gluey syrup which registers 115°C/239°F on the sugar thermometer. Whisk the egg yolks to blend. Gradually pour in the hot syrup, whisking constantl until the mixture cools to finger-heat. Beat the softened butter to a cream and fold it into the custard. (You can do all these things in a food processor.) Fold in half the praline, and put the crea to one side until it has cooled and solidified.

Assemble the cake. Start with a layer of meringue and spread it carefully with a quarter of the carame cream. Place a meringue layer on top, spread with th same volume of cream, and top with the third meringue layer. Smooth the rest of the caramel cream over the top and sides. Finish with a thick coating of the remaining praline. Store in a cool plac for a day and a night to allow the flavours to marry.

This cake freezes brilliantly and needs only an hour or two to defrost – allow just enough time to enable to be cut with a hot knife.

The gastronomy of the ancient kingdoms of Castile and Leon – castle country, defended to the death, homeland of the language as well as of the nation's oldest university – is, as might be expected, as sophisticated in the cities as it is down-to-earth in the countryside. Watered by the Duero, the land has been under cultivation since the earliest times by large-scale landowners and is Spain's main wheat-growing area. Only war and famine interrupt so important a responsibility as the making of wheat into bread. The Romans praised the good bread of Iberia. Proper country bread, that is; round for portability and with a dense, speckled, cream-coloured crumb protected by the thick brown crust which comes from the fierce heat of a wood-fired oven. Bread which, because it's made as it should be, dries out but never rots. Not the fluffy excuses for bread they sell in the bakeries of the town, but pan macho – unemasculated, with nothing taken out – raised with a sourdough leavening and made with flour which has not been bleached but has a pinch of lime in it to strengthen bones and teeth. Food for a working man and his wife, the first thing a baby ever tastes, the last he remembers at the end. Far more than a foodstuff, bread is sacred, blessed by Mother Church in case anyone should doubt its holiness, the stuff of life itself.

While bread is the mainstay of the country people, it's all the better when paired with the magnificent hams of Salamanca. Any Spaniard will tell you that – in much the same way that the Caspian has caviar and the Périgord has truffles – Salamanca has ham. It also has Spain's most venerable university, a wealth of beautiful medieval buildings made of golden stone, a large population of students and a reputation for having held the line against the Inquisition. Which, as it happens, is not so far from the knuckle. Public pork-eating once had a purpose. People who didn't eat pork, reasoned the Grand Inquisitor, must either be Muslims or Jews. Public ham-eating, it followed, was a demonstration of Christian allegiance – or a cunning ploy, depending on what decision was required.

After the day's work is done, Salamancans continue to gather in their elegantly proportioned central square for the evening's socialising, moving from bar to bar, mitigating the effects of good Christian wine with a nibble of Christian pig. While the prosperous citizens could afford the best bits, the rest was sold off cheap to the poor – in a university city, the students and the eateries they frequented. In the bars and restaurants of Salamanca you can taste the best Ibérico hams that money can buy. If you're poor and canny, you can sample delicious dishes of ears, snout, tail, blood-pudding, tripe, brains, sweetbreads. And all for free, since the bars attract customers through the quality of the tapa – the 'lid' that keeps the flies out of the liquor – which comes free with the glass.

Although most Ibérico pigs are reared in Extremadura, Salamanca is one of the main salting centres. Production processes have changed little over the years. Slaughter is strictly seasonal – mid to late winter, depending on the acorns. Once salted, the haunches are hung in airy attics, where the fat melts during the day and solidifies at night, massaging itself even further into the lean. The hams are then transferred to underground caverns, where they attract wild yeasts which cover the exterior with multi-coloured blooms – scarlet, ultramarine, saffron – which trigger the process of fermentation essential to flavour. The hams lose moisture as they gain in density.

Cellaring can last from eighteen months to five years – more, if the ham is very large. In contrast, salt-cured hams made from sty pigs of the modern breeds – serrano, prosciutto di Parma and elsewhere are ready within the year and, like wines which must be drunk young, can never achieve the complexity of an Ibérico.

The olive groves of Avila provide excellent oil – among the best you'll find in Spain – as well as sufficient forest-cover to shelter deer and wild boar. Segovia specialises in roast meat – beef, lamb and pork. The great city of Burgos has delicious junket, *coajada*, eaten with honey and almonds, and roast piglet – *cochinillo* – for a celebration.

To the north of the territory, the rocky lip which marks the edge of the Castilian plateau – a wilderness of deep ravines, high cliffs, boulders and forest – sheltered the monasteries which provided Christian Spain with a source of spiritual strength during the long Muslim ascendancy. One such sanctuary is the monastery of Santo Domingo de Silas. Approached from the north and east, the monastic enclave and its village are hidden high in a lunar landscape littered with huge boulders and rocky ravines crusted with cistus scrub. Such territory is easy to defend – as, being the first line of defence against the Moors, it was obliged to be. From the south and west, the approach is across the wide plains of Castile, rolling wheat fields as far as the eye can see, the land the monastic orders of warrior knights were sworn to defend. Santo Domingo is on the pilgrim's road to Santiago de Compostela, a source of revenue since many of the pilgrims were rich and could pay for their creature comforts without jeopardising their immortal souls. The monastic kitchen had a reputation for excellence. Even though the monks were obliged to follow the rules of fast as well as feast, these were not so strict as to discourage gluttony.

Fine wine, excellent bread, roast meat – all these good things are the gifts of God. All are found in abundance in Leon and Castile.

Rocky landscape in the Albarracín mountains

pan candeal castellana
castilian sourdough bread

Once tasted, Spanish country bread is never forgotten: made with flour milled by the baker himself, raised with sourdough and baked in a wood-fired oven, it has a close-textured, creamy-white crumb with a golden-brown crust. Its depth is measured in finger-widths. Bread of this kind – artisan-produced, sold from the mouth of the oven or the back of a van to those who know and understand its value – is priced according to weight. The customers wouldn't give a fig for fluffiness or ready-slicing. Nor would they consider any other kind of bread – unless to compare the merits of of the bread of one village with that of another - this one has a freckled crumb and a chestnut crust, the other has a cream-coloured crumb and a crust of a beautiful burnished gold. Country bread is round for ease of transport: round edges can better survive a bumpy ride on a donkey. Town bread is baked in a tin, since square edges slice more conveniently for sandwiches.

Makes 2 x 1kg (2lb) loaves

2kg (4½lb) strong unbleached flour
1 heaped tablespoon salt

In a bowl, work 110g (4oz) of the flour with its own weight of warm water to make a thick cream. Cover and set aside in a warm place for 24 hours. Work in another 110g (4oz) of the flour and its own weight of water. Set aside in a warm place for another 24 hours to bubble and ferment. This is your starter dough, which lightens the bread.

Weigh out 225g (8oz) of the starter dough (freeze the extra – it'll revive with warm water) and work with 750g (1lb 10oz) flour and enough warm water – about 600ml (1 pint) – to make a soft, very wet dough. Cover and leave overnight in a warm place. Knead in another 750g (1lb 10oz) flour, the salt and about 350ml (12fl oz) warm water. Knead vigorously – push and twist with the heel of your palm and hooked fingers – until elastic and smooth. Cover and set aside for an hour or two until it has doubled in size, by which time it should be spongy enough to bounce back when you prod it.

Tip it out again onto the floured board and punch it vigorously with your knuckles to distribute the air bubbles. Divide the dough in two, knead each piece into a ball and flatten them into thick fat cakes about the size of a dinner plate. Transfer to a baking tray dusted with flour and criss-cross the tops with a sharp knife. Cover with a clean cloth and set in a warm place until they have recovered their volume – 40–60 minutes.

Preheat the oven to 240°C/475°F/gas mark 9.

Slip the tray gently into the oven (the loaves deflate easily at this vulnerable moment). Bake for 15 minutes at this maximum temperature, after which you can do what you like – they won't feel a thing. Turn the oven down to 180°C/350°F/gas mark 4 and bake for another 40–45 minutes, until the loaves are nicely browned and sound hollow when you tap the base. Wait until they have cooled completely before you cut them. This bread will dry out rather than go mouldy and can be used for gazpachos and other preparations made with dried-out bread. For breakfast, it's at its best singed on a little camping grill set over the gas flame rather than popped in the toaster: the roughness of the caramelised crumb takes well to a rub of garlic and a trickle of olive oil

It's even better if the oil is the *flor*, flower, a sweet golden oil which flows from the weight of the olives alone, and the garlic is from a string you have grown and plaited yourself. Garlic discourages witches and keeps blight away from orange trees – useful attributes.

judías con almendras
green beans with spiced almonds

Vegetables are always served as a separate dish in Spain, never piled on the same plate as the meat. They usually appear after the main course, though they can sometimes arrive at the start of the meal as part of a selection of tapas. Small green beans, rather than large runner beans, are suitable for this dish. In summer, when the chickpeas are still small and tender, country housewives sometimes make it with fresh green chickpea-pods, but these are rarely sold in the marketplace.

Serves 4 as a starter or side dish

450g (1lb) green beans, topped and tailed
2 tablespoons flaked almonds
2 tablespoons olive oil
1 teaspoon cumin seeds
Juice of 1 lemon
1 teaspoon hot pimentón (Spanish paprika)
Rock or sea salt

Bring a pan of salted water to the boil. Cook the beans until tender but still green and firm: 4–5 minutes.

Meanwhile, fry the flaked almonds in the olive oil for a few seconds only or you will burn both the nuts and the oil. Sprinkle in the cumin. Remove from the heat, add the lemon juice and the pimentón and toss to coat the almonds.

Drain the beans and toss with the contents of the frying pan. Season with a little rough salt.

Gerald Brenan, settled in Spain in the 1950s, appreciated the virtues of Castilian bread: 'Almost everyone agrees about the excellence of Spanish bread. The loaf is very close textured, but it has a taste and sweetness like no other bread in the world. This, I imagine, is because the grain is entirely ripe before being harvested. Besides loaves we had roscos, or rolls made in the form of rings, and tortas, which are flat cakes made with wheat flour, sugar and oil. The poor, and sometimes the rich too, ate maize bread, and in the mountain farms they ate black bread made of rye: for shepherds it had the advantage of not going stale.

'Two dishes unknown to Western cooking are made with stale bread, though in more primitive times they were common enough: the first of these is gachas, a porridge of wheat flour simmered in water which used to be known in England as hasty pudding. In the villages it was taken with fried sardines, tomatoes and pimentos. The second is migas, a sort of porridge but fried in olive oil, garlic and water, which could be made either of wheat or maizeflour, or breadcrumbs. The poor eat it with the invariable sardines, while the rich like to pour hot chocolate over it. My landlord took it with both hot chocolate and fish, stirred up well together.'

The plains of Avila

olla podrida
stupendous bean-pot

Castile always has to have the best of everything, and the Castilian olla podrida is probably the mother of all bean-pots. I won't enter into a discussion of the origin of the name except to say that, directly translated, olla means an earthenware cooking pot of a particular shape – round-bellied and narrow of neck – and podrida means rotten. Since *podrido en plata* – stinking with silver – is a description of the seriously rich, this may be taken as an admiring reference to the luxuriousness of the dish rather than a perjorative comment on its composition.

Serves 4–6

450g (1lb) dried white beans
1 pig's trotter, split
1 pig's ear, scrubbed and singed
110g (4oz) pork ribs (salted, if possible)
225g (8oz) smoked streaky bacon (in a single piece)
225g (8oz) chorizo
1 quartered onion, stuck with 2–3 cloves
1–2 large carrots, scraped and cut into chunks
225g (8oz) cecina (dried beef-ham) – if unavailable, pastrami or fresh lean beef
225g (8oz) morcilla (black pudding)
Salt and pepper

To finish (optional)
Parsley and garlic, finely chopped together

Put the beans to soak overnight in plenty of cold, unsalted water. In another bowl, soak the pork bits – trotter, ear and ribs – in salted water overnight. The next day, drain the beans and the meats, scrubbing the pork skin with salt until perfectly white and clean.

Put the beans, pork, bacon and chorizo in a roomy boiling pot (a proper olla, if you can lay your hands on one), add the onion, carrots and enough water to cover generously, bring to the boil, skim off any grey foam which rises, turn down the heat and leave to cook very gently – the bubbles should only just break the surface – for 1–2 hours, until the beans are perfectly soft and the pork is tender. If you need to add water, make sure it's boiling.

Meanwhile, bring the beef-ham (or replacement) to the boil in another pan; transfer it to the bean-pot as soon as it's tender.

When the beans are nearly soft, add the morcilla. Make sure everything returns to the boil after you've added something new. Taste and season – you shouldn't need much salt. Finish, if you like, with a handful of parsley chopped with garlic. Serve the beans and broth as a first course, the meats afterwards. Good with a few pickled chillies or a shake of chilli sauce.

pollo rebozado
breadcrumbed chicken

Fried chicken enclosed in a crisp jacket of breadcrumbs: a practical use of leftover bread, and one which makes a luxury such as chicken go further. One smallish bird will happily serve six.

Serves 6

1 roasting chicken, jointed small (use a hammer to tap the knife through the bones)
About 4 tablespoons seasoned flour
2 eggs
2 tablespoons milk
About 4 tablespoons breadcrumbs
1 tablespoon pimentón (Spanish paprika)
1 teaspoon dried thyme
Olive oil, for frying
Salt and freshly ground pepper

Put the chicken joints and the seasoned flour in a polythene bag and shake to coat the joints lightly with flour. Shake off any excess.

Put the eggs and milk in a deep plate and blend with a fork. Spread the breadcrumbs in another plate and season with pimentón, thyme and pepper. Dip the chicken first in the egg and then in the breadcrumbs, pressing to make a jacket. Mend any gaps with another dip in the egg and breadcrumbs.

Heat enough oil in a heavy frying pan just to submerge the chicken joints. As soon as it's lightly hazed with blue, slip in as many of the chicken joints as will not cause the oil temperature to drop – bubbles should form around the coating immediately. Fry gently until the coating is crisp and the chicken cooked through. The oil should not be too hot as the chicken must be thoroughly cooked by the time the breadcrumbs are golden. If you're in any doubt, pop them in a medium oven to finish cooking. Drain on kitchen paper, and serve, if you like, with crisply fried chips and a fresh tomato sauce.

guiso de venado con vino
venison cooked in red wine

An aromatic venison stew from the hunting fores[t] of Avila. Tender venison fillet can be grilled over charcoal in the open fireplace, but the rest is bett[er] cooked gently in a pot. It can be prepared ahead, freezes perfectly, and is even better reheated.

Serves 5–6

900g (2lb) boned stewing venison (shoulder or leg[)] trimmed and cut into cubes
2 tablespoons seasoned flour
4 tablespoons olive oil
1 tablespoon diced serrano ham or gammon
2–3 garlic cloves, skinned and crushed
1 mild Spanish onion, finely chopped
1 carrot, scraped and diced
2–3 sticks green celery, chopped
1 tablespoon pimentón (Spanish paprika) or 1 dri[ed] red pepper, de-seeded and torn
1/2 teaspoon crushed peppercorns
425ml (3/4 pint) red wine
2 bay leaves
1 thyme sprig
Salt

Toss the diced venison in the seasoned flour – give [a] light dusting rather than a thick coat. Heat the oil i[n a] heavy casserole and add the meat. Fry over a high heat until it takes a little colour, then push to one s[ide] and add the diced ham, garlic, onion, carrot and celery. Fry gently until the onion is soft and golden. Stir in the pimentón and peppercorns. Add the win[e] and enough water just to submerge the meat, tuck [in] the herbs, season with salt and bring back to the bo[il].

Turn down the heat, put the lid on tightly and leave[to] simmer very gently either on top of the stove or in [a] low oven preheated to 150°C/300°F/gas mark 2 for 1 1/2–2 hours, until the meat is very tender. Check every now and then and add a little more boiling water if necessary. Serve on toasted bread or piled o[n] a heap of piping hot chips fried in olive oil.

cabrito asado al horno de leña

milk-fed kid roasted in a wood-fired oven

Don Emerito of the pilgrims' hostelry in Santo Domingo de Silas, whose recipe this is, says kid is better than lamb because it's juicier. Of the four quarters of the kid, he advises that the ones with the kidneys are the best. The wood for the oven – the fire is lit on the base of the oven and the ash and charcoal brushed as soon as the brickwork is white-hot – should if possible be oak, either holm or scrub. The roasting dish should be earthen-ware, the kind which holds the heat. Now you know it all.

To share between 4

1 milk-fed kid, 4–5kg (9–11lb), no more, quartered
Roughly ground rock salt – crystals rather than flakes
Lemon juice
Fresh pork lard, dripping or goose fat

Preheat the oven to 200°C/400°F/gas mark 6.

Arrange each quarter of kid in its own earthenware baking dish: if you don't own such vessels, individual gratin dishes of a suitable size will do. Sprinkle the meat with salt and a few drops of lemon juice. Put into the oven and keep the heat high for 1½ hours, so that the meat roasts rather than stews. Then spread with a little lard and cook for another 30 minutes, keeping an eye on it to make sure it doesn't burn.

Serve immediately with its juices and chunks of country bread, ideally locally made sourdough bread. For happiness and peace of mind, you need no more than good red wine to wash it down and a conscience soothed by Gregorian chant.

Santo Domingo

The monastery of Santo Domingo de Silas still has twenty monks, drawn by the solitude and the spiritual certainty of following the old ways. Vespers are sung in the church each evening at seven sharp. On an ordinary day, this takes thirty minutes, right on the nail. On a feast day, High Mass, an altogether more lengthy undertaking, replaces the evening's brief worship. But what draws the tourist buses as well as the devout is that the services are all sung in Gregorian chant.

Happily for modern visitors who might otherwise have had to rely on short commons at the monastery – the small community being unable to support the vast kitchens, vegetable-gardens and barnyards of the Order's heyday – several of the town's pilgrim-hostelries have been restored to cater to the tourists. Foremost among these is the Hotel Tres Coronas, a medieval glory which forms one side of the central square, a place of culinary pilgrimage in its own right, whose chef-proprietor, Don Emerito Martín, is the town's mayor.

Mayor Martín has earned himself a distinguished clientele. The prime minister José María Aznar himself, as well as Manuel Fraga, the leader of the opposition; businessmen from Burgos, Barcelona and Bilbao – in short, absolutely everyone who's anyone within a hundred miles comes to Emerito for one thing only, the succulent, crisp-skinned, exquisitely tender, milk-fed kid he roasts in the wood-fired bread-oven which warms the hotel dining room. Only Emerito knows exactly the moment at which the meat should be placed in the oven, heated to the right temperature by a fire whose embers must be raked out before the baking can start. The milk-fed kid comes from flocks which have pastured these mountains since long before the Christian armies defeated the Moors – and that, as everyone knows, was scarcely yesterday.

frite de Pedraza
roasted lamb ribs

This speciality of the walled citadel of Pedraza de la Sierra, in the mountains near Segovia, makes the best of one of the cheaper cuts of lamb. It reheats well and freezes perfectly.

Serves 4

900g (2lb) breast of lamb
2 tablespoons olive oil
6 garlic cloves, skinned and crushed with
  1 teaspoon salt
1 tablespoon pimentón (Spanish paprika)
1 teaspoon marjoram or oregano
2 tablespoons chopped parsley
2 tablespoon wine vinegar
Salt and pepper or chilli flakes

Trim the excess fat from the lamb (not too much: this is a rich, oily little dish) and cut into bite-sized. Heat the oil in an earthenware casserole or heavy cooking pot, add the meat and turn it in the hot oil until it takes a little colour. Add the garlic and salt, and fry gently for a few minutes more. Stir in the pimentón, herbs and vinegar and add a glass of water. Bring to the boil, turn down the heat, put the lid on tightly and leave to simmer very slowly for 1–1½ hours until the meat is tender and the juices have practically all cooked away. Remove the lid for the final 5 minutes, to evaporate any extra liquid. Serve with plain rice or crisp-fried chips or potatoes roasted in the cooking juices.

tortas de aceite
flaky olive oil biscuits

These light, delicate, flaky pastry-cookies are rather like sweet water biscuits. They're a children's treat, sold wrapped in wax paper – traditionally a speciality of Christmas, like so many good things.

Makes about a dozen

300ml (½ pint) light olive oil
1 teaspoon fennel seeds or aniseeds
About 450g (1lb) plain flour
1 teaspoon ground cinnamon
75g (3oz) sugar
1 teaspoon finely grated lemon zest
4 tablespoons white wine

To finish
Sugar, for dusting
50g (2oz) blanched, slivered almonds (optional)

Mix the oil with the fennel seeds or aniseeds and leave to infuse for an hour or two.

Preheat the oven to 200°C/400°F/gas mark 6.

Sift the flour and cinnamon into a bowl and mix in the sugar and lemon zest. Work in enough oil and wine to make a softish dough – use a wooden spoon or the hook of your hand. Break off walnut-sized pieces of the dough and pat or roll them out on a floured board into discs the size of a saucer.

Transfer to well-oiled baking trays, dust with sugar and sprinkle with the optional slivered almonds. Bake for 10–15 minutes until puffy, crisp and blistered black in places. Transfer to a wire rack to cool.

cuajada a la manera de Burgos
junket with honey & nu

The delicious sheep's milk junket you could buy i Burgos – it came in pretty little half-glazed terracotta pots – was the family treat when we were passing through the beautiful cathedral tow on our way to the Channel ports in the school holidays. The area is known for a particularly goo white sheep's milk cheese, queso de Burgos, usually eaten fresh, and the junket is the first stage in the cheese-making process.

Serves 4–6

600ml (1 pint) fresh full-cream milk (in default of sheep's milk, cow's or goat's will do)
150ml (¼ pint) single cream
3–4 drops rennet or crushed rennet tablets (from a good chemist or grocer)

To finish
1 teaspoon ground cinnamon
4 tablespoons roughly cracked shelled walnuts or hazelnuts
4 tablespoons runny honey – orange blossom or chestnut

Bring the milk and cream to the boil and then let cool to finger warmth. Stir in the rennet and pour the mixture into individual pottery jars. Leave it to set in a cool place – 2 or 3 hours will do the trick. Finish with a sprinkling of cinnamon and serve topped with a spoonful each of nuts and honey.

la mancha & madrid

The windswept plateau of La Mancha is dotted, as Cervantes' readers would expect, with Don Quixote's windmills. Baking-hot summers give way to icy winters. Nine months' hell and three months' freeze, as the natives put it. This is shepherding country, a land of dun-fleeced flocks which roam the dusty plains, sheep whose milk goes for the making of manchego, Spain's most famous cheese.

The emblem of the national capital, Madrid, the heart of the region, is a brown bear in an arbutus tree. Hard to believe, as you speed down the motorway which streaks across this vast expanse of red earth, that this land was not so long ago heavily forested, cleared in places for the growing of vines for wine and wheat for bread, with fortified towns surrounded by woodland.

The country food is muscular – *fuerte*, strong – with sophisticated city cooking left to the smart folk in Madrid. Toledo holds its own in the culinary stakes with roast suckling-pig, an alternative use for the baker's oven, which draws its Sunday audience from Madrid as well as the surrounding countryside. The presence of so many windmills indicates that this is – or was – a wheat-growing area. Bread is eaten with manchego cheese, best when matured for a year or more – even better when, as I have had it in a bar in Seville, matured under olive oil until it has the bite and fragrance of Parmesan. Or you might prefer to spread your bread with the rich fat of the cosseted sty-pigs which every household once kept to eat up the scraps. When stale and unpalatable otherwise, bread is used to make gazpacho, a bread porridge eaten hot in winter and cold in summer, which in this part of the world sometimes includes game meat, or a shepherd's dish of migas – softened crumbs refried with garlic.

Bread is also the automatic accompaniment for egg dishes of all kinds – tortillas, revueltos (scrambled eggs), *duelos-y-quebrantos* (wounds and suffering – eggs cooked with chorizo), a dish immortalised by Cervantes as Don Quixote's favourite breakfast. And

bread rolls – bolillos (little bolsters) – arrive unasked with the pisto manchego, aromatic summer vegetables gently cooked in olive oil. Maize is grown to feed poultry and the barnyard birds as well as the human population when there's nothing else around.

Wheat is not the only material sent to the miller. Flours milled from lentils, chickpeas, maize and, most unusual since found nowhere el[se] that I know of, *harina de almortas*, a flour milled from the seeds of th[e] blue vetch, a member the pea family. Lacking gluten, these are use[d] to make gachas, a soft porridge cooked with pork bits, serrano ham, chorizo or simply finished with a lick of olive oil and a sliver of garl[ic].

The cash crop of La Mancha – after the sale of manchego cheese – i[s] saffron. More of the precious spice – some seventy per cent of worl[d] production – is grown here than anywhere else on earth , including [the] land of origin, somewhere on the plains of Mesopotamia: saffron is nothing if not romantic. Spain has the Phoenicians to thank for the introduction of the crop, and the Moors for teaching its virtues. Saffron – the tiny stamens of *Crocus sativus*, three to each bloom – must be hand-cropped and hand-sorted, a labour-intensive busines[s] as with so much else that is good. In times of shortage, the cost, weight for weight, has risen to more than that of gold; even today it [is] still the most expensive spice on the shelf. But then you need very little – a knife tip is enough to colour rice or perfume a stew.

The wines of La Mancha – the strong reds of Valdepeñas, the elegan[t] wines of Toledo and Manzanares – are used as a cooking liquor for pork, poultry and game as well as to warm the heart in the cold winters and cool the brow in the heat of summer. Wine is always

even if only a handful of olives and a crust of bread. Even so, the
poorest landless peasant knows exactly what defines the quality of
the bread and excellence of the olives. Every Spaniard understands
that the raw materials dictate the quality of the dinner – and none
knows this better than the inhabitants of her capital city.

I was only just a teenager when my stepfather was posted to the
British Embassy in Madrid. Happily for me, our apartment was just
down the way from the city's main covered market which ran six
days a week, winter and summer. It was here that my mother's cook
shopped daily, trailing me in her wake. The morning treat was a
paper cone of churros – dough fritters hot from the frying vat – to
dip in a cup of hot chocolate as thick as lentil soup. At lunchtime
there were tapas to be sampled free with a glass of lemonade in
which the bartender would splash a drop of wine, while my minder,
too busy gossiping to pay much attention, took a nip of anis brandy
for her health. In the evening I would be sent across the street with a

cows were still kept for milking in the centre of the city; their
tranquil heads visible through the open stable door, their warm
breath mingling with the scent of fresh hay in the milking parlour.

On the occasions when my mother had decided to throw one of her
diplomatic gatherings – cocktail parties were the thing at the time –
I spent all day in the kitchen helping arrange the little canapés I
was later to hand round to the guests. The hot things were the most
exciting – miniature versions of what I most enjoyed: little squares
of potato tortilla, tiny pasties filled with tuna and tomato, cheese
fritters, croquetas made with a creamy bechamel flavoured with
ham. Better still – because the cook was, as she was fond of
explaining, overworked, underpaid and lacking a kitchenmaid – this
was the only time, on pain of not telling my mother, I was allowed
to help in the kitchen. I have never needed to learn how to flip a
tortilla, fritter a fish or roll a croqueta – these are the things every
Spanish child learns at mother's elbow. Me too.

Windmills in La Mancha

churros madrileños
doughnut fritters

1 tablespoon olive oil
1 teaspoon salt
About 275g (10oz) strong bread flour
Oil, for frying

To finish
Caster sugar, for dusting (optional)

Bring 600ml (1 pint) water, the oil and salt to the bo[...]
in a roomy saucepan. As soon as it's bubbling, beat [...]
the flour a fistful at a time until you have a smooth[...]
soft dough ball which leaves the sides of the pan
clean. Allow to cool.

For the homely version – leave the fancy piping to t[...]
professionals – pack the dough into a large star-
shaped piping-syringe, the kind you'd use for a
biscuit dough. The opening should be about as wide[...]
as your thumb. Lay a clean cloth on the table and
dust it with flour. Pipe out half a dozen finger-lengt[...]
churros – don't do them all at once or they'll form [...]
skin and burst when they encounter the hot oil.

Meanwhile, heat a deep pan of frying oil – this is on[...]
of the few moments when the Spanish cook reaches[...]
for the deep-fryer. When the oil is good and hot and
lightly hazed with blue, slip in the first batch of
churros and fry until golden. If the oil is too hot, the
centres will remain raw; if too cool, the churros will
break up in the oil. Transfer to kitchen paper to drai[...]
While the first ones are cooking, pipe out another
half-dozen lengths and transfer them to the oil.
Continue until all are done. Practice makes perfect.
Hand the sugar around separately (people who like t[...]
dunk their churros in their morning coffee or hot
chocolate usually sweeten the drink rather than the
churro).

If you'd like to try a potato dough, replace half the
flour with mashed potato. Potato churros are always
ridged, short and thick.

Every Madrileño's favourite breakfast, these long,
thin, tubular batter-fritters are sold by weight
piping hot from the frying kiosk in the corner of
every market throughout the land. In Madrid the
visit to the churreria is as much a part of the
morning ritual as the visit to the corner café for a
cup of hot chocolate or milky coffee – *café con leche*
– into which the churro is dipped. Where there is a
choice, certain stands are always much better
patronised than others. Each churreria has its own
technique for attracting customers: the deftness
with which the oversized piping-syringe is
handled, the theatricality of the cook, maybe a
particular shape – single circles instead of the
usual snail shape which is snipped into short
lengths. While the basic dough is a simple batter
mix, potato is sometimes added – if this is so, the
churro is pushed through a ridged syringe and the
fritters are short and straight. The notice *hay
churros* in a café window probably means
someone's prepared to fry up ready-made churros
from the deep-freeze – better than a stale
ensaimada, but not as enlivening as queuing for
the real thing.

Serves 4

Spanish markets are wonderful places for a child such as I was when my family lived in Madrid – every stall-holder treats you to a little taste of his wares, and never mind that every old lady pinches your cheek. What's black and blue when there's a mouthful of olive to be sampled, a scrap of cheese, a sliver of ham? In the main covered market there was a whole section devoted to fish – sloped marble slabs heaped with boxes of pale pink prawns, silvery sardines, clams, spiky sea snails, a slithering mass of unidentifiable multi-coloured sea creatures, live crabs, writhing eels, the heads of swordfish and tuna proudly displayed beside the steaks of flesh.

Another aisle was dedicated to meat. The butchers used huge cleavers to slice across the muscle, chopping the bones for soup, offering their customers nothing identifiable as a steak or a chop – until you came to the innards heaped beside them in glistening piles of whose identity there could be no doubt. Liver, kidneys, brains, testicles, tripe of every shape and colour – all for sale to those who couldn't afford *filete*, the generic name for everything which wasn't guts. There were stalls, too, which sold nothing but *embutidos* – the salt-cured products of the pig: chorizo, morcilla, dark-skinned hams shining with golden fat, hunks of bone, ears and trotters buried in salt.

The egg lady sold the egg-producers as well as their produce, pulling up a squawking bundle of feathers from the crate beside her. Our cook, if she had a puchero in mind, would casually tuck her choice under her arm and carry it, protesting loudly, all the way home. On my mother's instruction she would shoo me out of the kitchen before I could see her do the deed which led to the pot.

Nevertheless, I well remember a handful of unborn eggs, little golden globes, which she quite casually slipped in the broth and insisted I eat since they'd make my hair curl – an unnecessary precaution, as it happened.

Fish on display in a Madrid market

buñuelos de queso
cheese fritters

Here is something interesting to do with manchego cheese after it's dried out at the end of winter. Manchego, named after the region in which it's made, is a mature sheep's milk cheese whose fame has spread far beyond its land of origin and which represented, in the old days, a way of paying the rent. Just mix and fry – so simple.

Serves 4–6 as a tapa

4 large eggs
4 tablespoons milk
4 heaped tablespoons plain flour
4 heaped tablespoons grated manchego or any
    other hard cheese
1 tablespoon chopped parsley
1 tablespoon grated onion
1 teaspoon hot pimentón (Spanish paprika) or
    chilli powder
Salt and pepper
Oil, for frying

Whisk the eggs and milk together. Gradually work in the flour and cheese, beating to prevent lumps. Add the parsley, onion and paprika. Season with salt and pepper.

Heat two fingers' depth of oil in a frying pan, or heat up the deep-fryer (if you use one). When the surface is lightly hazed with blue, drop in teaspoons of the mixture – not too many at a time or the oil temperature will drop and the fritters will be heavy. Fry until they puff up, crisp and turn golden brown, flipping them to cook the other side – if they burst, drop the oil temperature a little. Transfer to kitchen paper to drain. Continue until the mixture is all used up.

Serve hot from the pan. Good with a dipping-sauce of chopped fresh tomato spiked with chilli.

tortilla española
potato omelette

The Spanish omelette is a thick, round, juicy egg-cake into which have been folded a variety of other ingredients which allow it to hold its shape: that of the light iron pan in which it's cooked. When making a tortilla, the volume of vegetables should be roughly the same as the volume of egg. If the tortilla is bolster-shaped – rolled over in the French style – it's designated French: *tortilla francesa*. Whatever culinary skills she may otherwise lack, every Spanish housewife makes a beautiful tortilla. It's served hot, warm or cool, though never cold, and appears at any meal at any time of day. Tucked into a bread roll, it's the field worker's midday break; schoolchildren take a portion, wrapped carefully in a square of sugar paper, for their lunch; toothless old grannies live on it; cut into neat little squares speared with a toothpick, it's served as a tapa in every bar.

Serves 4 as a starter, 8 as a tapa

4 medium potatoes
1 thick slice of Spanish onion, finely chopped
4 large eggs
Salt
Olive oil

Peel and dice the potatoes, or slice or chip.

In a small bowl, use a fork to beat the eggs with salt and pepper.

Heat a tortilla pan (Spanish housewives keep a light raw-iron frying pan for the purpose). Failing this, whatever you'd use to cook a French omelette will do. Heat enough olive oil in the pan to submerge the potatoes. Fry gently until perfectly soft – don't let them crisp or take colour. Just before the end of the cooking, salt lightly and add the onion. Transfer the potatoes and onion to a sieve set over a bowl to cool and catch the drippings.

Stir the cooled potatoes and onion into the eggs. Season with salt and pepper. Pour all but a tablespoon of the oil out of the pan, and reheat. Tip in the egg mixture, lifting the edges to allow the uncooked egg to run underneath. Fry gently – if the heat is too high, the base will be leathery. As soon as it begins to set, put the lid on loosely to aid the process. When the surface looks set, it's time to turn it. Be brave. Pop a plate over the top and invert the whole thing in one movement, so the tortilla lands cooked side uppermost. Easy. Reheat the pan – you may need a little more oil (use the drippings) – and slip the tortilla back in, cooked side uppermost. Use a spatula to build up a deep straight edge. As soon as it begins to feel firm when you press the top with your finger – it should remain juicy in the middle – slip it out onto a plate and pat off the excess oil with kitchen paper.

Serve warm, quartered as a starter or cut into small squares to serve as a tapa.

ensalada de remolacha
beetroot salad

Mediterranean cooks can buy bunches of beetroot complete with their leaves. In this recipe the leaves are cooked like spinach and dressed with vinegar, while the sweet roots are dressed with garlic and oil.

Serves 4–6

900g (2lb) beetroot
Salt
2–3 tablespoons wine vinegar
2–3 garlic cloves, skinned and cut into slivers
2 tablespoons chopped parsley
About 4 tablespoons olive oil
1/2 teaspoon cumin seeds

Trim off the beetroot leaves and reserve, leaving a generous hank of stalk on the roots. Rinse the earth off the beetroot but leave them whole – don't scrub or cut. Cook them in plenty of boiling water until perfectly tender: 40–60 minutes. Shred the leaves and stalks and rinse thoroughly. Don't shake them dry but put them, lightly salted, in a covered pan and cook them in the water which clings to the leaves for 5 minutes or until they are soft. Dress with the vinegar.

Drain the roots and slip off the skins as soon as they're cool enough to handle. Dice, dress with the garlic, parsley and olive oil and fold in the leaves. Finish with a sprinkling of cumin seeds and a little more olive oil.

machacón
hot potato salad

This cheap and cheerful dish from La Mancha is made with new potatoes in summer and mature potatoes in the winter – and the winters in La Mancha are hard. The inclusion of something salty and fishy – anchovies, salt-herring – is not essential, but does wonders for the flavour. A little soaked bacalao left over from another recipe would be even better – just blister it for a moment in a dry pan, then flake.

Serves 4 as a starter

900g (2lb) floury potatoes (all roughly the
   same size)

The sauce
2 large tomatoes, de-seeded and diced
1 green pepper, de-seeded and diced
2 tablespoons diced cucumber
2 tablespoons lemon juice
4 tablespoons olive oil
1 teaspoon cumin seeds, roasted in a dry pan
1 dried chilli, de-seeded and torn
1/2 teaspoon salt

To finish
2–3 salted anchovy fillets or herring or bacalao,
   flaked (*optional*)

Scrub the potatoes and cook in just enough boiling salted water to cover, until soft: 20–30 minutes, depending on their size. Drain them thoroughly.

Meanwhile, mix the sauce ingredients and leave in a warm place for the flavours to develop. Shake the hot potatoes so they split a little. Dress them with the sauce and finish with the optional flaked fish.

asadillo
roasted red peppers and tomatoes

A dish of caramelised peppers and tomatoes, nothing complicated, as served as a tapa at the Venta del Quixote, Puerto Lapis, near Aranjuez, where Cervantes' heroic cavalier tilted at windmills.

Serves 4 as a starter

4 red peppers
6 tablespoons olive oil
1 garlic clove, skinned and chopped
2 large, perfectly ripe beef tomatoes, sliced
Salt and pepper
1 teaspoon dried marjoram or oregano

Roast the peppers, whole and with their stalks still in place, over a gas flame or under the grill until the skin bubbles and blisters black (the kitchen fills with the most delicious aroma). Leave in a plastic bag for 10 minutes to loosen the skin. Carefully scrape off every scrap of skin, then hull, de-seed and cut into strips.

Pour 1 tablespoon of the olive oil into each of four individual earthenware cazuelas or gratin dishes. Arrange the peppers, garlic and tomatoes in layers, seasoning as you go. Sprinkle with the rest of the oil and the herb. Roast at a high heat either on the stove or in the oven – preheated to 230°C/450°F/gas mark 8 – for about 20–25 minutes, until the tomato is reduced to a jammy scarlet sauce.

Serve with toasted country bread and a few slices of serrano ham.

boquerones en vinagre
vinegar-pickled
anchovies

The fresh anchovy looks like a small slender sardine, lacks discernable scales and has a dark kingfisher-blue stripe down its flanks. In this familiar recipe – you find it in every tapa bar in every corner of Spain – the little fish are given a light pickling in salt and vinegar, a method used, in pre-refrigeration days, to add shelf-life to small fish which could not be eaten fresh. The result was so good it has remained on the menu ever since. Good after two days, even better after three, it keeps for a week in the fridge.

Serves 8 as a tapa

450g (1lb) fresh anchovies
2–3 garlic cloves, skinned and sliced
salt
2 tablespoons sherry vinegar

To finish
olive oil
chopped parsley

Rinse the anchovies – they have no scales to worry about – and gut them by pushing your finger through the soft belly. Pull the head of each fish firmly down through the belly towards the tail. This will bring the spine with it and leave the fish split in a butterfly shape, all in one movement.

Lay the opened fish flesh upwards in a single layer in a dish. Sprinkle with the garlic and a little salt. Mix the vinegar with its own volume of water – sherry vinegar is powerful stuff – and pour it over the fish. Cover with foil and leave in the fridge to marinate for 24–48 hours. Drain before serving and finish with the merest thread of olive oil and a sprinkling of parsley. Serve as a tapa with bread and green olives.

The garlic of La Mancha

The region has the reputation for the best garlic, an industry centred on Las Pedroñeras, where they weave the creamy-fleshed, purple-streaked bulbs into handsome plaits for export to other, less fortunate places. Every year, every man, woman and child in Spain eats at least 1.3kg (3lb) of garlic. It's the distinguishing flavour of the cooking of the Mediterranean – the pot-herb without which no cocido or bean-pot is complete. Garlic has disinfectant and healing properties, hence its use as a remedy against witches and werewolves. It was – still is – considered an effective water-purifier: pilgrims on the road to Santiago would squeeze garlic juice into the well-water to make sure it had not been contaminated. Andalusia's ajo blanco, a refreshment made with almond milk flavoured strongly with garlic, is a Moorish refinement on the theme. Babies are given a little taste on the tongue to settle their tummies; in the winter, infused in broth, it's sipped as a cold cure.

Saffron crocuses blooming near Membrillo, La Mancha

pez espada en salsa de azafrán
swordfish in saffron sauce

Both swordfish and fresh tuna are widely available inland, since their great size makes them ideal for transportation. They are treated more like meat than fish, and are often served as the main course in a meal. Recipes which suit swordfish work just as well with tuna.

Serves 4

4 thick swordfish steaks
About 1 tablespoon seasoned flour
6 tablespoons olive oil
2 onions, finely sliced
2 garlic cloves, skinned and finely chopped
4 tablespoons pine-kernels
1 egg yolk
1 glass dry sherry or white wine
Strip of lemon zest
1 bay leaf
1/4 teaspoon saffron threads, toasted in a dry pan
Salt and pepper

Salt the swordfish steaks lightly, dust with flour to protect the delicate flesh, and fry them in 1 spoonful of the olive oil on both sides until gilded and firm (2–3 minutes per side), then reserve.

Heat the remaining olive oil in the frying pan and fry the onions and garlic gently until they soften and gild – don't let them brown. Push them to one side and fry the pine-kernels until golden, then remove the pan from the heat. Whisk the egg yolk with the sherry or wine and stir it into the onions. Return to a low heat, add the lemon zest, bay leaf and saffron and stir until the mixture thickens to a cream – don't let it curdle. Remove the lemon zest and bay leaf and spoon the sauce over the swordfish. Good with a side dish of migas (roughly torn bread fried golden in olive oil).

The vineyards of La Mancha

tomates rellenos con piñones
tomatoes stuffed with pine-kernels

remember as a child sitting in the sunshine in
Madrid's Retiro Park, poking out with a stick the
nuts buried inside the pine-cones and using a rock
to get at the oily little seeds inside – a task which
could easily take all day. Make this with the large,
firm, field-ripened Mediterranean beef tomatoes
you can buy in the summer. The sweetness of the
tomato is balanced by the pungency of garlic and
the resinous flavour of the pine-kernels.

Serves 4 as a tapa

large tomatoes
tablespoons olive oil
tablespoons pine-kernels
2–3 garlic cloves, skinned and finely chopped
tablespoons fresh breadcrumbs
tablespoon chopped fresh marjoram
teaspoon ground allspice
Salt and pepper

Cut the tomatoes in half right through the equator.
Scoop out the seeds and discard. Hollow out the
shells, reserving the scrapings.

Preheat the oven to 180°C/350°F/gas mark 4.

Warm 2 tablespoons of the olive oil in a small frying
pan, add the pine-kernels and let them take colour.
Stir in the garlic, breadcrumbs, marjoram and
allspice and fry until all the oil is absorbed and the
breadcrumbs have crisped a little. Stir in the
reserved tomato scrapings, mashing to break them
down a little, and season with salt and pepper.

Arrange the tomato shells in a baking dish. Stuff
them with the breadcrumb mixture and trickle with
the rest of the oil. Bake for 25–30 minutes, until the
tomatoes are soft but not yet collapsed. Serve at
room temperature in their cooking dish.

pastel de higado
liver pâté

A rough country pâté. Serve it as a main dish, hot
with mashed potatoes in the winter, cold with a
salad in the summer.

Serves 6

450g (1lb) pig's liver
450g (1lb) pork shoulder
225g (8oz) pork belly
1 tablespoon diced serrano ham
1 garlic clove, skinned and finely chopped
1 tablespoon chopped parsley
1 teaspoon ground allspice
1 glass dry sherry
2 tablespoons fresh pork lard or olive oil
1 tablespoon chopped onion
1 egg, beaten with a fork
4 tablespoons dry breadcrumbs
Salt and pepper
2–3 bay leaves

Mince or chop the liver and pork together. Work in
the remaining ingredients, except for the bay leaves,
and season with salt and pepper.

Preheat the oven to 180°C/350°F/gas mark 4.

Line a rectangular baking dish or loaf tin with foil,
shiny side inwards, leaving a generous flap for
folding over the top. Pack in the mixture, top with
the bay leaves and fold over the foil to enclose. Set
the tin in a roasting tin – a bain-marie – with
enough boiling water to come halfway up the sides.
Bake for 1–1¼ hours, until the juices run clear
when you push a skewer through the middle. Allow
to cool and place a weight on top. Set it in the fridge
overnight to firm. Slice with a sharp knife dipped in
boiling water and serve at room temperature.

Good with red peppers in oil and a potato salad (see
p. 124).

duelos y quebrantos
scrambled eggs with chorizo

The name literally means 'wounds-and-suffering',
a reference to what happens when the pimentón
in the chorizo bleeds into the eggs, streaking them
scarlet. In Cervantes' tale of outdated chivalry, this
was Don Quixote's Saturday night treat – and the
closest to a battlefield the heroic knight would
ever be. Failing chorizo, use diced serrano ham,
a tablespoon of pimentón and add another
2 tablespoons of lard or olive oil.

Serves 4

2 links (about 225g/8oz) soft chorizo (picante, for
  preference)
2 tablespoons fresh pork lard or olive oil
4 tablespoons diced stale bread
8 eggs, beaten with a fork to blend
1/2 teaspoon chilli flakes (optional)
Salt

Slice the chorizo thickly and fry it in the lard or oil
in a frying pan. Cook until the fat runs and the
chorizo begins to brown. Add the diced bread and
toss it over the heat until it crisps and browns. Stir
in the eggs, season with salt and chilli if liked, and
scramble the eggs with the rich scarlet juices. As
soon as they begin to set, remove the pan from the
eat.

Serve immediately or the eggs will harden.

pisto manchego
slow-cooked summer vegetables

Perfect with manchego cheese and country bread. The essential ingredients are the aubergine, the garlic and the olive oil – everything else is negotiable.

Serves 4–6

tablespoons olive oil
firm aubergines, diced
-3 garlic cloves, skinned and chopped
Spanish onion, finely sliced
red peppers, de-seeded and diced
medium courgettes, sliced
50g (1lb) ripe tomatoes, scalded, skinned
and chopped
teaspoon crumbled dried oregano
alt
ot pimentón (Spanish paprika) or chilli powder

Warm 2 tablespoons of the oil in a frying pan and gently fry the diced aubergines, sprinkled with a pinch of salt, until they soften and take a little colour. Be patient: first they soak up oil like a sponge, then they release it again, then they begin to fry a second time. Transfer to a sieve placed over a bowl to catch the drippings. Add the rest of the oil to the pan, fry the garlic and onion, salted lightly, until just caramelised and transfer to the sieve. Add the drippings to the pan. Fry the peppers, transfer them to the sieve, put the drippings back in the pan, then repeat with the courgettes.

Reheat the remaining drippings and add the tomatoes. Bubble up, add the oregano and season with salt and pimentón or chilli. Add the vegetables from the sieve. Cook gently over a low heat for 10 minutes. Remove the lid, turn up the heat and give it a good bubble – the finished dish should be jammy rather than watery. Serve at room temperature, as part of a selection of tapas; as a main course, pop a fried egg on top or a handful of flaked, pre-soaked salt-cod or salt-cured tuna – *mojama*.

codornices con ajo
deep-fried spatchcocked quails with garlic

Farmed quail have now more or less replaced songbirds on the Mediterranean menu – just as well, since everything from blue tits to thrushes used to be trapped for the pot.

Serves 4 as a main course, 8 as a tapa

8 quail, prepared
1 small glass dry white wine
12 garlic cloves, unskinned but crushed
Salt and pepper
Olive oil, for frying

Split the quails right down the back, from vent to neck. Flatten them like squashed frogs. Put them to marinate in the wine, garlic, salt and pepper for a few hours. Drain, reserving the garlic, and pat them dry.

In a heavy pan, heat enough oil to submerge the birds. When it is lightly hazed with blue, put in as many of the quails as the pan will take in a single layer, garlic and all. Be warned: the oil will spit. Fry the birds until the skin and all the little bones are brown and crisp.

Sprinkle with rough salt and serve each bird skin side up on a thick slice of country bread.

pichones a la toledana
pigeons cooked in red wine

A recipe from the walled city of Toledo, once hidden in woodland, where a lively population of pigeons grows plump on the produce of the surrounding farmland, vineyards and olive groves.

Serves 4

8 tablespoons olive oil
4 pigeons, prepared
2 large Spanish onions, diced
16 garlic cloves, unskinned but crushed
2 glasses red wine
1 tablespoon wine vinegar
2 bay leaves
1–2 thyme sprigs
$1/2$ teaspoon crushed peppercorns
1 teaspoon ground allspice
Salt

Heat half the oil in a heavy casserole large enough to accommodate the pigeons. Turn the birds in the hot oil until the skin browns a little, then remove and reserve. Add the remaining oil, reheat the pan and fry the onions and garlic cloves until they soften and gild a little. Return the birds to the pan with the wine, vinegar, herbs and spices. Bring to the boil, turn down the heat, put the lid on tightly and leave to simmer for 50–60 minutes, until the pigeons are perfectly tender and the juices reduced to a few spoonfuls.

Serve one bird per person, making sure each has its share of garlic cloves – creamy and mild when slow-cooked like this.

galianos
game casserole with raisins and saffron

Madrid's coat of arms is a bear in an arbutus tree – which tells you that the whole region was once heavily forested. The aristocracy hunted deer and wild boar; the rural poor made do with the rabbit and anything else they could catch – though only when the landlord wasn't about. Galianos is what you do with the poacher's bag. Since the age of game is uncertain, long slow cooking is a wise precaution. The inclusion of a splash of vinegar helps to tenderise the meat – an old huntsman's trick.

Serves 6–8

2 wild rabbits (or 1 domestic rabbit)
4 partridges or 8 quail, prepared
6 tablespoons olive oil
1 thick slice of serrano ham fat (or unsmoked streaky bacon), diced
12 garlic cloves, skinned and roughly crushed
Sea salt and pepper
2 tablespoons raisins
1 short cinnamon stick
1/2 teaspoon saffron threads
1 tablespoon pimentón (Spanish paprika)
2 tablespoons wine vinegar

Pick over the game, removing any stray feathers or fur. With a sharp knife, lift off the fine transparent membrane which covers each rabbit's saddle – if you don't, the meat will never tenderise. Using a hammer to tap through the little bones, joint the rabbits into pieces which can be easily taken up in the fingers. Split the partridges in two if using; the quail can be left whole.

Heat the oil in a roomy casserole and put in as many of the joints as can be accommodated in a single layer. Fry until they take a little colour, removing each batch as soon as it's done. Add the diced ham fat and garlic to the pan juices and fry for a moment. Return the meat to the casserole, season with salt and pepper and add the raisins, cinnamon, saffron, pimentón, vinegar and a glass of water.

Bring to the boil, turn down the heat, put the lid on tightly and leave to simmer gently either on top of the stove or in a preheated oven at 170°C/325°F/gas mark 3 for 1¹/₂–2 hours, until the meat is practically dropping off the bones. If you need to add a little more water, make sure it's boiling. Serve with bread or boiled floury potatoes.

callos a la madrileña
tripe with chickpeas

Innards – variety meats – and mince are the mea[t] of the urban poor. The richer we are, the less we eat of what our ancestors would have considered great delicacies. As for tripe, you either love it or hate it. If the latter, use diced pork belly instead. Spain tripe is not machine-steamed, so it has a much more gluey texture and robust flavour whi[ch] can stand up to plenty of chilli in the sauce. Sinc[e] all that is available to most of us is the pallid, precooked tripe which has had all its distinction removed, the sauce adds character.

Serves 4–6

450g (1lb) chickpeas, soaked overnight
450 g (1lb) prepared tripe
2–3 garlic cloves, skinned and crushed
1–2 bay leaves
1 dried red pepper, de-seeded, or 1 tablespoon pimentón (Spanish paprika)
1/2 teaspoon crushed black peppercorns

The sauce
6 tablespoons olive oil
2 large Spanish onions, chopped
1 red pepper, de-seeded and diced
1 link chorizo, about 125g (4oz), sliced (choose picante rather than mild)
1–2 tablespoons diced serrano ham or a short length serrano ham bone
450g (1lb) canned tomatoes or fresh tomatoes, scalded, skinned and chopped
1–2 dried chillies or 1/2 teaspoon cayenne
1 glass red wine
Salt

cocido madrileño
chickpeas and chicken

Drain the chickpeas and put them in a roomy pan with enough water to cover generously. Bring to the boil, skim off the grey scum that rises and add the tripe, garlic, bay leaves, dried red pepper or pimentón and peppercorns – no salt. Bring back to a rolling boil, turn down the heat a little and leave to bubble steadily for 1–2½ hours (some chickpeas take longer than others). Don't let the pot come off the boil until the chickpeas are soft. If you need to add water, make sure it is boiling.

Meanwhile, make the sauce. Heat the olive oil in a frying pan and gently fry the onions and the red pepper until the vegetables soften and gild a little. Add the chorizo and let it fry for a moment. Add the ham, tomatoes, chillies or cayenne and red wine, and let it bubble up, mashing the tomatoes with a spoon. Simmer gently for 20 minutes or so, until you have a rich, thick sauce and add salt if needed.

Tip the sauce into the pot with the tripe and chickpeas and give it a stir. Cook all together gently for another 15 minutes to marry the flavours. Serve with plenty of bread and a plain salad, accompanied by the robust red wine of Valdepeñas.

A cocido, in common with any of the robust one-pot dishes based on pulses, is always served at midday since it takes all afternoon to digest. In the form in which it's prepared in Madrid, the broth is strengthened by the addition of a boiling fowl – a well-exercised old hen past her egg-laying days. It is usual, too, to include the neck and feet. Any unborn eggs found inside the cavity – bright yellow with a wonderfully creamy texture – are slipped in to poach briefly at the end.

Serves 6

450g (1lb) chickpeas, soaked overnight
1 small boiling fowl, jointed (a roasting chicken will do)
1 whole head of garlic
1–2 short lengths serrano ham bone or unsmoked bacon hock
2 dried red peppers or 1 tablespoon mild pimentón (Spanish paprika)
1 large onion, cut into chunks
1–2 mature carrots, scraped and cut into chunks
3–4 sticks green celery (or outer stalks white celery), chopped
2 tablespoons olive oil
1–2 bay leaves
Few parsley stalks
¼ teaspoon roughly crushed black peppercorns
1–2 links, about 125–225g (4–8oz), chorizo (optional)

To finish
2 medium turnips, peeled and cut into chunks
2 large potatoes, peeled and cut into chunks
Salt
2 generous handfuls shredded greens (spinach, chard, cabbage)
About 225g/8oz morcilla (black pudding), cut into chunks (optional)

Drain the chickpeas and transfer them to a roomy pot with about 2 litres (3½ pints) fresh water. Check over the boiling fowl, removing any stray feathers, rinse and add to the pot. Bring to the boil and skim off any grey foam that rises. Hold the whole garlic head in a flame to char the paper covering and roast the cloves a little, and add to the pot along with the rest of the ingredients except the optional chorizo.

Bring all back to the boil and then turn down to a fast simmer. Put the lid on loosely and don't let the broth come off a gentle bubble. You may need to add extra boiling water during the course of the cooking. Chickpeas are variable in the length of time they need to soften – they can take anything from 1½ to 3 hours to cook. If all you have is a few joints of roasting chicken, add these after the first hour, along with the optional chorizo. Return all to the boil rapidly, then leave to bubble gently until the chickpeas are perfectly tender.

To finish, add the turnips, potatoes and salt to taste – chickpeas never soften properly if salt is added before they're tender. Let it bubble for 10 minutes, then stir in the greens. Turn up the heat to return all to the boil, and simmer for another 10 minutes, until the potatoes are soft and the greens tender. Meanwhile, slice the optional black pudding and either slip it into the broth, or fry until crisp and add a slice to each serving (my favourite way, but then I always was a foreigner).

It is usual to serve the broth and chickpeas first as a soup, with the vegetables as a second course and the meat third – saving the best until last. In my household, we dished it up all together in deep soup plates and ate it with a fork and spoon. Leftover broth can be saved to make croquetas (see p. 105).

albóndigas en salsa
meatballs in tomato sauce

A dish of the urban poor (the rural poor very rarely had access to meat), this was a way of making inferior cuts of meat both tender and tasty while stretching the volume with breadcrumbs. Call it the Spanish equivalent of the British banger. In the cities, the butcher would sell the prime cuts to the affluent bourgeousie, while the offcuts, put through the mincer, could be sold to everyone else. The meat can be lamb or beef or a mixture, but pork is usually included for the richness of its fat. There is a modern fashion for chicken albóndigas, but they are a bit bland. The proportion of breadcrumbs to meat varies according to the housewife's purse – feel free to vary it likewise. Have your butcher put the meat through the mincer twice – in Spain, if you tell the butcher what you intend to prepare, this is done automatically.

Serves 6–8

The meatballs
450g (1lb) minced lamb, veal or beef
225g (8oz) minced pork
1 egg, beaten with a fork
4 heaped tablespoons fresh breadcrumbs
1 garlic clove, skinned and very finely chopped
1/2 large mild onion, grated or very finely chopped
1 tablespoon chopped parsley
1 teaspoon ground cumin
1 teaspoon ground coriander
Salt and pepper

To finish
Flour, for dusting
2–3 tablespoons olive oil, for frying

The sauce
2–3 tablespoons olive oil
1 red pepper, de-seeded and finely chopped
1 large mild onion, cut in fine slivers (half-moons)

1 garlic clove, skinned and finely chopped
1kg (2 1/4lb) ripe tomatoes, scalded, skinned and chopped (or canned tomatoes)
4 tablespoons dry sherry or white wine
1–2 short cinnamon sticks
Sugar

Work together thoroughly all the meatball ingredients. Have a plate of seasoned flour ready beside you. With wet hands (keep a bowl of warm water handy for rinsing your fingers), form the mixture into little bite-sized balls, rolling each one lightly in seasoned flour. Heat the oil in a frying pan, slip in the meatballs and fry until firm, turning carefully to brown each one all over.

Meanwhile, make the sauce. In a heavy frying pan, heat the oil and fry the red pepper, onion and garlic gently until they soften – don't let them brown. Add the tomatoes, wine and cinnamon, bubble up, season with salt and a little sugar, turn down the heat and leave to simmer and reduce for 20 minutes or so. Add the meatballs to the sauce, leave to bubble up, turn down the heat and cook gently until tender – 20–25 minutes. Serve with saffron rice or crisp chip fried in olive oil.

pastel de la reina
almond and quince tart

Sophisticated enough for a queen – even Reina Sophia herself – the crisp buttery pastry base is spread with quince paste and topped with a creamy almond custard.

Serves 6–8

The pastry
350g (12oz) flour
75g (3oz) icing sugar
225g (8oz) butter
1 egg yolk, to bind

The filling
175g (6oz) blanched almonds
75g (3oz) butter
75g (3oz) sugar
3 egg yolks
1 teaspoon grated orange zest
1 pinch ground cinnamon
1 large glass amontillado sherry

To finish
2–3 tablespoons membrillo (quince paste)

Sift the flour into a bowl with the sugar. Using the tips of your fingers, rub the butter into the flour until the mixture looks like fine breadcrumbs. Work in enough egg yolk to make a softish dough. Roll with short firm strokes, and use to line an 18cm (7in) tart tin. Line with foil, shiny side down, sprinkle with a few dry beans or grains of rice and bake blind for 10–15 minutes, until dry and sandy. Remove the foil and allow to cool. Preheat the oven to 150°C/300°F/gas mark 2.

Meanwhile, make the filling. Drop the almonds in a food processor and chop thoroughly – don't reduce them to a powder – or pound in a mortar. Add the rest of the filling ingredients and blend thoroughly. Melt the membrillo until just soft and spread it over the pastry. Pour in the filling and transfer the tart to the oven. Bake slowly for about 1½ hours until the filling is set and the pastry crisp and golden.

helado de azafrán
saffron ice cream

A delicate ice cream flavoured with La Mancha's most profitable crop, the stamens of the saffron crocus, a flavouring much appreciated by the Moors who cooled their ices with snow water from the mountains.

Makes about 1 litre (1¾ pints)

300ml (½ pint) full-cream milk
½ teaspoon saffron threads, lightly toasted in a dry pan
4 egg yolks
4 tablespoons sugar
300ml (½ pint) double cream

Bring the milk to the boil with the saffron. Remove the pan from the heat and let it infuse for 10 minutes.

Liquidise the milk and saffron with the egg yolks and sugar. The result should be a wonderful singing yellow. Pour the mixture into a china bowl set over simmering water, and whisk until it thickens to a custard that will just coat the back of a wooden spoon. Let the custard cool and whisk in the cream.

Freeze as usual – easier if you have an ice cream machine, though the ice-making compartment of the fridge will do. If not using a machine, allow the ice to freeze until nearly solid, then beat it thoroughly to incorporate as much air as possible. Bring it out of the freezer and into the fridge 30 minutes before you are ready to serve to allow it to soften a little.

May festival celebrations in Madrid

scrubland dotted with holm and kermes oaks, the dehesa – pig territory, to those in the know. The culinary habit is much influenced by a long history of trade with Portugal – particularly in pigs, since Portuguese pigs fattened on acorns fetch far higher prices in Spain than they ever do in their native land. Those parts of the countryside not used for profitable pig-husbandry are shepherding territory. Dishes include a caldereta of slow-cooked lamb with wine and ample use of game in slow-cooked stews – including lizard, I'm told. Though the underlying tradition is the cooking of necessity – a peasant cuisine, and poor peasants at that – a richer vein of monastery dishes surfaces in the towns and villages which serviced the religious communities. Their specialities include game stews enriched with ham fat. Above all, Extremadura is the land of the pig.

There are hams and there are hams, and there are the hams prepared with the haunches of semi-wild pigs of the ancient Ibérico breed. It's subjective, of course, like all good things, but these are simply the hams by which all others are judged. Scratch any Andaluz or Castilian or Catalan or Basque, and you'll find not only a man who knows his hams, but also a man (it's a man thing, really) willing to share his knowledge. Prepared, indeed, to back his

judgement with sharpened ham knives in a scrub-oak forest at dawn. We're talking here of salt-cured, wind-dried mountain hams prepared without the application of heat or smoke. You will know the Ibérico ham by the ebony hoof, the narrowness of ankle, the elegant elongated shape of the whole haunch while still on

during the cellaring.

Naturally, there's more to a pig than a pair of hams. Although the all-important buttocks are traditionally handed over to the men, the women deal with the rest of the beast – the loin and shoulder, the belly meat and bacon, the blood and the innards and all the other bits and bobs which go into the salt-drawer or are used to make chorizos, salchichas and blood puddings. These, along with the trimmings and sawn-up remnants of the ham bone – those who remember the hardships of the Civil War will tell of the bone being rented out to different households – go to strengthen the soups and enrich the bean and vegetable stews which provide the midday mea for the farming communities of all Iberia.

Extremadura's other claim to gastronomic fame reflects her early adventurings in the New World. The first conquistadors were recruited, not necessarily voluntarily, from the poverty-stricken population of Extremadura. When the survivors returned home they were laden not only with gold and silver but also with a taste for a particular New World flavour, the chilli pepper, Capsicum annuum an its related species, the seasoning which not only most resembles the oriental peppercorn but has the capacity to turn everything it touches a sunny scarlet. Better still, they carried a handful of seeds home in their pockets. When these were planted in the fertile earth of northern Extramadura, they flourished.

From these small beginnings grew an industry. Today practically every Spanish savoury dish has at least some contact with the capsicum, whether in fresh, dried or powdered form. Chorizos and morcillas would not be the same without it.

The varieties brought home by the conquistadors were the ancestor of all European peppers, both mild and fiery. They did not have the

Olive trees dotting the rolling hills of Extremadura

heat bred out of them until the middle of the nineteenth century. Until then – though the secret of drying and milling the fruits to make a seasoning powder was already known by the seventeenth century – all pimentón was fiery. The main advantage was that it was a home-grown spice – no need for expensive imports – and could be used to add colour, fire and a little extra shelf-life to *embutidos* – Spain's salted and wind-dried pork products.

After many centuries of careful breeding, the capsicums grown for the pimentón industry centred on La Vera are purpose-bred: each has a greater or lesser degree of heat or colour. Small, round bell peppers (lantern-shaped descendants of the Mexican strain) are grown for the mild pimentón dulce; a long, pointed, larger variety supplies a medium-heat, sweet-sour pimentón agridulce; the hottest, pimentón picante, is made from a blend of several different varieties bred from the triangular chile de arbol, the Chilean native. Almost the entire population of the area around La Vera is engaged in the production

of pimentón: either growing it and tending it on the floodplain of the Rio Tiétar; gathering it – a labour-intensive and back-breaking business – in the fields from September to November; or overseeing the smoke-drying which takes place in the purpose-built smoke-houses that ring the fields.

The smoking is what makes La Vera's pimentón different from all other paprika-like products. Those of Hungary and of Murcia are traditionally dehydrated in sunshine. Originally it was a matter of climate: the addition of smoke to the curing process is traditionally a sign of damp winters. Later it became a matter of excellence and taste. There's both knowledge and skill in the smoking process: oak wood is the only possible fuel and the peppers must be turned at just the right moment to take just the right amount of smoke. Which pimentón you choose depends on your own particular taste – just as you choose the amount of pepper you add to a dish. The heat in the chilli is addictive: you have been warned.

pescado en adobo rebozado
breadcrumbed fish

A practical way to deal with perishable fresh fish – marinating it in lemon and garlic adds a Mediterranean flavour as well as allowing it to keep longer.

Serves 4 as a starter

4 thin-cut steaks or fillets firm white fish
   (swordfish, monkfish, tuna, cod, haddock)
Juice of 1 lemon
1 garlic clove, skinned and chopped
Salt and pepper
1 egg, beaten with 1 tablespoon white wine
3–4 tablespoons fine breadcrumbs
Oil, for frying (olive and sunflower are a good mix)

Put the fish steaks to marinate for an hour or two in the lemon juice and garlic, salt and pepper. Remove them and drain well. Dip the steaks in the beaten egg, then coat them firmly with breadcrumbs. Heat the oil until it is lightly hazed with blue. Fry the steaks 2 or 3 at a time so that the oil temperature does not cool too much. Drain on kitchen paper. Serve with chips fried crisp in olive oil.

pollo asado relleno con migas extremeñas
roast chicken with crisp bread stuffing

Chicken is a luxury, making this a party dish suitable for a fiesta or, in these more affluent times, Sunday lunch. On ordinary days the migas would be eaten on their own, maybe topped with a fried egg – a fry-up with a difference.

Serves 4

1 free-range chicken or 4 poussins
Salt and pepper
2 tablespoons olive oil

The migas
125g (4oz) solid country bread, at least 3 days old
About 4 tablespoons olive oil
50g (2oz) smoked streaky bacon, diced
2 garlic cloves, skinned and crushed
1 dried mild pepper, de-seeded and torn,
   or 1 tablespoon pimentón (Spanish paprika)

Wipe the chicken and remove any stray feathers. Season it inside and out, rub with olive oil, place it in a roasting tin and set aside. Don't put it back in the fridge: the chicken should be at room temperature when it goes into the oven.

Meanwhile, crumble the bread roughly – you don't need fine breadcrumbs – and sprinkle with salted water. Leave to swell for 10 minutes, then squeeze dry.

Preheat the oven to 180°C/350°F/gas mark 4.

Heat the oil in a frying pan and fry the bacon until the fat begins to run. Stir in the breadcrumbs and garlic and let them take up all the oil. Fry gently until the breadcrumbs crisp and gild. Stir in the crumbled red peppers or pimentón, then remove from the heat. Pack the breadcrumbs into the chicken cavity.

Transfer the chicken to the oven and roast for about an hour, basting regularly, until the skin is brown and crisp and the juices run clear – test by pushing a skewer through the thigh. Joint neatly and serve each portion with a spoonful of stuffing.

puchero de castañas con garbanzos
chestnut and chickpea hotpot

The chemical structure of the chestnut is very similar to that of the potato, a New World import which, being quicker and easier to grow, replaced it in the puchero pot. The beauty of the chestnut is that in dried form – it doesn't last long if it's not rehydrated – it takes the same length of time to cook as the chickpea, which means that once you've set the pot on the stove, no further attention is needed. If you're using fresh chestnuts, skin them first and stir them in 10 minutes before the end of cooking.

Serves 6

450g (1lb) chickpeas, soaked overnight
225g (8oz) dried chestnuts, soaked overnight
short length serrano ham bone (or bacon knuckle)
225g (8oz) smoked streaky bacon, diced
2-3 garlic cloves, skinned and crushed
2-3 sticks green celery, chopped
2 smoked dried pimento peppers, de-seeded and torn
2-3 cloves
1 bay leaf
1/2 teaspoon crushed peppercorns

To finish
2 tablespoons olive oil
salt
4 hardboiled eggs
chopped fresh coriander or parsley
handful wild fungi – boletus, chanterelles and several of the edible amanita are all gathered in their season in the chestnut woods (optional but good)
olive oil, for frying (optional)
1/2 teaspoon dried thyme (optional)

Drain the chickpeas and chestnuts and put them in a roomy casserole or saucepan with the rest of the ingredients. Pour in enough fresh water to cover everything generously. Bring to the boil, turn down the heat a little and leave to bubble gently for 1½–2 hours until the chickpeas and chestnuts are perfectly soft, adding boiling water when necessary and making sure the pot never comes off the boil. The dish should be soupy rather than dry.

Stir in the olive oil and let it bubble up again – the broth will form a creamy emulsion with the oil and no one will believe you haven't thickened it. Taste and add salt.

Finish with quartered hardboiled eggs and a sprinkling of chopped fresh coriander or parsley. To make it special, stir in a handful of wild mushrooms fried in a little olive oil and seasoned with thyme, salt and pepper.

huevos al plato con jamón
eggs with serrano ham

Eggs are served as a first course at midday, or as a light meal in the evening. Spaniards lunch prodigiously well if they can, and have a relatively light supper.

Serves 4

4 tablespoons olive oil
4 slices of serrano ham
8 free-range eggs
Freshly ground pepper

You will need four small earthenware heatproof dishes.

Pour 1 tablespoon olive oil into each individual dish and put them straight onto direct heat. When the oil is smoking hot, lay a slice of ham in each dish and crack in two eggs per slice. Fry for 3–4 minutes to set the white. Give each dish a turn of the pepper mill, then serve. The eggs will continue to cook in their dish.

Serve with fresh bread and a cos-lettuce and tomato salad.

picada de pez de tierra
aubergine dip

Aubergine purée enriched with oil and garlic, fast-day food for the meatless days of the Roman Catholic calendar, eaten with bread. The aubergine – *pez de tierra*, earth-fish – was the rural household's replacement for the expensive imported salt cod – *pez de monte*, mountain fish – which was the fasting-food of choice for the landlord and the prosperous citizens of the towns. The aubergine, a member of the deadly nightshade family indigenous to the region, is valued as a meat substitute, doubly prized because it can be dried for storage.

Serves 4

2 large, firm aubergines or 225g (8oz) dried
   aubergines
6 tablespoons olive oil
3–4 cloves garlic, skinned and roughly chopped
1/2 teaspoon coriander seeds, crushed
Salt

To finish
1 tablespoon smoked paprika

Hull the aubergines and cut them into chunks – don't bother with salting and rinsing.

Heat the oil in a roomy frying pan. Add the garlic and cook it for a minute or two. Add the aubergines and the crushed coriander and salt lightly. Fry, turning as each side cooks, until perfectly soft – about 10 minutes on a medium heat. Pour the contents of the pan into the food processor and reduce it all to a speckled purée, or use a pestle and mortar. Pile in a bowl and finish with a sprinkling of paprika.

Serve at room temperature with bread for dipping.

patas de cerdo con ajo y perejil
grilled pigs' trotters with garlic and parsley

Pigs' trotters are much appreciated in pig territory, where they make a cheap and delicious meal, needing only long slow cooking to soften them – preparation time is minimal. The trotters can be prepared in advance and grilled when you are ready.

Serves 4

4 pigs' trotters, split lengthways
1 onion
1 carrot
1 bay leaf
4 peppercorns, crushed
1 glass sherry
1 teaspoon salt

To finish
2–3 tablespoons fresh breadcrumbs
1 tablespoon chopped parsley
1 garlic clove, skinned and chopped
Salt and pepper
2 tablespoons olive oil

Wash the pig's trotters and scrub them well. Tie them together in pairs. Put the trotters and aromatics in a saucepan that will just accommodate them, then pour in the sherry and enough water to submerge the trotters to a depth of 1 finger. Add the salt.

Bring to the boil and keep boiling steadily for 30 minutes. Top up with boiling water, turn down the heat, put the lid on tightly and leave to simmer very gently for 5 hours, until the trotters are soft and the bones are dropping out. Check the water level every now and then, and add boiling water if necessary.

Let the trotters cool in their liquid before you drain them. Arrange them in a grill pan, sprinkle with breadcrumbs, parsley, garlic, salt and pepper and trickle the oil over the top.

Reheat in the oven, and then finish them under the grill to gild and crisp the topping.

There are 40 million pigs in Spain, of which ten per cent are béricos, members of an ancient race of foraging pigs When you first come across them in their feeding grounds – as you surely will n Extremadura – you will have trouble distinguishing them among he silvery trunks of the trees and the grey mass of the rocks. They are large, hump-backed and move surprisingly fast on the dainty black trotters which have earned them their nickname of *pata negra*. Their skin, though of an elephant grey, is furred with bristles whose colour ranges from ebony black to russet red. Their territory follows the Ruta de la Plata, the Silver Road – named after the metal-workers who embellished the cathedrals of Catholic Spain – north to south along the line of the Portuguese border. Poignantly, these grey ghosts in a terracotta landscape survived partly because of the Moors, whose presence quite literally saved their bacon, and partly for their adaptability to the territory – a land of barren winters and inhospitable summers in which no other crop was viable.

The fat of the hams of Extremadura is the colour of melted topazes, said traveller Richard Ford, surveying the territory in the 1850s. The meat is dark and velvety, with a dense texture. Visible in the fibres is a delicate butteriness that comes from the absorption of the fat by the flesh during the long and gentle curing. In the dry days of summer, the ibérico puts on very little weight, subsisting on roots and tubers and sleeping away its days. But as soon as the acorns fall, a foraging pig can double its weight in a month, storing up fat in the flesh – making the meat appear lean, but rendering it wonderfully rich. The meat of a pig which has been fed on a diet of acorns develops a light sprinkling of little white specks, faintly gritty to the teeth and reminiscent of the texture of a Roquefort cheese. The bloom which forms on the rind of an ibérico ham – the skin and exposed surfaces of the meat – is produced by the same wild yeast, *Penicillium roquefortii*, which thrives wherever it can find a food source.

Fortunately for their keepers, who often suffer from drought themselves, ibérico pigs require very little water. Given a choice, the pig is a fastidious eater – his tastes are exactly the same as his master's. The holm oak which makes the dehesa such a desirable place for a pig to live yields acorns which are small, dark and sweet and taste like chestnuts, though no one would willingly eat pig food – famine rations – if he can eat ham.

There is no guarantee that each and every pata negra ham will be identical. This is not a factory product but the work of men. As with great wines which develop a little differently in every bottle, to the connoisseur every ham will be subtly different from every other – even the left and right haunch of the same pig will have their own small differences. A reputable curing-house will be able to guarantee the excellence of its product – commercial considerations demand reliability – but to the expert, each ham each ham is a surprise. Texture, scent, flavour – each part of every ham has its own particular character. Inexpert cutting can ruin a good ham: it should always be cut from the bone in short, fine, almost transparent strips which follow the grain, never deboned and sliced by machine.

potaje de lentejas con chorizo y morcilla
lentils with chorizo and black pudding

A one-pot stew for a cold day, relatively quick to prepare since lentils are the only pulses which don't need soaking. The enrichment and flavouring are whatever comes to hand – a length of ham bone, chorizo, a link of black pudding. The family version when we lived in Spain was prepared with our own home-made marjoram-flavoured chorizos, a product of the yearly pig-matanza, a somewhat traumatic event in which all our neighbours assisted. For a more sophisticated contrast of flavour and texture, hold back a few slices of chorizo and morcilla to crisp with a handful of croûtons.

Serves 6–8

250g (8oz) green lentils
I whole head garlic
Short length serrano ham bone or 1 tablespoon
  chopped serrano scraps
1–2 links, about 125–225g (4–8oz), soft chorizo
1–2 links, about 125–225g (4–8oz), morcilla
  (black pudding)
1 onion, chopped
2–3 sticks green celery, chopped
1 large tomato, diced

1 dried mild red pepper (preferably ñora),
  de-seeded and torn
1/2 teaspoon crushed peppercorns
1/2 teaspoon crushed coriander seeds
1 bay leaf
2–3 cloves

To finish
1 large potato (about 450g/1lb), peeled and diced
2 handfuls shredded cabbage, chard or
  tagarninas (thistle rosettes, gathered from the
  wild in spring)
2 tablespoons virgin olive oil
Salt

Pick over the lentils and remove any tiny stones. Singe the garlic head, holding it in the gas flame or popping it on the electric ring to char the papery covering. Put all the ingredients in a large pot with 1 litre (1 3/4 pints) water, bring to the boil, turn down the heat, put the lid on loosely and leave to bubble gently for 30 minutes.

Add the potato, bring back to the boil, turn down to a simmer and leave for another 20 minutes. Lentils need about 40 minutes' cooking in all, after which they should be quite soft – if they're old, they take little longer. Top up with boiling water if necessary. When the lentils and potatoes are perfectly tender and floury, stir in the shredded greens, add the olive oil, bubble up again and cook for another 5 minutes. Taste and season.

Serve in deep soup plates, with bread for mopping or (even better) with a scattering of crisp migas – cubes of stale bread – fried in manteca colorado, a deliciously creamy pork lard, coloured and flavoured with pimentón.

caldereta extremeña
slow-cooked lamb with wine and chilli

A dish for a celebration. A whole milk-fed lamb will serve four. If the lamb is more mature, use the whole shoulder and have the butcher chop it into chunks right across the bone. Milk-fed kid will give stickier, richer juices but a less delicate flavour.

Serves 4

1 milk-fed lamb, quartered, or 1 shoulder of lamb, chopped into portions through the bone
Salt
2 tablespoons olive oil
1 thick slice of lamb's liver (if using milk-fed lamb, the whole liver)
1 thick slice of country bread
4 garlic cloves, unskinned but crushed
1–2 dried chillies, de-seeded and torn
2 glasses robust red wine
1 tablespoon pimentón (Spanish paprika)
1 tablespoon wine vinegar

Wipe the meat and salt it lightly. Heat 2 tablespoons of the oil in a roomy casserole and add the meat. Fry it over a high heat until it takes colour on all sides, then remove and reserve. Fry the liver in the oily pan drippings (don't over-cook: it should remain quite pink), remove and reserve. Add the rest of the oil to the pan, fry the bread until crisp and golden, then remove and reserve. Return the reserved lamb to the casserole and turn it in the hot drippings with the garlic. Add the chillies, wine and a glass of water and let bubble up. Turn down the heat, put the lid on tightly and cook gently until the lamb is perfectly tender: 40–60 minutes.

Meanwhile, in a food processor or with a pestle and mortar, pound to a paste the reserved liver, fried bread, pimentón and 1 tablespoon water. Stir the paste into the lamb juices as soon as the lamb is tender, bring it to the boil briefly, and sharpen the sauce with vinegar and salt.

arroz con leche, almendras y pasas
rice pudding with almonds and raisins

A plain dessert but good, this is never eaten hot but always served chilled, summer and winter. For a special treat, sweeten it with the glorious chestnut honey from the slopes of the Sierra Morena.

Serves 6

225g (8oz) round-grain rice
1 litre (1¾ pints) full-cream milk
short cinnamon stick
Curl of lemon zest
2 tablespoons chopped blanched almonds
2 tablespoons raisins or sultanas
4 tablespoons liquid honey

To finish
Single cream
Ground cinnamon

Soak the rice for 10 minutes or so in enough cold water to cover. Drain and rinse in a colander.

In a roomy pan, bring the milk to the boil with the cinnamon and lemon zest. Then stir in the rice, almonds, raisins or sultanas and honey and cook gently for about 30 minutes until the rice is perfectly tender and the milk almost all absorbed. Remove the cinnamon stick and lemon zest.

Transfer to a serving bowl or spoon into individual glass dishes and leave to cool. Refrigerate overnight. Finish with a thin layer of cream and a dusting of ground cinnamon.

polvorones
crumbly almond cookies

A Christmas treat, crumbly, soft and rich (the literal translation of the name is 'dusties'), these come wrapped up in scraps of tissue paper and are sold throughout the land. The shortening is pure white lard, a speciality of pig territory, mild and sweet and made by melting pork fat very slowly in the lowest possible oven with a little water to keep it from browning. Since the lard is soft, this is a beaten rather than a rubbed-in cookie dough.

Makes about 30 cookies

225g (8oz) flour
110g (4oz) blanched almonds, roughly ground
1 teaspoon ground cinnamon
1 teaspoon ground cardamom
225g (8oz) fresh white lard, softened
110g (4oz) icing sugar

Sift the flour into the ground almonds and mix in the spices. Beat the lard with the sugar until light and fluffy – easiest in a food processor. Work in the flour and nut mixture and 1–2 tablespoons cold water until you have a ball of soft dough. Cover with a clean cloth, and leave to rest for an hour in a cool place to firm up.

Heat the oven to 180°C/350°F/gas mark 4.

Roll the dough out to twice the thickness of a £1 coin. Cut out neat little rounds with a biscuit cutter and transfer to a well-buttered baking sheet. Press together the scraps with the tips of your fingers and cut out as many more rounds as you can.

Bake for 15–20 minutes, until pale gold. Transfer gently to a wire rack and leave to cool. The end result is like very soft, crumbly shortbread. Wrap in scraps of tissue paper before storing in an airtight tin.

A group of volcanic islands moored in the tropical waters some sixty miles off the coast of Africa, the Canaries achieved prosperity as a stepping stone for the transatlantic trade between Europe and the Americas. They were mapped early in Europe's history. In Roman times Ptolemy and Plutarch, noting reports of pockets of fertility in what seemed at first sight little more than a giant lava-field, called them the Fortunate Islands.

My first glimpse of the gun-metal cliffs of the archipelago was as a child, more years ago than I care to admit, when my family made the Atlantic crossing on the HMS *Andes*, the only way to reach the southern Americas in those days. My stepfather, a diplomat on his first posting, was on his way to the embassy in Montevideo, capital of Uruguay. We were, I later learned, following the path taken by the greatest sailor of all time, Francisco Magellan, captain of the first ship to circumnavigate the globe.

The liner was huge, as tall as a skyscraper – or it seemed to me – and we were unable to dock at Tenerife, the islands' capital. Instead, we rocked gently on our anchors within sight of the waving palm fronds on the sea-front. We were waiting, the purser told us, for the delivery of stores for the ocean crossing. From what looked like a line of deserted quays, a swarm of little boats, open-bellied, piled high with island produce, swooped towards us through the swell. Lines were secured, ropes thrown and huge open-topped baskets laden with multi-coloured foodstuffs began to rise and fall against the deep curve of the ship's side. Neither my brother nor I, children of wartime, had ever seen anything like it. We had never tasted so much as a bunch of grapes, let alone the great heaps of green coconuts, scarlet mangoes, purple figs and, most astonishing of all, bundles of fat green sticks one of the crew told us was sugar-cane, riding up and down on the ocean swell.

CANARY ISLANDS
LANZAROTE
LA PALMA
FUERTE VENTURA
Santa Cruz
de Tenerife
LA GOMERA
Las Palmas
TENERIFE
EL HIERRO
GRAN CANARIA

It was not until many years later that I made landfall on th islands. I was reminded of that early contact as soon as the perfumes reached my nostrils drifting across on the breeze, the toasty scent of sugar-cane, spicy breath of tobacco leaves dryin on the rooftops, the fragrance of jasmine and roses.

The tranquillity of the indigenous population, the Gualches, was fir disturbed during the thirteenth and fourteenth centuries by trader in search of slaves. Contemporary accounts describe a cave-dwellin people who dressed in skins, kept dogs, raised sheep, pigs and goat and planted a few crops. They also mummified their dead, allowing palaeontologists to identify characteristics which point to the Berbers of North Africa, though the presence of fair-skinned, blond individuals seems incompatible with the theory of an exclusively African origin. The islands' history is troubled – those who escaped the attentions of the slavers were just as likely to perish in a volcanic eruption or as a result of drought – and there are none of pure Gualche blood remaining. Perhaps new techniques will reveal the secrets of their genealogy, although it can never unravel all the strands that form a nation.

The earliest European settlers were Normans. The natives gave them a run for their money for more than a century – waging an effective form of guerrilla warfare from their mountain fastnesses until, in 1498, six years after the opening up of the Americas, Tenerife fell to the Spanish crown, providing the monarchs with a much-needed Atlantic base from which to explore the new lands beyond the sunse

The cooking of the Gualches, as it survives to this day, was simple and largely vegetarian. Padre Espinosa, chronicler of Spain's ventures in the New World, explained the situation a century or later: 'The cooking of the Canaries has clearly preserved much of the Gualcho habit. The mainlanders have added to it, but it is also necessary to highlight the "bridge" with the Americas which has brought the New World vegetables and established them on the islands, notably potatoes and tomatoes.'

Culinary historian Carlos Pascual, writing in the 1970s, also identifies the mysterious Gualches as responsible for what makes the food of the islands different: 'The cooking of the Canaries is without doubt the most exotic of Spain's cuisines, and not simply for geographical but for historical reasons, since the islands were relatively recently added to the dominions and the origins of the earlier inhabitants remain shadowy. Many of the vegetables derive from the Americas. The tomato grown on the islands is superlatively sweet and aromatic, its export contributing one of the principal sources of wealth. The bananas of the Canary islands, planted in the place of the walnut trees in which the island's breed of red-bristled pigs were fattened, are also more fragrant and less woolly than those of America. The most remarkable preparation, gofio, recalls in some respects the couscous of the African mainland. The grain with which it's made can be wheat, barley, maize or chickpeas which are toasted and milled to a powder. After it's prepared in the form of a porridge much like the classical alcuzcusu of Arab origin, it is rolled into a ball and carried to the fields in a container which keeps it soft.'

Further evidence of otherness is to be found in chicken sauced with pistachios, the inclusion of raisins and almonds in the black pudding, but especially among the desserts – gofios sweetened with honey, sweet potatoes and yams cooked with sugar, bananas used in fritters and pies. Nor do the islanders lack for alcoholic refreshment. The traditional wine grape is the honey-sweet Malvoisie, and an excellent rum is distilled as a by-product of the sugar-cane industry established by the Arabs.

The islanders, too, have had a considerable influence on the cooking of the Americas, particularly Venezuela and Cuba, to which many emigrated in times of famine – a not infrequent occurrence when the rains failed. Returning when times were easier, they brought with them a lightness of spirit, a taste for African rhythms and yet more exotic ingredients: passionfruit, papaya, avocados and cacao, the raw material of chocolate. Another of their imports was tobacco – a weed which flourished mightily on the islands – along with enough expertise to roll a fine cigar.

Fields and vineyards in the dark volcanic soil of northern Lanzarote

potaje de berros
watercress soup with pork and beans

The refreshing pepperiness of the watercress is perfectly balanced by the smooth creaminess of the beans and potatoes. For a vegetarian version, omit the pork and finish the soup with extra olive oil.

Serves 4–6

125g (4oz) dried white beans, soaked overnight
1 thick slice of pork belly or unsmoked streaky bacon
225g (8oz) watercress
2 garlic cloves
1 teaspoon salt crystals
450g (1lb) potatoes
Salt and pepper
2 tablespoons olive oil

Drain the beans and put them in a soup pot with the pork or bacon. Add enough cold water to cover the beans to a depth of two fingers – about 1.5 litres (2½ pints). Bring to the boil, skim off any grey foam that rises, turn down the heat and leave to bubble gently for 1–2 hours, depending on the age and type of the beans.

Meanwhile rinse and finely chop the watercress, reserving a few sprigs, crush the garlic with the salt, and peel and dice the potatoes. When the beans are tender but still holding their shape, remove the pork or bacon and reserve. Add the potatoes to the bean-pot. Bring back to the boil, stir in the watercress and the garlic crushed with the salt, and cook for another 20 minutes or so, until the potatoes are perfectly soft. You may need more water – the soup shouldn't be too thick. Mash a little to thicken lightly.

Meanwhile, remove and discard the skin from the pork or bacon, and cut the rest into small cubes. Fry the cubes of meat gently in the olive oil until they crisp and gild. Finish the soup with the contents of the frying pan and the reserved watercress sprigs.

papas arrugadas
salt-wrinkled potatoes with two sauces

The wrinkled skins of the title are the result of a closed-pot, minimum-liquid method of cooking – technique which mirrors the effect of the earth-oven, popular in the potato's land of origin, the uplands of Peru. The Canaries are rich in ancient varieties of potato, a result of early contact with the New World. Among the very small varieties suitable for this dish are the pink-skinned ojitos, the Tenerife black (papa negra) and the little bonitas of Gran Canaria. Here they're served with the two dipping sauces typical of the islands.

Serves 4

1.7kg (4lb) small new potatoes
Salt

The red mojo

2–3 small dried chillies, de-seeded
4–5 garlic cloves
1 teaspoon rough salt
1 tablespoon pimentón (Spanish paprika)
1 teaspoon cumin seeds
150ml (¼ pint) olive oil
2 tablespoons red wine vinegar

The green mojo

1 fresh green chilli, de-seeded and finely chopped
4–5 garlic cloves
1 teaspoon rough salt
1 teaspoon cumin seeds
150ml (¼ pint) olive oil
2 tablespoons white wine vinegar

sancocho canario
sweet potato, chickpea and sweetcorn hot-pot

inse the potatoes but don't scrub or skin. Put them
n a heavy pan with enough water to half-cover. Add
 tablespoon of salt, put the lid on tightly and set
ver a low heat until all the water has evaporated –
tir them halfway through (after about 15 minutes)
o allow the uppermost potatoes to feel the heat at
he base. When they're tender, remove the lid and
ry them over the heat for a few minutes, until the
kins wrinkle and crust with salt.

Meanwhile make the mojos. In a liquidiser or pestle
nd mortar, combine all the red mojo ingredients
xcept the oil and vinegar and crush to a paste.
Work in the oil – it should form a thick emulsion –
dd the vinegar and enough water to dilute to a
ipping consistency. Repeat this process with the
reen mojo ingredients.

erve the wrinkled potatoes with the two sauces. It's
icest if you eat them with your fingers, squishing
he soft flesh between finger and thumb to allow the
otato to absorb the sauce.

A one-pot stew which takes its name from its
Chilean equivalent and is distinguished from the
cocidos of the mainland by the presence of three of
the New World's more unusual vegetables: sweet
potato, pumpkin and sweetcorn. You can also
include beans, potatoes, dried or fresh figs and
grapes. In this version it's finished with mint, a
Moorish herb little known on the mainland. It may
or may not include a piece of pork, salted or fresh.
If so, add it to the chickpeas at the beginning of the
cooking. This is traditionally eaten with gofio, a
porridge made with toasted, milled grains.

Serves 4–6

225g (8oz) chickpeas, soaked overnight
6 garlic cloves
1/2 teaspoon saffron threads, lightly toasted in
   a dry pan (don't let it burn)
900g (2lb) tomatoes, scalded, skinned and chopped
1 tablespoon raisins
450g (1lb) sweet potatoes, peeled and cut into chunks

1 thick slice of pumpkin, peeled and cut into
chunks
2–3 fresh sweetcorn cobs, thickly sliced
Salt and pepper

To finish (optional)
Handful mint – the leaves from 3–4 stalks
2 tablespoons toasted almonds, roughly chopped

Drain the chickpeas and bring them to the boil in
plenty of water in a roomy stewpot. Skim off the grey
foam that rises. Add the garlic and saffron (no salt)
and return to the boil. Cook without letting it come
off the boil until the chickpeas are perfectly tender,
1½–2 hours, adding boiling water when needed – the
finished stew should be soupy rather than dry.

Stir in the chopped tomatoes and raisins and let
bubble up again. Add the chopped vegetables in the
order given, reheating the broth between each
addition. Taste and season with salt and pepper.

Finish each portion with the optional mint leaves
and chopped toasted almonds. (The Canary Islanders
have a Moorish fondness for raisins and almonds in
savoury dishes – their black pudding includes both.)

To present it in the traditional way, serve the broth
first with soft balls of polenta – the closest you're
likely to get (unless you're an islander) to gofio. The
traditional grain food of the islands, gofio is a porridge
made by toasting whole unmilled grains – wheat,
barley or maize – with a little salt. The grains are then
milled to a coarse flour, mixed with water and cooked
until firm enough to be scooped up in the fingers and
formed into little balls for popping into the mouth, in
much the same way as a Moroccan diner would
prepare a mouthful of couscous.

Haystacks in Lanzarote

the fruits of the canaries

My brother and I, war babies on the way to South America in the early 1950s, watched in wonder as the supply boats put out from the quayside at Tenerife to trade with the purser of our ocean liner. Could they really be bananas, those bright yellow fingers which smelled of spring flowers and clustered thick as bees on stalks as tall as a man? Could those scarlet fruits as big as a fist really be tomatoes? And over there, in a heap on the heaving deck, was a fruit known as a custard apple which, as one of the sailors showed us, could be split open to reveal creamy flesh and jet-black pips and which, we learned, tasted sweet as honey. Beside them were boxes of velvety black grapes, shiny green olives, almonds still encased in their green furry jackets, ivory-fleshed onions, rosy-skinned garlics, lemons, limes. Here too were the American natives, the vegetables and fruits which were soon to replace the carrots and potatoes of our wartime larder: passionfruit, silky-tasselled sweetcorn, knobbly yams, yellow-fleshed sweet potatoes, round green marrows which could sit neatly in your palm, golden pumpkins, capsicums – peppers both fiery and mild, green and red, lantern-shaped and pointed; the fierce little habañeros which make your eyes water just from the scent. And everywhere, wafted upwards on the breeze or carried on the skin of the saleswomen themselves, was the warmth of cumin, the rankness of leaf coriander, the sunshine and scents of the souk.

quesadilla de plátanos
banana cheesecake

This delectably fattening treat is a speciality of the days of romeria, the midsummer pilgrimage during which the guardian of the water source – the Virgin, who takes care of her congregation by ensuring the wellspring never runs dry – is carried down to take her place in the church below. This time is considered particularly holy because of the presence of the Mother of God: prayers and supplications are accepted, weddings celebrated, children baptised, so sweet things are appropriate, the richer and more sumptuous the better.

Serves 6–8

The pastry
150g (5oz) flour
1/2 teaspoon ground cinnamon
Pinch nutmeg
1 tablespoon caster sugar
110g (4oz) cold butter, grated

The filling
3 ripe bananas, skinned and chopped
450g (1lb) fresh curd cheese
3 egg yolks
Squeeze of lime or lemon juice

Mix the flour with the spices and sugar and stir in the grated butter. Rub delicately with your fingertips to amalgamate the fat with the flour, then work in enough iced water to give a softish dough. Let it rest for 10 minutes. Roll out the pastry lightly with small strokes – the idea is to press it out rather than stretch it, which would result in a shrunken casing.

Use the pastry to line a 20cm (8in) tart tin with a removable base. Let it rest for another 10 minutes. Meanwhile, preheat the oven to 200°C/400°F/gas mark 6.

Prick the base of the pastry case with a fork. Line the case with foil, weight with a few dried beans or rice and bake for 15 minutes to set the pastry. Remove the foil and weights and slip the pie case back into the oven for another 10 minutes to set the surface. Remove and leave to cool. Turn the oven down to 170°C/325°F/gas mark 3.

Beat the filling ingredients to a smooth cream either by hand or in a food processer. Tip the filling into the cooled pastry case – take care not to let it overflow or the pastry will be soggy. Bake for 40–50 minutes, until the filling is just set.

Overleaf: The Douro river at Oporto

dulce de boniato
sweet potato and rum cream

Both sweet potatoes and yams are treated as dessert ingredients, cooked and mashed with honey or sugar and eaten with fresh curds or cream. This sophisticated version is from the capital, Tenerife.

Serves 4–6

450g (1lb) sweet potatoes, peeled and cut into chunks
2 tablespoons raisins
4 tablespoons rum
4 egg yolks
425ml (¾ pint) full-cream milk
110g (4oz) sugar

To finish:
150ml (1/4 pint) double cream, lightly whipped
1 tablespoon toasted almonds, slivered

Cook the potatoes in enough boiling water to cover until perfectly soft – or leave them unpeeled and bake in the oven. While the potatoes are cooking, set the raisins to soak in the rum. Drain the potatoes (or scoop them out of their skins), and mash thoroughly to a smooth purée.

Whisk together the egg yolks, milk and sugar in a bowl. Set the bowl over a pan of boiling water and whisk until the mixture thickens to a custard.

Fold in the sweet potato purée, the raisins and rum, spoon into a glass bowl or individual sundae glasses, swirl in the whipped cream and top with slivered toasted almonds.

portugal

Salt-cod, hams and sausages, sturdy breads, one-pot stews and fortifying soups: the traditional cooking of Portugal is robust. Nor, as might be supposed, is it just a less sophisticated little sister of the Spanish tradition. Although the two countries are adjacent, the almost impenetrable emptiness of the inland mountainous district has kept Portugal divided from its neighbour for centuries. This can be explained only by geography – though even here the boundaries are not obvious.

Portugal's eastern frontier runs down one side of Iberia's central plateau, 1000m (3000ft) above sea level, but lacks any natural indication of its limits. Since the slope is westward, the rivers which rise in the mountains of Spain run to the Atlantic rather than the Mediterranean, and the slope is steep enough for the waters of the upper reaches to move at a pace too swift for navigation. These rivers form deep valleys which broaden to fertile floodplains the closer they get to the ocean. Travel and trade are therefore obliged to move across rather than up and down – west to east rather than north to south. Portugal's situation is almost as if she sits at the edge of a tipped-up plate: her population is concentrated along the coast, leaving the harsh terrains of the upland regions sparsely populated, and it is this lack of accessibility that provides a natural barrier against invaders.

Although the cooks of Portugal and Spain rely on the same basic ingredients – pork products, fish, rice and pulses, tomatoes and peppers, olive oil and garlic – the cooking methods, utensils and combinations of Portugal are distinctively her own. No one makes better soups than the Portuguese, and when it comes to stews, no one has a surer hand with the spicings – after all, it was Portuguese sailors who first sailed round the Cape of Good Hope, establishing a sea route to the Orient, and Portuguese adventurers who first dropped anchor on the southern landmass of the New World.

It was, too, Portuguese shipwrights who designed and built the caravel – the first vessel capable of sailing both with and against the wind. This manoeuvrability was crucial to the great voyages of the fifteenth century which opened up the southern sea routes to the spice trade. Easy access to the west coast of Africa provided Portugal

Boats carrying port barrels on the Douro

not only with the foundations of a colonial empire, but also with a source of the slave labour with which to colonise the New World.

These days Portugal looks across the Atlantic for its cultural energy. There are 10 million inhabitants in Portugal, 180 million in Brazil. As one of the merchants of Oporto put it to me, 'Our vitality comes from over the ocean. The New World rejuvenates us – it's a window wide open. You have only to listen to our music. Portuguese fado is sad, a lament – but Brazilian music is full of joy.'

The Portuguese were – remain at heart – a sea-faring nation. The narrow coastline and mountainous interior obliged the inhabitants to seek fame and fortune elsewhere. While most returned from their travels with exotic ingredients and unfamiliar culinary tricks, many remained to make new lives in new lands. All over the world there are emigrant populations of Portuguese who, by returning frequently to their homeland, have contributed to a flexible culinary habit. Necessity, too, dictates imaginative combinations: Portuguese housewives cook pork with shellfish, ham with trout, salt-cod with eggs and olives. Three elements have contributed to a istinctive national cuisine: the need to victual ships with salt-reserved stores for the long sea voyages – most particularly salt-od, bacalhau; ease of access to eastern spices – not only dried tores such as cloves and cinnamon, but fresh leaf-coriander, a aste acquired from trade links with Japan and unknown elsewhere n Europe (and certainly not in Spain, where only the dried seed is raditionally used); and, finally and most significantly, the sunny egetables of the New World – tomato and peppers (both sweet and iery), pumpkins and squashes, potatoes, haricot beans and maize – ll of which were unknown in the Old World before contact was established with the New.

he salt-cod dish most usually encountered in restaurants is olinhos de bacalhau, little fritters made of soaked salt-cod beaten vith mashed potato, bound with egg, flavoured with onion and parsley (lots) and eaten with a hot sauce, piri-piri, which takes its name from its main ingredient, a vicious little scarlet chilli grown in Angola, Portugal's one-time colony.

Bread is the staple of the diet, but rice – grown in paddy fields up and down the west coast – is also popular. Usually it's cooked plainly in the oriental way as an accompaniment to a main dish, rather than as in Spain, with other flavouring ingredients to provide the centrepiece of a meal. Somewhat unusually, it's often served with (rather than as an alternative to) potatoes. And one of the few desserts the Portuguese housewife makes at home is a creamy rice pudding flavoured with cinnamon.

Portuguese olive oil is traditionally strongly flavoured. The practical difficulties of gathering the fruit from inaccessible olive groves meant that the harvest was not taken immediately for pressing, out had to wait until enough quantity had been gathered. The result is a light fermentation and a kick like a mule. You either love it or you hate it.

Pork-curing and sausage-making remain cottage industries, and each region has its own preferences. The best ham – most esteemed by the natives – is presunto, dry-cured in salt with garlic and paprika, then smoked to a dark mahogany. The most popular cured sausage is the chouriço – paprika-spiced, very garlicky, excellent for grilling and adding distinction to a stew.

Portuguese housewives rarely make their own cakes and pastries, preferring to order them from the local pastelaria. Favourites are teeth-achingly sugary confections – doces de ovos – made with egg yolks alone, since the whites went to refining the wine. The confectioner's art was learned from the Moors, the colonial power in the southern regions for five centuries, and remains the province of professionals. For a finale to everyday meals, there's fresh fruit of astonishing splendour – enormous apples, giant pears, peaches as round and firm as tennis balls. In the wine-growing areas up the Douro valley, the fig trees are so heavily laden that the fruits hang in bridal bouquets right down to the ground.

Portugal considers herself a Mediterranean nation, though she has no Mediterranean seaboard. This feeling rests entirely on culture and history. Nostalgia is part of the Portuguese soul. Although emigration was the only option for the landless, the colonists returned home as soon as they'd made their fortunes, bringing foreign habits with them. Marie Noele Kelly, a keen observer of Portuguese culture and landscape in the 1950s, explained the roots: 'There is still an essential harmony between the Portuguese and his land, a sense of pride in things earthy and an obstinate contentment with ways of life which were old and familiar when Virgil wrote his *Eclogues*.'

Change is inevitable. No-one wants to live in a museum. And once things begin to vanish, it's in the Portuguese nature to long for their return. In the 1980s and early '90s, the remoteness and beauty of the Alentejo attracted a new generation of settlers, good-lifers escaping the political and social confusion which followed the fall of Salazar's dictatorship. The area they chose is one of the most depopulated of all, with a coastline lacking natural harbours and too wild and windy for sun-seekers, while much of the inland region is mountainous and heavily forested

Changing times in the countryside – the drift to the towns, the disappearance of subsistence agriculture, a vanishing way of life –

Torre dos Clerigos, Oporto, 1837, by James Holland

Portugal of 1992 – is as practical as she is beautiful, and that her family is from hardworking Porto.

The herdade – the name given in the south of Portugal for what in the north would be called a quinta – stands at the head of a little valley, red-earthed, half-hidden in cistus scrub among rolling hills, tranquil, cool and beautiful. All around are newly planted terraces of cork trees, the result of grants from Brussels, and tall stands of eucalyptus ready for pulping to feed the paper trade. Monica and Alfredo's three children go to the local school, picked up and brought home every day from the end of the short drive by a bus which brings, in return, a couple of local ladies to wash and clean.

Alfredo's basic training was in vegetarian cooking, working in a community with Indian and Goan cooks – a strong influence on Portugal's culinary traditions – supplemented by catering in Lisbon for private parties. Meanwhile he continued to paint his big vibrant abstracts – red and ochre and blue, the colours of the landscape – as his alternative winter work. 'I headed off for Australia and cooked at Fins in Byron Bay on the Queensland border. I came back and married, and I thought we'd have a better life in Australia. And then I had a sell-out painting exhibition in Lisbon and I thought – let's give the old country a chance. I wanted somewhere where the children could have a good life. I looked and looked and nearly gave up, and then a friend said, you have to come and look at this place. And that was that.'

The first evening of my visit, we are at table with a dozen young professionals, fortyish, down from Oporto for the Easter holiday with their children. All the guests are from the hardworking north, looking for a little early sunshine. Portugal is an enthusiastic subscriber to the European Union and there is talk round the table of how hard you have to work to maintain your family income, the lack of childcare for working mothers, the high rates of unemployment among young people with university degrees who cannot export their skills because of the language. Nevertheless, says one of our number, there are 180 million in Brazil and all of them speak Portuguese, and that's before you get to Angola and Guinea.

required the escapees to earn a living directly or indirectly from the tourist trade, much of it internal. Among those who have made a success of what is at best a risky enterprise are Alfredo and Monica Moreira da Silva of the Herdade da Matina in Alto Alentejo, a guest-house with a reputation for good food – updated traditional, just like their way of life. It helps, too, that Lisbon-bred Alfredo is an established artist as well as a talented cook, and that Monica – Miss

We eat sourdough bread from a local farmhouse, good bread with a yellowish crumb, a rough texture, chewy, with a tender, crisp crust. Everyone agrees it tastes the way bread should taste, how it used to taste, and all the rarer since few of the farmhouses still do their own baking. 'It's the same all over, even in Tras Os Montes,' says someone. 'We're losing our rural culinary traditions because there are no large families to cook for any more, and the recipes aren't written down.'

The bread is delivered daily by a woman who collects it from a farmer's wife who still bakes. She delivers it to the farms that no longer bake; no money changes hands: she accepts payment in eggs which she then takes to market. Everyone agrees that this was usually the way it was done, and even town-dwellers could expect to eat good country bread baked with properly milled flour in a wood oven, although this too was changing. Although, as one of the other guests points out, it's to do with women going out to work in offices where once they stayed at home. And the men have no idea what to do. For instance, explains the husband, he can't cook rice because when his wife tells him to put in a handful, his hand is much bigger than hers, so how is he to know? 'What do I do? I cook pasta instead. Eight minutes and it's ready.'

This produces a reaction I've encountered before in Portugal. Questions about any dish – ingredients, method, regionality – always produce a much-thumbed copy of Cozinha Tradicional Portuguesa, Maria de Lourdes Modesto's mammoth contribution to Portugal's national identity, first published in 1982 and now in its nineteenth edition. Poring over the recipes simply triggers more discussion about how someone's mother or grandmother had done it differently. This is not, I am assured, in order to cast doubt on the great work, but simply to demonstrate the variations between different villages or households or even particular cooks, so that I am left in no doubt of the possibilities. Whether Maria Modesto has changed the way Portuguese cooks actually cook is impossible to tell: though to some extent, considering the book's wide popularity, it must be assumed that it has.

No matter. Everything changes all the time. Cozinha Tradicional Portuguesa was assembled at a time of change. The colonies were lost, the dictatorship banished and democracy was on the way – and with it the loss of an ancient way of life which, although few would wish to endure its hardships, protected much that was good. Communities which had survived on subsistence farming found themselves in a cash economy, families who had once worked the land together lost their younger and fitter members to the newly industrialised cities. At around this time, fearing the disappearance from her native land of a centuries-old oral tradition, Senhora Modesto set about collecting the regional recipes of her countrywomen. After twenty years' labour, initially undertaken as a result of a televised appeal in 1961 during a Portuguese regional cookery and confectionery contest, her files were filled with over 2000 recipes and she was faced with the task of narrowing the list to 800 – more than enough for any cook's lifetime.

Her criteria for selection, sensibly, were that the recipes should be both representative and authentic. Historical and geographical contexts are supplied. Towns and villages from which the recipes derive are often named. The result is a remarkable work of reference which has, to a large extent, bridged the gap between what granny knew and what modern cooks require. The author is in no doubt of its purpose, to encourage people to continue to cook: 'Home cooking gives us a sense of identity, a sense of being that expresses itself in all its diversity and exuberance in our traditional recipes. I therefore look upon this book as a sort of broadside fired in defence of our culinary heritage and against the insidious invasion of that impersonal, dull and monotonous "international cuisine" into our homes.'

Indeed. It's possible that Maria Modesto's magnum opus has kept alive regional culinary traditions which were bound to vanish in the sunshine of democracy like snow in summer. It is also possible that, by publishing a book which has now become Portugal's universal culinary bible, she's altered the way that people cook. There are no simple answers. People provide their own.

oporto & the douro

The people of Portugal's most northerly province are hard-working and thrifty. The locals say, with some justification, that Oporto earns what Lisbon spends. They have the look of their neighbours to the north, Galicia's Celts, and the bagpipes of the Celts are played at the midsummer romerías and festivities of the church.

As soon as the mighty Douro becomes navigable enough for trade to have been established, the slopes of the valley are dotted with small whitewashed villages, aproned by olive groves, vegetable gardens and orchards. The steepest slopes have been hacked laboriously into terraces for vineyards, each vine dropped into its own little hand-crafted pocket of soil. The land here is the most expensive in Portugal: impossible to imagine the labour which went into its creation. It is generous to those who treat it with respect. The vineyard terraces are edged with olive trees whose fruits are milled for oil during the winter months when the wine presses are idle. The lower slopes where the vines cannot thrive are planted with potatoes, rows of dark-leafed cabbage, carrots, leeks as fat as a man's arm. The narrow lanes which give access to the terraces are shaded by avenues of fruit trees – apples, almonds, peaches, plums, quinces, pears, figs – the raw material of the preserved-fruit trade. The pig is king of the rural table, doubly valued as winter stores and as a trade item for the salt-barrellers of Oporto who supplied the ocean-going ships with victuals for the long Atlantic voyage. Pig-slaughtering time runs from November to March, when rural households put up their year's supplies of chouriço and ham, *presunto*. Fish from sea and river is eaten in spring and summer, salt-cod in winter. The fasting dish of Christmas Eve is salt-cod with potatoes, onions and eggs, with *couve galega*, turnip greens, piled high on the side. The meal after midnight mass includes sweet things and wine – honey, pumpkin pies, sonhos, nut cookies made with pine-kernels; raisins, hazelnuts, almonds, apples, quinces are winter's treats.

Cork trees stripped of their bark stand in a field of sunflowers

The miracle is that the steep canyons cut by the waters can be cultivated at all. This, at any rate, was the view of my self-appointed guide to the city of Oporto, a medical man with a passion for the gastronomy of his native land. The one thing the politicians of Lisbon and the businessmen of Oporto share is an enthusiasm for the good things of life: wine, women, food. And literature, of course.

'We read because of the climate,' he explains as we share a midday meal of Porto's two most famous dishes, salt-cod fritters and tripe with beans. 'No one goes outside in winter unless they have good reason. We read everything – Somerset Maugham, William Faulkner, Harry Potter.' The view from the restored waterfront of the old harbour is of a jumble of warehouses where, in the old days, the salters and barrellers victualled the merchant-adventurers of the transatlantic trade. These days, smart new warehouses

ccommodate the port-blenders who work their alchemy on the
ouro wines. It was not the wines, however, that interested my
ompanion so much as my knowledge of J. K. Rowling's masterwork.

Do you know the location of Hogwarts School?' he asks hopefully.
No? A pity. That is not to say we don't appreciate our own. We have
many great Portuguese writers and poets. Many of us come to it
ter, after we have had some experience. We live on the edge of the
orld and we like to travel first, at least in our minds. Our Nobel
rizewinner, Jose Seramago, author of *Memorial do Convento*, didn't
ublish anything until he was forty. Then he had a quarrel with the
linister for Culture and went off to live in Spain. What can you do?
Ve are a quarrelsome people.'

The Portuguese temperament is very passionate. You have only to
sten to our music and you will understand how strongly we feel.
bout food as well as everything else. You will have been told, I'm
ure, that we have 365 recipes for salt-cod, one for every day of the
ear. This is not true. We have as many recipes for salt-cod as there
re cooks in Portugal. And this will be so until there are no more
ooks left and we have nothing but Macdonald's to eat. And that will
e the end of civilisation, which will be no more than we deserve.'
Quite so.

The links with Portugal's oldest ally are visible everywhere. English
ames are emblazoned all over the warehouses. The port-blenders
nderstood their market, took up residence over the shop, leaving
othing to chance. The vintners who supplied the blenders grew
rosperous on the trade, building themselves elegant manor houses
quintas – among the vineyards.

The labour in the vineyards is still Herculean. These days, plastic
oxes replace the heavy wicker baskets, but the grapes still have to
e hauled by hand from terrace to terrace down to the tracks where
the tractor and trailer, replacement for the old ox-cart, wait. Modern wineries, staffed by chemists as well as vintners, can now produce wines whose quality no longer requires the attention of Porto's blenders. Nevertheless the quinta owners feel the need to diversify, opening their homes to offer accommodation to visitors.

'There is a great need for cultural tourism, visitors who will come for the things other than what's on offer in the Algarve. The vineyards are an expression of our culture, our way of life,' says Antonio Sequer1a of the Quinto do Picota, one of the prime movers in a scheme to attract tourists to the district. 'We need the tourist dollars. Tourism is now essential to rural economies everywhere. What we need is high-value, low-density. The Douro is not a natural destination. We have very few restaurants or hotels – nothing much for the coach parties – but plenty for the educated visitor who wants to experience our way of life. Some of the quintas are luxurious, others more modest – but we all have a tradition of hospitality, and that is how we must survive. We can learn so much from each other – the Portuguese have always been travellers; we enjoy travellers' tales.'

The cooking of the quintas is the best in Portugal, or so the vintners will tell you. 'It's simple, naturally, but with everything straight from the garden, beautiful pork, water from the mountains for soups and broths, good bread – and, of course, our wonderful wines. How could anyone resist?'

lombo de porco
roast loin of pork with potatoes

Roast pork is the traditional Sunday lunch at the Quinta do Picota, where Antonio and Maria Sequera keep the roof on the family home by offering overnight accommodation to visitors sightseeing among the wineries. Tourists brought in by the new EU-funded, four-lane highway which runs up the Douro valley are essential to the survival of the manor houses, and the welcome is warm. Guests share the family table, which at weekends includes the grandchildren. A few of the quintas still keep a styful of pigs to eat up the household scraps, so the pork is excellent. Loin is the real treat, but if there are more guests, a leg will be roasted instead.

Serves 6–8

1 boned pork loin, weighing about 1.7kg (4lb)
Salt and pepper
300ml (1/2 pint) dry white wine
150ml (1/4 pint) virgin olive oil
4–5 garlic cloves, skinned and roughly chopped
2–3 bay leaves, crumbled

To finish
8–10 waxy yellow-fleshed potatoes (oblong rather than round)

Season the pork with salt and pepper and settle it in a casserole with the wine, olive oil, garlic and bay leaves. Cover it with a cloth and leave it overnight in a cool larder to marinate. Preheat the oven to 180°C/350°F/gas mark 4 (bread-baking heat).

Scrape the potatoes and quarter them lengthwise. Tuck them around the meat, turning to coat with the marinade. Roast uncovered for 1½–2 hours, basting regularly and turning the potatoes to crisp them all over. Serve with a salad of ripe tomatoes and mild onion, and plain oven-baked rice.

bolinhos de bacalhau
salt-cod fritters with parsley and onion

The salt-cod fritter is a contentious subject. This recipe was taught me by Lucinda Oliveira, who was born in the late 1950s in the little village of Boa Aldea near the town of Viseu in the highlands of Beira Alta. The family was landless and poor, and Lucinda went to work in the salt-cod business in the port of Lisbon when she was just fourteen, staying there until her marriage ten years later. 'I went to work on the boats, just like a man, with my elder sister, because there was money in the bacalhau trade, salting and packing cod for sending away to other countries. We went in little boats to the big boats to bring the cod back to the factory, where we unloaded the fish from big baskets. And then we salted it and laid it out in layers on flat racks in the open air. And every evening, unless it was high summer, we had to bring the fish back in and put it in the hot room so that it went on drying. There was one wage for men, another for women, and another for children. We all did the same work, though. Often the little children worked harder than any of us.'

As well as demonstrating her recipe for salt-cod fritters, she also explained how to choose the main ingredient. 'When I buy it now, I look carefully. To be good, the flesh must be pure white. If it has a yellow tinge, that is not good. And if you can see pink down the spine, that is because it was not properly dried before it was packed and sent away.'

Note: If bacalhau is unobtainable, fillets of any firm-fleshed white fish, or smoked salmon or haddock, give good results.

Serves 6–8

450g (1lb) middle-cut salt-cod (bacalhau), soaked in several changes of water for 48 hours
450g (1lb) floury potatoes, scrubbed
1 large mild onion, grated
4 tablespoons flat-leaf parsley, chopped
Freshly ground pepper or chilli flakes
3 medium free-range eggs
Olive oil, for deep-frying

To serve
Piri-piri sauce (or any hot chilli sauce)

When the bacalhau is perfectly rehydrated and plump, drain it.

Bring the potatoes to the boil in plenty of water. Place the fish on top, bring it back to the boil, put the lid on and leave to cook for 20 minutes or so, until the potatoes are perfectly tender. Lift off the fish and reserve. Drain the potatoes and skin them as soon as they're cool enough to handle. Meanwhile, skin and de-bone the fish – use a pair of tweezers, feeling the flesh with your fingers – and flake the flesh with a fork. Mash the potatoes thoroughly with the grated onion and parsley, season with pepper or chilli, mix in the flaked fish and beat in the eggs.

Heat a heavy frying pan and add enough oil to submerge the fritters. As soon as it's lightly hazed with blue – test by dropping in a cube of bread: bubbles should form round it immediately – drop in teaspoons of the fritter mixture, a few at a time. Wait until they bob up, then flick them over. Remove and drain on kitchen paper. Continue until the mixture is all used up. Serve immediately, with a bottle of piri-piri sauce on the side.

tripas a moda do Porto
tripe with chicken, chouriço and beans

arroz no forno
oven-baked rice

The citizens of the industrious harbour city of Porto were known as tripe-eaters, a distinction they share with the inhabitants of Cork, Marseilles and every other city which supplied ships on the transatlantic trade route. While the salt-barrellers took part of their wages in tripe and innards (a by-product of their trade) and cooked them frugally with beans, the merchant-victuallers could afford to add choicer flavourings – salt-cured ham, chouriço, a joint or two of boiling fowl – to the plainer fare of their workers. Porto has a reputation for keeping its purse well-buttoned.

Serves 8–10

900g (2lb) veal tripe, well washed and scrubbed (but not steamed and bleached)
Salt
1 calf's foot, scrubbed and split (or a veal-bone, sawn into lengths)
900g (2lb) dried white haricot beans, soaked overnight
1/2 boiling chicken
225g (8oz) chouriço
225g (8oz) smoked salt-cured ham, diced
2 large carrots, scraped and cut into chunks
1 large onion, chopped
1 parsley sprig
1 bay leaf
1 lemon
1/2 teaspoon black peppercorns

To finish
1 large onion, thinly sliced
1 tablespoon lard or olive oil
1 handful parsley, finely chopped

Scrub the tripe with salt and lemon, cut into squares and put into a roomy pan with the calf's foot. Add enough water to cover generously. Bring to the boil, skim off the grey foam which rises, add 1 tablespoon salt and cook for 2 hours, adding boiling water if necessary, until the stock is rich and glutinous and the tripe perfectly tender.

Meanwhile, in another pan, cook the soaked beans with the rest of the ingredients with enough water to cover, until perfectly tender – about 1 1/2 hours. Combine the contents of both pans and simmer for another 30 minutes to marry the flavours.

Meanwhile, prepare the finishing ingredients: very gently fry the sliced onion in the lard or oil until lightly browned – allow a full 30 minutes – then stir the contents of the frying pan into the beans. Finish with a handful of chopped parsley.

Rice almost always accompanies meat dishes even if potatoes are also on the menu. Since Portuguese rice paddies were a product of trade with the Orient, Carolina, a grain which is neither long nor short but oval, is the preferred rice, though long-grain is available as an alternative. In Spain, where rice was first planted by the Romans, round-grain is the rice of choice. Long-grain and Carolina cook dry and fluffy, while round-grain is best left with nutty little heart and served juicy.

Serves 6–8 as an accompaniment

700g (1 1/2lb) Carolina or long-grain rice
4–5 tablespoons olive oil
2 garlic cloves, skinned and finely chopped
1 tablespoon sea salt

Measure the volume of the rice – use a glass or cup – and then measure out 2 1/2 times its volume of water.

Preheat the oven 180°C/350°F/gas mark 4.

Heat the oil gently in a flame-proof casserole, add the rice and turn it in the hot (but not smoking) oil until the grains become opaque – 2–3 minutes. Add the measured water, the garlic and salt, bring to the boil and let bubble gently for 15 minutes. Transfer to the oven and cook for another 15–20 minutes, until the top layer gilds a little. For an *arroz sucio* (dirty rice), include a chopped tomato or two.

úplicas de pinhos
pine-nut prayers

ine-nuts are to Portuguese confectioners what
monds are to the confectioners of Spain: a
arvest free for the gathering, requiring no more
an time, patience, a strong arm and a sharp
one to crack the shells. *Obreiras* – rice paper
ommunion wafers (unsanctified, of course, but
idely available in commercial bakeries and very
uch part of the baker's stock-in-trade) – are used
 prevent the cookies sticking to the baking sheet.
ce paper or non-stick baking parchment will also
 the trick.

akes about 18 cookies

0g (4oz) pine-kernels, crushed
5g (3oz) finely milled cornmeal (polenta)
5g (1oz) flour
0g (4oz) caster sugar
tablespoon ground aniseed
eggs, whisked until fluffy

 finish
ine-kernels

eheat the oven to 200°C/400°F/gas mark 6.

ix the dry ingredients together, then fold in the
hisked eggs. Drop teaspoons of the mixture onto a
ned baking sheet, allowing plenty of room for
em to spread, and finish each with a pine-kernel
 three.

ake for 20–25 minutes, until crisp-edged and
rown. Transfer to a wire rack to cool. Good with
ne of Portugal's many eggy desserts: *oves moles,*
igas doces, toucinho-do-céu.

This is the land between two mighty rivers: the Minho, which forms the border with Galicia, and the Douro, which empties itself into the ocean at Oporto. Although both find their source in Spain's high central plateau, their characters are very different: the Minho is stately, slow and smooth, while the Douro rushes helter-skelter down deep ravines on its way to the sea. Two lesser, gentler rivers, the Cavado and the Lima, water the region's heartland. On the eastern border are the mountains of the Marão and the Geré. To the south are bustling market towns, ancient seats of learning and places of both religious and secular pilgrimage.

The regon's principal port, Viana del Castelo, a busy merchant harbour in the days of Portugal's maritime ascendancy, has converted itself into the Minho's main resort town. Spread along the wooded slopes at the mouth of the Lima estuary within reach of the best of the northern beaches, it was, in former times, a hub of the Atlantic trade – a past which endowed the citizens with an elegant town centre and a repertoire of excellent salt-cod dishes.

The regional capital, the ancient city of Braga which overlooks the floodplain of the Lima and protects the Atlantic approaches, was founded by the Celts and established by the Romans, who made it the capital of Roman Gallaecia. Over-run by the Visigoths and annexed by the Moors, in its history it mirrors that of Portugal itself. A cathedral city and ecclesiastical centre of pilgrimage, it is described proudly by its citizens as the Portuguese Rome. As a cosmopolitan centre, Braga is well-provided with public eating places, among them nineteenth-century cafes which serve food throughout the day. Regional specialities include chestnut soup, *caldo de castanhas* –

ENTRE DOURO E MINHO
Minho
Viana do Castelo
Braga
Guimaraes

appropriately, since the chestnut is the potato of the Celts, a foodst of vital importance in the pre-Columban era – and *rabanadas*, eggy bread, served with a luxurious sauce flavoured with cinnamon.

The region's second city, Guimaraes, is the Minho's industrial centr as well as the seat of her university. As the founding city of the Portuguese nation – Portugal's first monarch, Alfonso Henrique, wa born here in 1110 and it was from here that the Reconquest, the campaign to rid the land of its Moorish overlords, was launched – Guimaraes considers herself the cradle of Portugal's nationhood, though the honour of providing the first capital actually went to Coimbra. No matter. Every monument – medieval to the present da – bears a legend which needs no translation: *Portugal nasceu aqui*. Regional specialities include what might be considered – along with the omnipresent salt-cod – Portugal's national dishes: a feijao, the haricot-and-pork-bit bean-pot without which no regional culinary vocabulary is complete, and the definitive version (according to the locals) of that rich, tooth-achingly sweet yolk-and-syrup confection *toucinho-do-céu*.

The northern landscape is wild and beautiful, with grey granite clif burnished by Atlantic mists, lush valleys and rolling hills. It is inhabited by a population which, in the rural areas, lives in much the same way as its forefathers did, where the ox can still be seen a beast of burden. In the early 1930s novelist and traveller Douglas Goldring admired its beauties while appreciating its wines: 'Due to abundant rainfall, it resembles a vast garden. Camellias and magnolias flourish and everywhere one sees the vines festooning t trees or forming green arbours, supported by pillars of granite, by the sides of the roads. These vines produce in perfection the slight acid but delicious and thirst-quenching "green wine" – *vinho verde* – for which Minho is famous. The population, mostly small peasant proprietors, is dense for Portugal, and the Minhoto [a native of the Minho] is much gayer. The arts of song and dance flourish; the

Women still wear their traditional red-banded shawls, striped skirts
and earrings of gold filigree; the men take pride in their long-horned
oxen and display their craftsmanship in the elaborated carving of
the heavy wooden yolks. In the hills the shepherds still wear their
traditional waterproof reed cloaks, coroças.'

Traveller Marie Noele Kelly enjoyed the life of the market at Ponte
de Lima in the 1950s:

'On the road I met leisurely groups of women carrying carefully
concealed goods on their heads. Each basket is covered by an
immaculate white towel under which you can find anything from
eggs to embroidery, poultry to painted earthen pots, cakes, piglets,
cabbages or nothing, for unmarried girls will walk twenty miles to a
fair with a carefully covered basket quite empty: their quarry is
different. The tempo of much of this market is set by the pace of

hundreds of oxen brought from the surrounding villages. Often
decorated with a big bunch of flowers, the patient eyes of the animal
shaded by roses, for roses are everywhere. There was order and
politeness, no hurry, and people at midday settled down to eat cooked
meals by charcoal fires, cattle to the right of the bridge, hens and
piglets to the left. The attitude of peasant to pigs is interesting: one
talks about pigs in a hush-hush manner, and prefixes all talk with a
"by your leave". Piglets are carefully washed to a lovely pink before
they are shown through a peep of basket or a fold of towel....Maize
bread or broa, thick and glutinous but its crust is delicious, is nearly
always cooked at home. They eat it with a bowl of sugared chicory at
sunrise; then dip it in soup at twelve and have it again when they
turn in. In good homes, bacalhao appears two or three times a week,
chicken at Christmas, at illness or childbirth. Cooking is à l'irlandaise
– one boils, one reboils, soups in which maize, coarse macaroni and
the heads of great cabbages, couve galega, are the staple diet.'

Monte de Santa Luzia, Viana do Castelo, Minho

a minho speciality

The lamprey is an eel-like fish equipped with a gaping sucker for a mouth and a lethal set of teeth. The best way to cook it is stewed in a sauce thickened with its own blood, or so says my friend from Oporto, an enthusiastic lamprey fisherman, 'But I expect you already know this from your readings. Your countrymen wrote many books at the time when travel in Portugal was fashionable, fifty or a hundred years ago. These days we have the tourists in the Algarve, but there's not the same interest in the rest of the country. People lie in the sun, drink our wine and go home. From Porto, too, we like to escape to the south whenever we can, though we prefer the countryside to the beach. Of course, we are quite happy to go to the harbour to eat fish or buy from the fishermen. We are very passionate about what we eat. People argue about where to find the freshest sardines, the fattest prawns, the best salt-fish – we salt other fish too, not only the cod. And we conserve our anchovies and sardines under our own good olive oil. We export them all over the world. We know exactly what's good and we don't mind telling everyone what we know.

'It's worse when whatever we're arguing about is something which is eaten nowhere else. There are many disputes among fishermen over which of our rivers has the best lampreys. My father says it's the Lima. My mother says it is the Minho. But my sister, who married a man from the mountains of Caramulo, says the best come from the River Dao. A good cook can tell the difference. Although fishermen catch them at other times and restaurants serve them, they're really only good in Lent, when they come up the rivers to spawn. They must come into the kitchen alive and the cook has to kill them herself because you have to save the blood to thicken the sauce.'

caldo verde
green broth with portuguese cabbage

The diagnostic ingredient in this simple but excellent soup – a dish many people consider to b typical Portuguese food and which is now found throughout the land – is a special variety of cabbage. A very dark green brassica, it can be harvested, like Brussels sprouts and curly kale, by stripping the leaves from the stalk without destroying the plant. It is identified as coming from Galicia, just across the border from the Minh – hence its name, galegas. The secret of a good caldo verde lies in slicing the coarse, chewy leaves as finely as possible so they cook rapidly in the broth without losing their brilliance of colour and pleasant chewiness. Portuguese housewives can buy a special instrument for shredding this cabbage or can buy it in the market ready-shredded. You may include a few slices of chouriç or any other smoked pork sausage, if you wish, but the flavour is purer and cleaner without.

Serves 6–8

4 large floury potatoes, peeled and cut into chunks
1 onion, finely chopped
Salt and pepper
450g (1lb) galegas (or curly kale or spring greens), rinsed and trimmed
2 tablespoons extra virgin olive oil

To *serve*
More olive oil
Piri-piri sauce

Put 2 litres (3½ pints) pure spring water in a roomy soup pot with the potatoes and onion. Bring to the boil, add salt and cook for 20 minutes or so, until the potatoes are perfectly tender.

Meanwhile, shred the cabbage – the only really important task, since the strands must be as thin as angel's tresses. Remove the hard white stalk and central vein of the leaves (not necessary if using tender spring greens) and shred as finely as possible. This is easier if you roll the leaves up into little bundles and cut firmly right across the grain.

Mash the potato into the broth to thicken it, season with pepper and check for salt, then stir in the oil. Bring the broth back to the boil and shower in the shredded cabbage, stirring so it feels the heat immediately. Let it bubble up fiercely for 3–4 minutes – just long enough to soften the greens but not long enough for them to be mushy. The cabbage should retain a little bite (the whole point of the fineness of the shredding).

Ladle the soup into bowls and serve steaming hot. Hand around extra olive oil and a bottle of piri-piri (see p. 207) for those who like a little heat, and serve with cornmeal bread and young wine – what else?

bacalhau a moda de Viana
salt-cod with onions, white wine and cabbage

A sophisticated salt-cod dish from the merchant-port of Viana de Castelo, which these days is the Minho's main resort town. The combination of slow-cooked onions (the town's housewives look for onions from Barcelos and Póvoa) and salty fish works well with the robustness of the cabbage, used in this recipe as a wrapper. The ladies of Viana do Castelo are as famous for their cooking as they are for their expertise with the needle, a skill most evident in the beautiful red costumes embroidered with glass beads they wear on feast days.

Serves 4–6

700g (1½lb) salt-cod or 4 thick steaks any fresh
   firm-fleshed white fish
900g (2lb) onions, finely sliced
4 tablespoons olive oil
1 green cabbage
900g (2lb) waxy potatoes, peeled and thickly sliced
1 glass vinho verde or any dry white wine
Salt and pepper

To finish
Parsley, finely chopped
Piri-piri sauce (optional)

If using salt-cod, cut it into four equal pieces and soak for 48 hours in several changes of fresh water, until perfectly de-salted and well plumped. Remove from the water but don't drain or dry (slip off the skin if you prefer). If using fresh fish, rinse, salt lightly and leave for a couple of hours in a colander for the flavour to develop.

Preheat the oven to 180°C/350°F/gas mark 4.

Set the onions to cook gently in the olive oil in a roomy frying pan. Allow 30 minutes: they should gild and soften but not brown. (This is the basic cebollada, the most important flavouring of the Portuguese kitchen.)

Trim the cabbage, removing and reserving four of the largest and most perfect outside leaves, and shred the heart. Nick out the thick stalk at the base of each of the four reserved leaves, flatten them with the blade of a heavy knife, and use them to wrap the fish steaks. Lay the little parcels on a baking tray and transfer to the oven for 20–30 minutes, until the wrappers are as dry and brown as tobacco leaves.

Meanwhile, set the potatoes to cook for 15 minutes or so, until tender, in a covered pan with the wine and enough water to cover. After 10 minutes, drop in the shredded cabbage and put the lid on tightly to allow the greens to cook in the steam.

Remove the potatoes and cabbage with a draining spoon and arrange them in a layer in a warm serving dish. Pour the cooking juices into the cebollada in the frying pan, taste and season, and let bubble up until you are left with a thick rich sauce. Pour the sauce over the potatoes and cabbage and top with the fish parcels, opened to reveal their contents. Sprinkle with a little finely chopped parsley and maybe a shake of piri-piri.

toucinho-do-céu
baked egg custard with almonds

The direct translation of the name is heavenly bac — a description which gives no indication of its delicacy. Every region, indeed every household, ha its own version of this popular dessert. Possible extra enrichments are well-pounded pork fat, lard ground almonds, butter.

Serves 8–10

450g (1lb) caster sugar, plus more for dusting
110g (4oz) blanched almonds, pounded
18 large egg yolks, blended with a fork
Butter, for greasing
2 tablespoons flour

Put the sugar in a heavy pan with 300ml (½ pint) water and stir gently over the heat until the crystal have dissolved to make a syrup. Let bubble gently until the syrup reaches the small-thread stage (103°C/217°F). The syrup will thicken a little and a droplet held between the finger and thumb forms a fine thread when the fingers are pulled apart (only this if you're used to working with boiling sugar). St in the pounded almonds, return to the boil and let bubble up for 2–3 minutes. Remove from the heat a leave to cool a little. Beat in the egg yolks and rehea gently, beating all the while, until the mixture thick a little – stop before it comes to the boil.

Preheat the oven to 230°C/450°F/gas mark 8.Butter baking tin with a capacity of about 1.5 litres (2½ pints). Sprinkle with a tablespoon of flour, pour in t custard and sprinkle with another tablespoon of flo Bake for 30–40 minutes, until a knife pushed into th heart comes out warm and dry. Shake off the excess flour, turn out of the mould, cut into slices and dust with caster sugar. To store, wrap in rice paper and keep in an airtight tin. It's good with a winter comp of apples and prunes or with peaches or slices of fr pear – a storable fruit which can be overwintered o beam, its stalk dipped in wax to seal in the sap.

bolo de família
polenta and orange cake

A sunny golden cake in which a proportion of the wheat flour is replaced by cornmeal, and olive oil is used instead of butter. Rough-ground polenta gives the crumb a nutty sweetness balanced by the acidity of the fruit, which should be small, sharp and juicy. Bitter oranges – otherwise known as marmalade or Seville oranges – are perfect. If they're out of season – you'll find them in January and February – use a sweet orange and a lemon instead. You really do need the acidity.

Serves 8

175g (6oz) self-raising flour
1 teaspoon baking powder
50g (2oz) coarse-ground polenta
225g (8oz) caster sugar
225ml (8fl oz) mild olive oil
4 medium eggs
Juice and finely grated zest of 2 bitter oranges

Preheat the oven to 170°C/325°F/gas mark 3. Sift the flour into a bowl with the baking powder and add the polenta and sugar, tossing lightly to mix. Make a dip in the middle and pour in the oil. Drop in the eggs and, using your hand at first, then a wooden spoon, mix thoroughly until there are no lumps left. Add the orange zest and juice (save a little for the tin) to give a mixture which drops softly from the spoon. You may need a little water if the mixture is too stiff.

Lightly grease a cake tin about 18cm (7in) square – a roasting tin is fine – and line the base with grease-proof paper. Brush the paper and the sides of the tin with orange juice. Drop the mixture into the tin, smoothing it into the corners and flattening the top. Bake for about 1¼ hours (check after an hour), until the cake is well risen, has shrunk from the sides and is firm to the finger. Let it rest for 10 minutes before gently transferring it to a wire rack and peeling off the paper. Slice and serve with mid-morning coffee.

The two provinces of northeastern Portugal, Alto Douro (the upper reaches of the Douro river) and Tras-os-Montes ('the land across the mountains') are bordered to the north by Galicia, much of whose culinary habit they share, and to the east by the ancient kingdom of Leon. Together they form a protective no-man's land between Spain and Portugal.

Tras-os-Montes is as remote and sparsely populated as anywhere on the Iberian peninsula. Swathes of heathery moorland provide pasturing for hardy flocks of sheep. While there is no natural border to define where Portugal ends and Spain begins, steep ravines and dense forest form a broad barrier which confines as well as defends. In these cold uplands, *terra fria*, centuries of isolation have

A walled field on the banks of the upper reaches of the Douro

bred self-sufficiency in the people in both body and soul. Smallholdings – *minifundha* – make subsistence farming the only possible way of life. The mountain-dwellers rarely live in isolated farmhouses, preferring the mutual support of village life. Small stone-built houses thatched with heather and straw – dwellings for man and beast – perch on stone pillars that raise the living area above the cobbled streets; during the long months of winter rains these serve more as conduits for the rushing waters than as passageways. The inhabitants, often cut off by snow, are intolerant interference and prefer to make decisions within their own communities. Many are descended from Jewish refugees, escapees from the Inquisition during the hard times which followed the Reconquest of Spain's southern lands.

The cooking of those places where a Jewish population settled reflects the religious prohibitions they brought with them, though these were, of necessity, masked. Rabbit, hare or partridge was used instead of pork to make chouriços, known in the region as alheiras, which were then hung in the fireplace to take the smoke, adding a further layer of indecipherability when the priest came to call. Since the food of these Sephardic refugees – *cristaos-novos*, new Christians was good, the tradition of using non-pork products in alheiras remained, although the pork has slipped back in – too good to lose.

Poet Sacheverell Sitwell, passing the summer of 1953 with Portuguese friends near Bragança, found much to enjoy in the region. The melons and smoked ham of Chaves were, he declared, the finest in the world, particularly when eaten together, cut very thin. He found the country people equally remarkable: 'The shepherds, sometimes to be seen in the streets of Chaves, wear straw raincoats which rustle as they walk and give them the look of toilers in a paddyfield from lacquer cabinet. Men and women alike wear birchwood sabots of huge size.' The regional capital is the royal city of Bragança, neat, compact, crowned by a magnificent ninth-century castle-keep with pretty palace at its heart. As befits a royal place of residence, game is on the menu: wild-boar stews – the wild pig is treated in much the same way as the tame, as the raw material for chouriços and presunto; a fine dish of partridge cooked with grapes; river trout wrapped in ham. The only other towns of any size are the hunting centre of Macedo de Cavaleiro, the market town of Vila Real, the spa town of Chaves and the border town of Miranda do Duero. Vila Real lies at the heart of a high boulder-strewn plateau which drew its wealth from granite and marble quarries, a harsh, cold land grazed by goats and softened at intervals by small farmsteads surrounded by orchards: the town's specialities include roast kid and a sugary treat, pasteis de Santa Clara. Chaves has excellent ham and a dish made with dried octopus brought up from the coast, cooked with potatoes and turnip greens. Miranda has spectacular almond blossom in the early spring and excellent veal, a by-product of the dairy industry.

Macedo de Cavaleiro, the centre for the hunting fraternity – the guns come from all over the world for the sport – specialises, naturally, in game dishes. At the Salazar Hotel (the inhabitants of these uplands don't easily change allegiance) in the middle of Macedo, mementos of past triumphs – boars' heads with ferocious tusks, dainty little deer – stare down from the walls. Toby jugs and British sporting prints, evidence of the Oldest Ally, line the shelves in the deep-carpeted dining room where lace-pinnied waitresses in black silk treat the guests to silver service. There's no shortage of clients: the lodge is newly refurbished Balmoral-style, with chandeliers, chintz upholstery and blazing fires in the brass-fendered grates. The food is, as the clients expect, simple, hearty

and plentiful. Appetisers are pared-down versions of the regional specialities: fingers of sheep's cheese, slices of smoked chouriço, a generous dish of home-pickled purply-green olives, bite-sized pasties filled with shredded bacalhau in a white sauce. A slice of hare pâté (rough, all-meat, no messing) comes with imported German pickles – gherkins, onions. An alheira made with game is fried crisp and served with boiled potatoes and turnip greens, grelos. Hare with rice – arroz com lebre – is as simple and perfect a rice dish as is to be found anywhere, being made with nothing more than the dense, rich, dark meat which has been stewed to make the broth in which the rice is cooked, with the blood stirred in at the end.

In the countryside the culinary highlights are based mostly on salted smoked pork from pigs (wild as well as tame) fattened on forest gleanings: game both feathered and furred; kid meat and goat's-milk cheese. Maize and chestnuts are the staples for both man and beast. Turnip tops and other robust members of the cabbage family provide the greens. Blood sausages and pork products enliven what remains a highly seasonal, locality-specific culinary habit. The region's feijoada – bean-pot – is made with white haricots and includes smoked meats, pig's head, trotters, ears and tails.

The southerly lands of the region, terra quente – hot lands – well watered by the Douro's tributaries, afford a good living for the few and employment for the rest. Here the climate is benevolent: the red alluvial soil supports vineyards and olive groves, orchards producing Mediterranean fruits such as peaches and oranges, and, in winter, melons ripen in the fields. The midday meal of the quintas, northern Portugal's manor houses, is traditionally a communal affair: the lord and lady share the same table, eating the same food out of the same dishes as their workers. Traditional rural life, dependent on the community's goodwill, permitted of nothing else.

sopa de alheiras de caçador
huntsman's broth

In the hunting district centred on Macedo de Cavaleiro, wild meat – rabbit, duck, partridge, hare, boar – often replaces butcher's meat. Although the idea of preparing your own is full of romance, the reality may be less so. Buy it, roast it and eat it with grelos and potatoes dressed with the juices when you find it. If not, a game casserole will have to do. If using hare, remove the bluish membrane which covers the legs and saddle – otherwise the meat will never be tender.

Serves 6 hungry hunters

2 partridges or 2 wild duck, jointed
2 rabbits or 1 young hare, jointed
1 salpicão (a particularly chunky chouriço) or
  smoked pork sausage
About 225g (8oz) presunto or smoked
  gammon, cut into cubes
900g (2lb) pork spare-ribs or pork belly, cut into
  chunks
1 glass Mateus Rosé or any dry rosé wine
Salt and pepper
A ladleful of conserved wild mushrooms (optional)
1 malagueta (chilli) pepper

To serve
6 thick slices of dense-crumbed, round country
  bread or plenty of boiled potatoes
500g (1lb) turnip greens or kale, shredded and
  cooked in very little salted water

Place all the meats in a large casserole, add 2 glasses of water, the glass of wine and, for a richer flavour if liked, the wild mushrooms. Season, bring to the boil, put the lid on tightly – seal with a flour and water paste if it doesn't fit properly – and cook gently either in the oven or on the top of the stove for 2 hours, until the meat is falling off the bones. Don't remove the lid unless you smell burning and need to add water, in which case the heat was too high – better luck next time.

Open the pot, take out a ladleful of the cooking broth and heat it with another glass of water and the malagueta pepper. Simmer for 10 minutes, then remove the pepper. Meanwhile, prepare the meats for serving. Slice the sausage and the pork. You may bone the game or not, as you please.

Heap the meats on the bread and hand the greens around separately. Or pile the meat on the greens and offer plain-boiled potatoes on the side. Hand around the peppery broth separately as a sauce. After the meal, go for a long walk in the woods – you've earned it.

arroz com lebre
hare with rice

To prepare a hare for the pot, don't forget to remove the fine bluish membrane which covers the back and hind legs – if you don't, the meat will never soften. You may add a pinch of saffron if you like, a somewhat Moorish taste acquired through trade with La Mancha. Duck, partridge, pigeon, pheasant, rabbit – or a mixed bag of whatever the guns bring home – can replace the hare.

A good sized hare feeds 8–10

1 hare, jointed and stripped of its outer membrane
225g (8oz) presunto or lean smoked bacon, in one
  piece
1 chouriço or linguiça
1 bay leaf
1/2 teaspoon peppercorns
2–3 cloves
Juice of 1 lemon (reserve the squeezed-out shell)
900g (2lb) medium-grain (Carolina) rice
Salt and pepper

To finish
The hare's blood, if you can get it (if not, 2 squares
  dark chocolate and a glass of red wine, beaten
  with 1 egg yolk)
Small knob butter
Handful parsley, chopped

Cook all the meats, seasoned with the bay leaf, peppercorns, cloves and the lemon zest, in a roomy boiling pot or ovenproof casserole with enough water to cover generously. Simmer until the game meat is perfectly tender – 1–2 hours, depending on the age of the beast (a hunter can tell the age of a hare by the softness of the claws and tearability of the ears). Remove the meats and reserve, de-boned or not, as you please.

Preheat the oven to 180°C/ 350°F/gas mark 4.

Meanwhile, wash, drain and measure the volume of the rice. Strain the broth, taste and season, and measure out twice the volume of broth to rice. Bring the measured broth to the boil in the pot, stir in the rice and lemon juice, return to the boil and transfer to an ovenproof casserole (if necessary). Bake for 30–40 minutes, until the broth has all been absorbed and the rice is tender. Stir in the hare's blood, or the chocolate, red wine and egg yolk mixture – both will set as soon as they touch the heat – remove half the rice, lay in the reserved meat, top with the remaining rice, dot with butter and cook for another 10 minutes or so, until prettily crisped and golden. Finish with a generous shower of parsley.

Wild flowers on one of the rare gentle landscapes of Tras-os-Montes

neither spain nor portugal?

The most famous of Tras-os-Montes' independent mountain villages – I was told of it in Lisbon – is Rio de Honor. High on the shoulder of the mountains, reached through a bleak landscape of moorland and pine forest, the village occupies an astonishingly fertile little valley, green and sheltered, with orchards lining the single-track road which leads across a hump-backed bridge into Spain. A steep huddle of wood-framed dwellings made of unmortared stone and a few modern bungalows perches neatly on either side of the frontier, half in Portugal, half in Spain. The inhabitants have taken advantage of this political no-man's land to run their own affairs without recourse to either government. The place is by no means bleak. A clear stream, tinkling brightly over rounded stones, runs through the middle; on either side of the stream a small floodplain planted with apple trees is grazed, at lambing time, by sheep; the vegetable patches are in full production and chickens pick their way daintily between the rows of beans, lettuces and carrots, searching for worms. Although there are some indications of tourism – an explanatory sign with the EEC ring of stars on a blue background, a local bar – there is far more evidence in the well-stocked store-sheds and neat fields of sprouting potatoes and maize of a self-sufficient way of life.

rutas a moda de Bragança
trout cooked in smoked ham overcoats

Wrapped in a deep red jacket of presunto and fried in bacon drippings, this is trout as they like it in the royal city of Bragança, seat of Portugal's monarchs. The smoky richness of the ham and golden fat makes this one of the most delicious ways of preparing delicate river fish. Smoked gammon will do at a pinch; you do need the smokiness for authenticity.

Serves 4

fine fat trout, gutted, heads left on

thin slices of lean presunto (smoked salt-cured ham)

thick slices of streaky bacon with plenty of fat, diced small

To serve

Waxy golden potatoes, plain-boiled with or without their jackets

Wrap the trout carefully in their ruby-red jackets and set aside. Heat the diced bacon in a heavy pan and fry gently until it yields up all its fat. Remove and reserve the crisp little scraps of crackling. Fry the trout gently in the drippings: allow about 10 minutes, turning the fish over once to brown the other side. It's done when the flesh feels firm to the finger. Serve with plain-boiled potatoes dressed with the reserved bits of crackling and the pan drippings.

broa
cornmeal bread

Broa, a bread made with yellow or white maize meal, is the daily grain food of the poorer regions of Portugal – mountain territory where the semi-wild pigs of the old ibérico breed provide a cash crop. It has a distinctive whitish crust which cracks to reveal a golden-brown crumb. Maize, a hardy grain, an introduction from the New World which proved a boon to upland farmers, is combined with wheat-flour in varying proportions. The higher the proportion of wheat flour, the lighter the loaf. Although this recipe uses a high proportion of wheat to cornmeal – 2:1 – broa is never dainty. It tastes good, though, and is an excellent keeper.

Makes 2 large loaves

900g (2lb) strong white unbleached flour
450g (1lb) fine-ground cornmeal (polenta)
1 teaspoon salt
25g (1oz) fresh yeast or 12g (1/2oz) dried (or
  1 quantity sourdough starter p.110)
About 1.2 litres (2 pints) warm water

To finish
Flour, for dusting
Oil or lard, for greasing

Sift the flour into a warm bowl and stir in the cornmeal and salt. Dissolve the fresh yeast in a cupful of the warm water and sprinkle with a spoonful of the flour.

Work the yeasty liquid into the flour, adding as much of the water as you need to make a soft, sticky, rather wet dough. Work the dough to stretch the gluten (push and tug), form it into a ball and dust with flour. Set it to rise under a damp cloth in a warm place for a couple of hours until more than doubled in bulk: you need well-risen dough with nice big bubbles to get a crisp light bread.

Dust your hands and the table with flour. Scoop out the dough and knock it down roughly with your fists to distribute the air. Cut the dough in half, work each piece into a ball and dust generously with flour. Transfer to a greased baking sheet, cover with a cloth and leave to rise again in a warm kitchen for 30 minutes.

Preheat the oven to 200°C/400°F/gas mark 6. Bake the bread for about 1 hour, until well-risen and hollow-sounding when you tap the base. Don't undercook the loaves, or they'll be heavy. Perfect with a spoonful of quiejo da serra (mountain cheese: ripe and runny in winter and spring, firm and pungent later in the year) or a few slivers of the region's magnificent salt-cured hams and sausages.

When stored in a cotton bag and hung in a current of air, home-baked bread dries out rather than growing a furry green jacket and rotting. In dried form, it provides the basis for dozens of different soaked-bread dishes, serving much the same function in Portugal as dried pasta in Italy.

migas doces
egg custard with walnuts and cinnamon

A rich, eggy Christmas speciality whose name translates as 'sweet breadcrumbs' but which is nothing more or less than a fluffy eggnog thickened with freshly gathered walnuts (the migas) and flavoured with cinnamon. Proportions for the custard are roughly 1½ tablespoons sugar to each egg. It's only worth making in quantity.

Serves 10–12

12 eggs
350g (12oz) sugar
Small glass white brandy or flavoured liqueur (optional)

To finish
225g (8oz) shelled fresh walnuts, skinned and roughly crushed
Ground cinnamon, for dusting

Whisk the eggs in a bowl with the sugar and the optional brandy until well blended and light. Set the bowl on a pan of simmering water and whisk over the heat until the mixture thickens like a sabayonne.

Remove from the heat and allow to cool a little. Fold in most of the walnuts, and pour into a bowl or individual glasses. Top with the remaining walnuts and finish with a generous powdering of cinnamon.

bolo de castanhas
chestnut cake

Chestnuts are a traditional autumn crop in the remote mountain areas of Tras-os-Montes. Once harvested, the nuts quickly go rancid and the gatherers took to burying them under a thick layer of earth, a decision which preserved their sweetness but made them vulnerable to the attentions of the wandering herds of Ibéricos, foraging pigs of the old black-foot breed.

Serves 6–8

650g (1lb 7oz) fresh chestnuts or 450g (1lb) can unsweetened chestnut purée
25g (1oz) butter
1 teaspoon ground cinnamon
3 eggs
150g (5oz) caster sugar

To finish
Icing sugar

If using fresh chestnuts, skin and boil in plenty of lightly salted water until soft – about 20 minutes. Drain and remove the soft inner skin as soon as the chestnuts are cool enough to handle. Pound them to a paste in a food processor or push them through a sieve. Beat in the butter and add the cinammon. If using chestnut purée, tip the contents of the can into a small pan and warm gently before you beat in the butter and cinnamon.

Preheat the oven to 180°C/350°F/gas mark 4 and line and butter a 20cm (8in) diameter cake tin.

Separate the eggs. Whisk the whites until stiff (stop before they go grainy) and reserve. Whisk the yolks until they begin to lighten and then gradually add the sugar, carrying on whisking until the mixture is light and white. Fold the chestnut purée into the yolk and sugar mixture, turning it well to blend, then fold in the whisked whites. Tip the mixture into the tin, smoothing the top, and bake for 40 minutes until firm and set. It will shrink back when you take it out of the oven.

Run a knife around the sides, tip it out onto a plate and leave it to cool. Dust with icing sugar. Fabulous with sliced peaches or fresh figs.

the cakes of alto douro

Poet Sacheverell Sitwell, touring the upper reaches of the Douro in the 1950s with his wife, went in search of a certain notorious cake prepared for the romería of Sao Gonçalo, patron saint of the town of Amarante. He wrote: 'We chose a restaurant which was also a confectioner's and looked at the cakes in the windows correctly labelled, as advertised in the guide-books, lerias, galhofas, papos de freira. On the way through the shop to the restaurant we asked for the special cakes made for the romería, and it is sad to say that even the name Sao Gonçalo aroused no response. But this is not to say this is not a pretence on their part. Sao Gonçalo, in fact, is the patron saint of marriages, and every confectioner in Amarante sells special cakes baked in the form of a phallus which the young men and women give as presents to each other. It must be the most strange survival of pagan times in all Europe, yet little is known of it.'

ribatejo

The broad slow-moving Tagus is the lifeblood of the Ribatejo, the river from whose banks the region gets its name. The territory is mostly low-lying meadow-lands interspersed with rice paddies, cattle-pasture and bull-ranches, though in modern times the citizens earn their keep from heavy industry. Factory chimneys may belch smoke over the ancient pastures, but the population still sees horses as an important contribution to human happiness. Horsemanship is the birthright of the countryman and the admiration of the town-dweller – serving both for pleasure and as a practical answer to the problem of herding cattle in wetlands. Bullfights, as in Spain, remain a national passion, though the mounted bullfighters of Portugal never pursue the bull to his death: man rides against bull for sport alone.

Poet Sacheverell Sitwell describes a bullfight on the banks of the Tejo in the 1950s:

'The dress of the bull-fighters is unlike that of the toreros of Cordoba and Seville. These are the campinos of the Ribatejo, in knee-breeches, white shirts, barretes verdes or green stocking-caps, and armed with tridents. We shall see them running to and fro at speed to herd the bulls, balancing their tridents. The horseman, meanwhile, has been handed his lance. He gallops towards the bull...allowing the bull to come after him; the bull standing his ground, he gathers his horse and himself and charges. The cavaleiro plants the dart in the bull's shoulder. The bull comes after him in a fury and just fails to catch him. The process is repeated again...when this is finished, the bull's death is often simulated with a wooden sword. But now comes the final feat of strength and skill when eight strongly built young men, the moços de forcado or heroes of the town, advance in Indian file. Their leader puts himself first and with arms folded meets the rush of the bull and allows himself to be lifted off his feet upon the horns. The others then close

on the bull in a wrestling, struggling mass, and after a moment or two the bull is brought to a dead standstill with the stoutest of the young men holding its tail...the bull trots out in the midst of his herd, uninjured, and the round is over.'

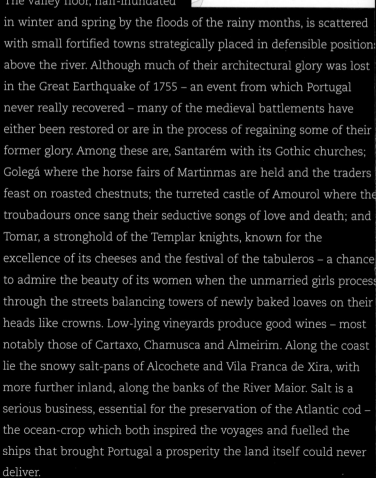

The valley floor, half-inundated in winter and spring by the floods of the rainy months, is scattered with small fortified towns strategically placed in defensible positions above the river. Although much of their architectural glory was lost in the Great Earthquake of 1755 – an event from which Portugal never really recovered – many of the medieval battlements have either been restored or are in the process of regaining some of their former glory. Among these are, Santarém with its Gothic churches; Golegá where the horse fairs of Martinmas are held and the traders feast on roasted chestnuts; the turreted castle of Amourol where the troubadours once sang their seductive songs of love and death; and Tomar, a stronghold of the Templar knights, known for the excellence of its cheeses and the festival of the tabuleros – a chance to admire the beauty of its women when the unmarried girls process through the streets balancing towers of newly baked loaves on their heads like crowns. Low-lying vineyards produce good wines – most notably those of Cartaxo, Chamusca and Almeirim. Along the coast lie the snowy salt-pans of Alcochete and Vila Franca de Xira, with more further inland, along the banks of the River Maior. Salt is a serious business, essential for the preservation of the Atlantic cod – the ocean-crop which both inspired the voyages and fuelled the ships that brought Portugal a prosperity the land itself could never deliver.

ince this is cattle country, veal is the festive meat of choice.
egetables grow well and are combined with pulses in main-course
ɔups such as the intriguingly named *sopa de pedra*, stone soup.

There is, too, since the land is prosperous, a strong tradition of
convent sweets, ladies' treats, eaten mid-morning with coffee or
served as dessert, or consumed, as the nuns intended, on the feast
days of female saints.

farmer herds bulls at Barroca, Ribatejo

sopa de pedra
stone soup

This is the most famous soup in the Portuguese repertoire (with the sole exception of caldo verde), perhaps because the name appeals to the nation's self-deprecating sense of humour. A main course red-bean soup which appears regularly on rural restaurant menus, this particular recipe is attributed by Maria Modesto, the Isabella Beeton of Portugal, to Jose Manuel Toucinho of the restaurant of the same name at Almeirim in the Ribatejo. It is best made with fresh red kidney beans, which don't need soaking. The inclusion of a stone is entirely optional but enjoyable as a notion.

Serves 4 heartily

450g (1lb) red kidney beans, fresh or soaked
   overnight
1 pig's ear (or similar-sized piece of pork skin),
   scraped and sliced
1 chouriço negro or morcela or similar blood
   sausage
1 thick slice of streaky bacon, diced small
2 large onions, finely sliced
1 whole head of garlic, separated into cloves and
   skinned
1 bay leaf
1/2 teaspoon crushed white peppercorns
Salt
3–4 large waxy potatoes, diced
Handful fresh coriander

To serve
1 smooth, rounded, river pebble of noticeable size

Put the beans in a roomy soup pot – if they've been soaked, drain them and give them a preliminary quick boil, then drain again. Add the pig's ear or pork skin, the sausage, bacon, onions, garlic and bay leaf and pour in enough fresh water to cover to a depth of two fingers. Bring to the boil, skim off any grey foam that rises, and season with the crushed white peppercorns and a little salt. Turn down the heat a little and keep the pot bubbling gently for as long as it takes to tenderise the beans: 1–2 hours. If you need to add water, make sure it's boiling. Remove and reserve the sausages. Add the potatoes and let bubble for another 15–20 minutes, until tender. Chop the coriander and stir it in.

Transfer the broth to a warm tureen in which you have placed the stone and return the sausage, neatly sliced, to the broth. For a more substantial dish, place thick slices of bread in the soup plates before you spoon in the broth.

couço com vitela assad
black-eyed peas with mint and roast veal

African legumes flavoured with Christian pork finished with Muslim mint: nutritionally the balance is perfect. If you can't find morcela, the spicy, chilli-spiked Portuguese blood pudding, use whatever black pudding you can find but add another stick of cinnamon and double the chilli. If you have no meat, serve the peas on thick slabs of toasted bread rubbed with oil and garlic.

Serves 6

450g (1lb) dried black-eyed peas
900g (2lb) boned rolled shoulder or leg of veal
Rough salt
2 lengths morcela (Portuguese black pudding)
1 onion, sliced into rings
1 short cinnamon stick
1/2 teaspoon dried, flaked chillies
4 tablespoons olive oil
2 bay leaves
1 glass young red or white wine (vinho verde)

To finish
Small bunch of mint

Soak the peas overnight in enough cold water to cover generously. Dip the veal in water, roll it in rough salt (the water allows the salt to stick) and leave in a bowl overnight.

Drain the peas and put them in a pot with the black pudding, onion, cinnamon and chillies. Bring to the boil, skim off any foam that rises, turn down the heat, add 2 tablespoons of the olive oil, put the lid on and leave to simmer gently for an hour or so, until the peas are perfectly tender; or transfer to a preheated oven at 180°C/350°F/gas mark 4 for about an hour.

Meanwhile, rinse the veal, pat it dry and put it in a pot – a Dutch oven is perfect – into which it just fits tir in the remaining oil, tuck in the bay leaves and add the wine. Transfer to the oven or set the pot over a low flame, turning the joint regularly to brown every side, and cook until perfectly tender. Allow to settle for 15 minutes before carving into thick slices. Stir the meat juices into the peas, heap on a warm plate and finish with a few sprigs of mint. Hand the meat around separately.

The Convent of Christ, Tomar, Ribatejo

pão-de-ló
light-as-a-feather sponge cake

Dependent for its lightness on nothing more than a thorough beating – at least an hour when made by hand – this classic Portuguese fatless sponge is traditionally baked in an earthenware casserole in a wood-fired oven. When cut into slices or squares and soaked in flavoured syrups, or layered with oves moles, a thick pouring custard (see opposite) it forms the basis of many classic desserts.

Makes 1 large cake

4 whole eggs and 8 egg-yolks
250g (9oz) caster sugar
150g (5oz) plain flour

Whisk the egg yolks and whites until fluffy – easiest with an electric mixer. Sprinkle in the sugar a spoonful at a time and carry on whisking until light and white: allow at least 20 minutes with an electric whisk, twice that by hand. Sift in the flour spoonful by spoonful, folding it in with a metal spoon to incorporate it into the mix without destroying the lightness.

Preheat the oven to 200°C/400°F/gas mark 6.

Line a 25cm (10in) diameter cake ring – a round baking tin with a funnel in the middle – with a double thickness of baking parchment. Tip in the mixture, smoothing it round with a metal spoon. Bake for 35–40 minutes, until well puffed and brown. Cover with foil, shiny side down, lower the heat to 180°C/350°F/gas mark 4 and bake for another 10 minutes to ensure it doesn't collapse when turned out. Allow to cool a little before tipping it out onto a wire rack, paper and all. Leave the paper in place until you're ready to cut the cake.

sopa dourada
golden custard

This is a Christmas dessert, though its fragrance, delicacy and relative simplicity – once you've baked the basic sponge cake and mastered the art of oves moles – make it popular as a party dessert throughout the year. The whites can go to make meringues, though in the convents, where most of Portugal's sweet confections were perfected, the whites would have been required for the day's baking of communion wafers. If it's not as thick as you would like – sugar-syrup custards are a little temperamental – do as they do in Portugal and stir in a handful of powdered almonds or a spoonful of pumpkin jam (see p.209).

Serves 8–10

750g (1lb 10oz) caster sugar
350g (12oz) sponge cake (pão-de-ló; see p. 180)
2 tablespoons orange-flower water
16 egg yolks

In a heavy-based pan, dissolve the sugar in 300ml (½ pint) water over a low heat and then boil rapidly until it reaches the thread stage (106°C/222°F) – use a sugar thermometer until you get used to the texture.

Meanwhile, cut the sponge cake into thick slices. As soon as the syrup is ready, dip each slice of cake into the hot syrup and remove with a draining spoon, allowing excess syrup to drain back into the pan, and arrange the slices on a serving dish. Return the pan to the heat, stir in the orange-flower water and bring the syrup back to the boil. Let it bubble it up rapidly until a drop on a saucer forms a skin and wrinkles when you push it with your finger.

Meanwhile, mix the yolks together with a knife, working in a little of the hot syrup. Beat in the rest of the syrup and pour the mixture back into the pan. Stir over a gentle heat until the mixture thickens to the consistency of soft confectioner's custard, known in Portugal as oves moles. Pour over the sponge slices and finish with flaked almonds and a dusting of cinnamon, or a sprinkling of diced crystallised fruit. In early summer, add a handful of the tiny, exquisitely fragrant wild strawberries gathered in the short season – the higher up the mountain, the later they ripen.

the mountain beiras & beira litoral

The two Mountain Beiras, Alta and Baixa, High and Low, are wild, romantic and as remote as anywhere can be in these days of four-lane highways and instant accessibility. Beira Litoral is the little sister of the coastal plain, the region's window on the outside world. At her heart is proud Coimbra, one of the four founding capitals of the Portuguese nation, a reality, however historical, no one is ever allowed to forget.

The River Tagus rises in the spine of Beira Baixa, the Serra da Estrela, whose eastern slopes, defended by castellated villages, hold the frontier against invasion from Spain – still, six centuries after the Reconquista, referred to by country people as the land of the Moors. The names of the towns – Castel Branco, Guarda, Monfortino – and their position on eminences along the rivers, reflect an awareness that threats from the east can be contained, but they never go away. The region is blessed with the wines of Maçao and water from the mineral springs of Foz da Serta and Unhais da Serra to dilute their effects. Monfortino has orchards as well as waters, the heathery uplands are full of partridge and hare – cooked with a little vinegar to soften the muscular flesh – and there're trout, lamprey and shad in the streams, excellent potatoes to eat with bacalha or mountain-fish, or beat with lard and colour with paprika, or flavour with olive oil and garlic. While sheep are kept for milk, wool and meat, the pig remains the most important of all – practically a member of the family, until the moment of truth when everything but the squeal disappears into the winter larder. Chouriço, a more economical preparation than ham since the whole pig can be used, goes into the boiling-pot with the beans, or is roasted and eaten with turnip greens.

The inhabitants of a region in which self-sufficiency is a necessity rather than an ideal have a tradition of hospitality to strangers – provided they come unarmed. No one, however poor, need go hung when there's a pot of soup simmering in the hearth and bread to mop it up. And for weddings and celebrations there's sucking-pig, exquisitely tender and crisp-skinned when basted with wine, brushed with cumin, nutmeg and garlic and roasted in the bread oven. Such pleasures are rare, and all the more appreciated for tha

Beira Alta's little capital, Viseu, its walled citadel scrubbed and polished and its cobbled streets newly pedestrianised, drew its prosperity from the Dao vineyards and the surrounding farmlands. Milk-sheep graze the orchards. Viseu is proud of its reputation for good food, although this is mainly to be found in the domestic kitchen. Why go out to eat when there's better to be had at home? The most remarkable cheese of the region – indeed of any region since it's the most famous in the land – is the sheep's milk cheese o Castel Branco. It is similar in presentation and consistency to a Swi vacherin (though to my mind more complex and deeper in flavour) it's just as seasonal. From late autumn to early spring – it comes to maturity just in time for Christmas – it's gorgeously runny and can only be eaten with a spoon. After that, it's aged into rounds like Parmesan and used for cooking.

Beira Litoral, as the name implies, is low-lying, divided from the ocean by a line of dunes and a rampart of pines, with the foothills o the Mountain Beiras rising behind. The houses – clustered in small villages or as single farmhouses dwarfed by their barns – all have overhanging eaves and are built on high ground. In the long rainy season which keeps the land fertile, there's always a danger of alluvial flooding. Along the coastal strip from Lisbon to Coimbra, inland from the cliffs and dunes, the undulating hills and valleys a dotted with smallholdings and orchards, a market garden for the cities of the coast. In spring, field workers bend double among the heat rows of emerging plantings – new potatoes, spring cabbages, lettuces, beans, peas. Still in place from last year are fat white stalks of overwintered leeks and thick green rows of parsley, the pot-herbs which flavoured winter's soups.

The region's capital, the bustling little university city of Coimbra, Portugal's oldest seat of learning, dominates the plain of the River Mondego and the approaches to the Mountain Beiras, the route taken by many an invader through the centuries. In the main shopping street, brightly lit pastry-shops alternate with bookshops and dusty emporiums selling mysterious kitchenware. The cake-shops are crammed, mid-morning, with smartly dressed ladies grabbing a mouthful at the counter – *pasteis de nata*, little heaps of cinnamon-dusted blancmange, sticky squares of *toucinho-do-céu*, slabs of walnut-studded spice-cake – proffered in a square of tissue paper for eating in the hand, or with a little cup of ferociously strong coffee and a glass of water for those less pressed for time. For those on a diet (or, like me, unable to choose), there are miniature versions of everything except the billowing waves of enormous meringues which fill the windows and overflow on to the glass shelves behind the counters. Maybe, in these secular times, the egg whites no longer needed for church wafers have nowhere else to go.

Coimbra's cuisine has a reputation for heartiness as well as sophistication, at least in the cake department, much of which has survived since medieval times, including a blancmange made with pounded chicken breast. But for those in search of something more substantial, the student café by the railway station serves man-sized portions of salt-cod blackened on the grill and slapped on a heap of roasted new potatoes crushed with oil and garlic. Hot sauce and more olive oil is provided on the formica tables. Salt is absent: no one needs extra salt.

Trade between the cities of the Atlantic has always been far easier than trade between the mountainous interior and the coast. A man from the Minho, provided with a means of crossing the river-mouths, could make his way to Cape St Vincent and scarcely be required to scale a cliff. The Mountain Beiras have far more in common with Tras-os-Montes and the wilderness of Alto Alentejo than the regions for which they serve as ramparts. The cities of the Atlantic littoral, Coimbra among them, are cosmopolitan by conquest, if not by design. Celts, Phoenicians, Greeks, Romans, Suevi, Moors all came by sea, and this has shaped the habit and the culture of the people.

View of Coimbra, nineteenth century, by James Holland

Portuguese babies

Traveller Ethel Hargrove offers insights into the principles of child-rearing in Coimbra c. 1914: 'In all classes the babies are very well dressed. So much so indeed that in the midst of poverty and want the little one's clothes are trimmed with lace and ribbons and the materials are often silk and velvet. All the parents' pride lies in the babies' frocks, and they are very affectionate, so much so that they spoil their children…You cannot scold them much and they are very quickly offended. Once they know how to eat, they sit at the grown-up people's table. The rich have no faith in feeding bottles or patent food and Portuguese babies are generally sent out to nurse. As to the peasant babies, they begin to eat Indian bread, sardines and olives and to drink wine while still very young. You must have noticed how very late quite tiny children go to bed. In fact they often pass their evenings with their mother and nurse at the neighbours' houses.'

beringelas fritas
aubergine fritters

This is the easiest and simplest of vegetable dishes, quickly prepared and very good if the raw materials are plump and fresh (check the hulls for signs of dryness and the flesh for sponginess). The addition of a little roughly ground semolina or cornmeal makes the coating crisper and compensates for the rougher texture of home-ground flour. To serve as a main-course vegetarian dish, double the quantity with thin slices of pumpkin or parsnip – *xerovias* – and serve with a *refolgada*, a heap of onions gently cooked in olive oil until golden and sweet as honey.

Serves 4

2 fine plump aubergines
4 tablespoons strong bread flour
2 eggs
1 teaspoon sea salt
Olive oil, for shallow-frying

Wipe and hull the aubergines and cut them into thin rounds – I usually do them on the diagonal.

Spread the flour on a plate and mix with the eggs and salt to make a runny paste.

Heat a finger's width of olive oil in a frying pan. As soon as a faint blue haze rises, dip a few of the slices of aubergine in the eggy paste and slip them into the hot oil: no more than will cover the surface. Fry until crisp, turning once, and transfer to kitchen paper to drain. Continue until all are done. In my family the fritters vanish as soon as they come out of the pan.

caldo do poveres
poor man's broth with greens

This is Portugal's minestrone, a fortifying combination of pasta and beans cooked in a bacon broth, finished with dark green winter cabbage. Prepared in the morning and eaten both at midday and in the evening in rural areas, it can be served either as a single plateful, or as two courses, with pasta, meat and greens first and broth afterwards.

Serves 6–8

200g (7oz) smoked bacon, chopped into bite-sized pieces, or a bacon hock
1 large carrot, scraped and chopped
1/2 teaspoon peppercorns
1–2 bay leaves
110g (4oz) pre-soaked dried haricot beans or fresh fava beans
110g (4oz) long-grain rice
2 large handfuls green leaves (cabbage, chard, turnip greens), shredded
110g (4oz) short tubular pasta – elbow macaroni is perfect
Salt
1–2 tablespoons extra virgin olive oil

Bring the bacon to the boil in about 1.5 litres (2½ pints) water with the carrot, peppercorns and a bay leaf and simmer gently for an hour, until the broth is well flavoured. Add the beans and simmer for another hour, until the beans are perfectly tender. Remove the soggy carrot and the bacon bone if using, add the rice and cook for another 10 minutes. Add the greens and the pasta, return to the boil and cook for another 20 minutes or so, until the pasta is soft and the broth has thickened. Taste and add salt if necessary.

Ladle into bowls and swirl a little olive oil into each serving. Hand round a bottle of piri-piri sauce (see p.207) for those who like a little heat, and serve with thick slices of freshly baked broa (see p.173).

chuletas de vitela da Beira
chops in parsley jackets

This elegant dish from the Beira Litoral is a refinement of the usual egg-and-breadcrumbing – the frugal housewife's trick that makes a little meat go a long way.

Serves 4

veal chops or escalopes
garlic clove, skinned and crushed
salt and pepper
glass white wine

To finish
large egg
tablespoons chopped parsley
4–5 tablespoons fresh breadcrumbs
Oil or pork lard, for frying

Flatten the chops or escalopes with the back of a heavy knife, lay them in a deep plate, add the garlic, salt and pepper, and pour over the wine. Leave for a few hours or overnight to imbibe the flavours.

When you're ready to serve, have ready three plates. In the first plate, mix the egg with its own volume of water; spread the parsley on the second; and place the breadcrumbs on the third. Drain the chops and dip them first in the egg, then the parsley, then the breadcrumbs, making sure all the surfaces are covered.

Heat a pan of oil or lard for shallow-frying. As soon as the surface is lightly hazed with blue, lay in the chops – no more than will cover the base of the pan. Fry gently, turning once, for 4–5 minutes each side, till the meat is firm and cooked right through, and the coating is crisp.

Serve with small, waxy, yellow potatoes cooked in their skins, crushed between your finger and thumb and tossed over the heat with olive oil and garlic.

manjar branco de Coimbra
velvety milk pudding with orange blossom

Manjar branco ('white food', also known as *teta de freira*, 'nun's nipple') is one of Portugal's most remarkable dishes, a medieval dessert which, in the classic version from Coimbra, includes pounded chicken breast. Comfort food, smooth and velvety, just the thing for babies as well as toothless old granddads. For authenticity you need four unglazed, flat-bottomed pottery dishes – failing that, any heat-proof, saucer-like containers will do.

Serves 4

110g (4oz) poached chicken breast
6 tablespoons chicken broth or water
110g (4oz) rice flour
500ml (18fl oz) creamy milk
110g (4oz) caster sugar
Pinch of salt
2 tablespoons orange-flower water (or 1 teaspoon grated orange zest)

Pound the chicken breast in a mortar (or use the food processor, including enough broth to allow the blades to work) until reduced to a smooth paste. Mix the chicken broth or water with the rice flour in a heavy saucepan, then whisk in the remaining ingredients and heat until the mixture begins to thicken, whisking throughout to avoid lumps. Divide half the mixture between four little dishes, and set aside to cool and form a skin. Spoon all but a third of the remaining mixture into each dish, mounding it up in the middle, and allow to cool again. Finish with the remaining mixture, piling it up as before – the result should be a soft, breast-like curve.

Preheat the oven to 200°C/400°F/gas mark 6.

Slip the little dishes into the hot oven for 20–25 minutes to brown lightly – a sprinkling of freckles, no more – and serve cool. Try with a handful of wild strawberries in summer or baked apples in winter.

doce de tomate
tomato jam with vanilla

A thick, deep crimson jam with a wonderful depth of flavour made in much the same way as the popular quince jam. Make it with firm-fleshed, sun-ripened Mediterranean fruits in their proper season, the end of summer. It's no use trying it at any other time of year, particularly with watery Dutch greenhouse stuff. Island or mountain-raised tomatoes are the sweetest: grown under harsh conditions – volcanic soil, salt-laden breezes – they are obliged to make the most of themselves to attract the limited population of pollinators and predators which spread their seed (the reason, after all, for their existence).

Makes about 3kg (6¹/₂lb)

1.7kg (4lb) firm-fleshed field-ripened tomatoes
1.7kg (4lb) unrefined (golden) sugar
A short length vanilla pod, split
Juice of 2 lemons

Scald, skin and chop the tomatoes. Push them through a sieve, which is easiest if you liquidise them briefly first (all you need to lose is the seeds – the jelly contains much of the vitamin C you wish, no doubt, to conserve).

Put the tomato pulp in a pan with the sugar. Heat gently, stirring until the sugar dissolves. Add the vanilla pod and lemon juice and leave to bubble until the mixture is satisfactorily thick and jammy: 1–2 hours, depending on the initial wateriness of the tomatoes and your preferred consistency for jam. Remove the vanilla pod (you can scrape in the seeds if you wish), then ladle into sterilised jars, seal and keep on a cool shelf, away from light and heat.

Use to sandwich together a sponge cake (pão-de-ló, see p. 180) or with a breakfast of toasted cornmeal broa drizzled with olive oil. It's nicest of all with a spoonful of runny *quiejo da serra* (mountain cheese).

Estremadura is the coastal region which includes Lisbon, the political and national capital. Cosmopolitan and sophisticated, Lisbon has access to all the dishes from other regions as well as those from its former colonies in Africa, Latin America and the East. Among truly local specialities the citizens will urge you not to miss are the grilled sardines (May to October only); grilled chorizos in the fado houses; and salt-cod in all its guises.

Fishing was, until competition for the Atlantic's resources dictated otherwise, a way of life as well a business for profit. In the 1950s Marie Noele Kelly reported on Lisbon's flourishing fish market: 'The varinas and peixeras, the fisherwomen, live all over Lisbon and go down to the quay on foot and shoeless. Before eight, a long line of them has already made their rendezvous with the river and met the saveiros, a type of boat very like those on the Bosphorus, or the fragatas all dressed in brown or réd sails bringing their catch along the moles. The sea fish is vigorous and often still alive. Great whitings, sharp swordfishes, heavy pink hakes, elegant sardines and the aristocratic soles all spill on to the quay. They eat ten times more fish in Lisbon than meat, and a fishless day is unheard of in the capital...A great deal of cooking [is done] in the open air under the protection of the seawalls. The menu? Either grilled sardines or a good fish stew with lashings of oil and boiled potatoes.'

Lisbon's wealthy citizens still like to eat the dishes that mama used to make. The surroundings may be more elegant than in days gone by, but the cooking remains. Smart new restaurants

The Harbour, Lisbon, early nineteenth century, by Charles Henry Seaforth

such as the Bario Alto's minimalist Papa Açorda – all blond wood, black leather and white nappery with handsome Armani-clad waiting-staff to match – serve updated traditional cooking presented in thoroughly unminimalist portions. Soft-shell crabs are deep-fried in batter and served on a purslane and dandelion salad; crisp-crusted slices of morcela come, as they should, with a heap of steaming *grelos*, turnip tops, green and fresh. But the most popular dish with the lunchtime crowd – politicians, media faces, local bigwigs – is the magnificent shrimp açorda, a culinary construction too delicious and complex to be described as a bread porridge. Let's call it a bread risotto, Portuguese-style.

The hinterland which supplies the city with all the good things that were once enjoyed so lavishly by the monks, the region of Estremadura, is formed from the peninsula to the north of Lisbon. Made up of a rocky coastal strip which includes the spa town of Caldas da Raina, it is mountainous at its heart, with the sanctuary of Our Lady of Fatima tucked into the northern serras and the walled royal hunting forest of Mafra sheltering a pack of semi-wild wolves, carefully tagged and observed. The main tourist developments stretch along the sheltered southern edge of the peninsula, all but drowning in high-rises the fishing harbour of Cascais.

The inshore fleet now operates mainly out of the picture-postcard harbour of Ericeira. The fishermen's whitewashed dwellings edge the cliff-tops, tumbling towards the bouldered causeways which break the swell. At Eastertime many of the fishermen's blue and yellow caiques are drawn up well out of harm's way on the sandy access road by the quay. Fishermen mend their nets beside the boats, knotting the filaments with gnarled fingers, and there's evidence of a limited catch on the washing lines where flatfish hang, suspended on sticks, to take the wind. In the marketplace the fish counters offer a few crates of sardines, a heap of purple-veined octopus shifting uneasily on the slab, prawns, anchovies, a bucket of clams. Nothing much, considering this is a Catholic country and it's Friday. In the dry-goods shop on the upper level there's a brisk trade in salt-cod, barrelled anchovies and unidentified dried flat-fish. In the pasticceria, however, the famous Sintra cheesecakes are on sale – little almond tarts, a bit like maids-of-honour – along with billowing towers of sponge cake, *pão-de-ló*, to be drenched in syrup and dosed with a thick egg custard in much the same way as the English trifle. The English learned much of the pastrymaker's art from Portugal – the links have always been strong.

In the 1950s Marie Noele Kelly described the peninsular harbour of Peniche as thronging with more than fifty black-tarred, half-moon fishing boats, each manned by at least sixteen sailors, unloading great baskets of swordfish which were rapidly salted on shore by the fishwives. Up the coast at Nazaré the sardine boats, each bearing a bright blue painted eye on either side of the prow, were hauled up the sandy beach by oxen. The whole community lived off nothing but the short season when the sardines shoaled; the fishwives – 'admirable, hieratic, draped in black capes under which seven petticoats swirl' – worked like demons, carrying, salting and boxing the fish. At Setubal she saw over forty canning factories in full production, though not all the catch went to the canneries; visitors could sample it on the beach, grilled over a little charcoal fire, food which, when eaten with a crust of maize bread, is 'a royal dish'.

Inland from the fishing villages, smallholders grow vegetables for the markets of Lisbon. Local restaurants serve robust soups and chips with grilled meat – steaks flamed over charcoal in the Brazilian way, a taste brought back to the motherland by repatriated Portuguese ex-colonisers, along with a taste for piri-piri, red-hot chilli sauce made with malagueta peppers. Fava beans are eaten both dried and fresh, combined with the fragrant little bulbs and fronds of slender-rooted wild fennel – a roadside crop which, like so many other good things, children once knew how to eat on the way to school.

fava e funcho
fennel and fava beans

This is a combination popular throughout the lan as well as in the capital. In winter it can be made with beans from the store-cupboard, soaked and cooked until tender with dried fennel stalks; in summer it's made with fresh beans and young fennel fronds grown in the wild. Bulb fennel will do – and if you can't find ones with plenty of green, substitute a handful of dill. It is good as a quick mid-morning snack, as a light supper, or as a first course with quartered hearts of lettuce, an grilled sardines (May to October only) to follow.

Serves 4

450g (1lb) broad beans
2 fennel bulbs, including the young fronds
4 tablespoons olive oil
1 thick slice of streaky bacon, diced
1 large bunch of spring onions, trimmed and
  chopped
A handful of dill, chopped (optional)

To finish
4 thin slices of cornbread (broa), toasted

Prepare the vegetables first. Shell the beans and skin them if they're a little on the leathery side. Trim the fennel bulbs, reserving the frondy ends, and slice vertically.

Heat the olive oil in a shallow heat-proof casserole, add the bacon and spring onions, stir over the heat for a few minutes, then add the vegetables, except for the fennel fronds. Season, bring to the boil, turn down the heat, cover loosely and simmer gently for 30–40 minutes, adding a few drops of water as needed. Let it bubble up to thicken the sauce, then stir in the chopped fennel fronds or dill. Spoon over slices of grilled wood-oven bread, or hand round the bread separately, as a mop.

arroz destroçido
ruined rice

This is everyone's favourite kitchen disaster: the onion and garlic is allowed to singe and blacken, imparting a delicious bitter-caramel flavour to the rice – hence the name.

Serves 4

450g (1lb) long-grain rice
1 onion, cut in slivers vertically or chopped
2–3 garlic cloves, skinned and cut in slivers
2 tablespoons olive oil
salt

Rinse the rice and reserve.

In a heavy pan – the kind you'd use to prepare a risotto – fry the onion and garlic gently in the olive oil until the pieces blacken at the edges. Don't lose your nerve, but stop before they turn to charcoal. Stir in the rice and fry for another few minutes, until the grains turn transparent. Add about 1 teaspoon of salt and enough water to submerge the rice to a depth of two fingers (in Portugal the general rule when cooking rice is to add its own volume of water plus 10 per cent). Let it bubble up, then turn down the heat and cook until the grains are soft and the water has all been absorbed. You may need to add a little more water.

Pile on a hot serving dish and serve with fried eggs or whatever else you please. Ruined rice is the only possible accompaniment for monkfish cooked with chickpeas (see right).

peixe-pescador com grão-de-bico
monkfish baked with chickpeas

Monkfish tail – poor man's lobster – is a firm-fleshed fish which can stand up to oven cooking and which combines well with pulses such as chickpeas. The alternative is black-eyed beans, a legume of African descent much used in Brazil, Portugal's former colony. In this unusual recipe the fish, skinned but left whole, is baked between a layer of apple and a layer of chickpeas spiced with cinnamon. Delicate diners might like their fish filleted – if so, reduce the length of time in the oven.

Serves 4

450g (1lb) chickpeas, soaked overnight
1 onion, sliced
1 short cinnamon stick
2–3 cloves
1/2 teaspoon crushed peppercorns
1 large waxy potato, peeled and sliced
1 tablespoon olive oil
1 large apple, peeled
700g (1 1/2lb) skinned monkfish tails

To finish
1 heaped tablespoon chopped parsley
1–2 garlic cloves, skinned and finely chopped
1–2 tablespoons olive oil

Drain the chickpeas and put them in a roomy pan with the sliced onion, cinnamon, cloves and crushed peppercorns. Add enough cold water to cover to a depth of two fingers, bring to the boil, turn down the heat and allow to bubble gently, without letting the pan come off the boil, until the chickpeas are perfectly soft – allow 1 1/2–2 hours. If you need to add more water, make sure it's boiling. When the chickpeas are tender, add the potato and cook until soft – another 15–20 minutes – then stir in the oil.

monastic riches

Lisbon's aristocracy all have links to the land, mostly crumbling family quintas in the wine regions visited once a year at harvest time. At Alcobaça, the Cistercian monastery where Dom Pedro and his mistress Dona Ines de Castro – Portugal's star-crossed lovers – are united in death, poet Sacheverell Sitwell wandered through the cloisters. Although he found the vast kitchens, once famed as a temple of gluttony, completely destroyed, the monks had left at least one gastronomic legacy, prolific orchards yielding plums, pears, apples and peaches of an astonishing size and succulence which enabled the town to establish a thriving fruit industry. William Beckford, in his Letters from Portugal and Italy (first published in the 1840s, but purporting to have been written in 1794), describes the monastic dining table as 'groaning with good things: mountains of game, lampreys, sausages as well as exotic foods brought from Brazil and Asia – swallows' nest soup and sharks' fin prepared by a Chinese lay brother according to the latest fashions from Macau'.

Preheat the oven to 180°C/350°F/gas mark 4. Slice the apple into a hot baking dish and place the monkfish tails on top. Cover with the chickpea and potato mixture, finish with chopped parsley, some garlic and a trickle of olive oil and bake for about 20 minutes, until the fish is perfectly opaque.

açorda de mariscos
bread risotto with prawns

Lisbon's açorda is made with fresh seafood – usually prawns – and a risotto-like texture is preferred. Although city folk prefer the elegance of white bread, cornbread broa makes a particularly good seafood açorda: the sweetness of the crumb works well with crustaceans.

Serves 4 as a main dish, 6–8 as a starter

450g (1lb) dried-out broa or any sturdy
  farmhouse bread
2 large onions or leeks
150ml (¼ pint) olive oil
1.7kg (4lb) ripe tomatoes
1 whole head of garlic, separated into cloves
  and skinned
1 teaspoon black peppercorns
1 teaspoon coriander seeds
1 teaspoon dried oregano
450g (1lb) large raw prawns, peeled or not, as
  you please
110g (4oz) chouriço, roughly sliced (optional)
1 tablespoon anchovy essence or 2–3
  canned anchovy fillets, crushed (optional)

To finish
A small knob of butter (optional)
Chopped fresh coriander – plenty

Tear the bread into bite-sized pieces. Set it to soak in a bowl of salted water for a couple of hours, then squeeze dry, using your hands.

Meanwhile, finely slice the onions or leeks and set to fry gently in half the olive oil until soft and golden – 30 minutes is not too long. Chop the tomatoes and set them to cook down to half their volume in a roomy stewpot with the rest of the olive oil and the garlic. Crush the peppercorns and coriander seeds in a mortar and add them to the tomatoes, along with the oregano.

When the tomatoes are well cooked down, push through a sieve, return to the pan and stir in the soaked, squeezed-out bread and 1 litre (1¾ pints) of fresh water. Let it bubble up and cook gently for another 20 minutes, then stir in the contents of the frying pan along with the prawns, the sliced chouriço, if using, and an optional dash of anchovies to bring up the fishy flavour. Cook for another 20 minutes, until the bread is perfectly amalgamated with the broth. Stir in a knob of butter and finish with a liberal scattering of fresh chopped coriander.

mousse de chocolate
chocolate mousse

More than a pleasure: a passion. Chocolate mousse to the Portuguese is like honey to a bear, cream to a cat. At the Papa Açorda, Lisbon's fashionably minimalist restaurant, the chocolate mousse is served from an enormouss ice-frosted steel bowl, a glorious scoop of brown, vanilla-scented sludge proffered on a huge wooden spoon. You scoop off what you want, and then they offer you seconds. Embarrassing – but what can you do but accept?

serves 4–6

350g (12oz) bitter dark chocolate (at least 70 per cent cocoa solids)
50g (2oz) unsalted butter
4 eggs, separated
A pinch of salt
2 tablespoons caster sugar (more if you like it sweeter)

Break the chocolate into smallish pieces and put it in a small bowl with the butter. Set the bowl over a panful of simmering water and leave to melt gently. Chocolate must be handled with kid gloves.)

Meanwhile, in a very clean bowl, whisk the egg whites with the salt until stiff. In another bowl, whisk the egg yolks with the sugar until light and fluffy. Fold the melted chocolate into the egg yolks and then delicately fold in the whites. Tip the mixture into a metal bowl (or, more conventionally, spoon it into a glass bowl or individual ramekins) and pop it briefly in the freezer to set. Nothing to it, really.

a thousand ways with bread

Portuguese tastes in food are formed at an early age – and bread is the first thing an infant puts in its mouth. Without good bread there is no açorda, no migas, no gaspacho – the dishes which define the rural regional table. Impossible to overestimate the significance of bread in the Portuguese heart. Treated with reverence, eaten every day and at every meal, and finally, when it's too hard to yield to the teeth, made into one of a thousand soaked-bread dishes which speak straight to the Portuguese soul. Country bread – dense-crumbed and baked in a wood-fired oven – is what you need. The kind of bread you can store in a cotton bag and hang from a hook, which loses moisture but never goes bad. In rural areas, where fuel was (still is, in the outlying districts) a precious commodity, bread was baked no more than once a week, and in sufficient quantity to be used in a bread dish the following week.

Within these limitations are many choices. The basic material can be served plain with no other dressing than a little oil and garlic; it can also be a vehicle for a small amount of something good – meat, chicken, game, fish or vegetables. When fresh food is in short supply in winter, store-cupboard staples – bacalhau, presunto, chouriço, morcela, farinheiras – are used as enhancements, though none is essential.

The difference between, say, a sopa seca and an açorda is as much in the heart as in the head. Only an insider can tell you which is which, and even those who know can disagree. All that can confidently be said is that each one depends on soaked bread. As a general rule – and there are exceptions – an açorda is a boiling-pot soup, a bread-thickened broth to which heat has been applied directly; migas are soaked breadcrumbs which are then heated with oil in a pan (sometimes to the point of crisping and browning, sometimes simply made into a soft pan-dumpling); ensopados or sopas are bread soups, spoon-food, usually eaten with more bread to sop up the broth; a gaspacho is a bread soup made by moistening torn-up bread with hot or cold water or broth; and a sopa seca, dry soup, is, well, a bread porridge. And then there are the various sweet bread fritters – fatias doradas, rabanadas, fidalgas – much loved by children as well as adults.

alentejo

The two regions of the Alentejo – Alto and Baixo, High and Low – stretch to the Spanish border in the east, the Atlantic in the west and the River Tagus in the north. Quite a territory. Relatively undeveloped, the cooking of the Alentejo remains close to its roots: soups fortified with pulses, rice cooked with tomato and wild oregano, a herb also used as a flavouring for a rural gaspacho. Other wild gatherings are purslane for soups and salads; lemon grass, an oriental import naturalised on riverbanks throughout the territory and used as a digestive infusion; pennyroyal, a member of the mint family used to flavour an açorda in combination with (or instead of) fresh coriander, the herb which defines the Alentejan cooking pot; and truffles of the summer variety, a woodland crop treated at times of hardship as a meat substitute. Cork forests and wheat fields – billowing seas of golden grain punctuated by the red-trunked, silvery-leafed cork-oaks among which the last of the old foraging breed of pigs feast on acorns – provided the people with a livelihood.

Sheep are kept for milk, wool and meat. 'The prevailing impression that the traveller carries away from the Alentejo is of remoteness,' wrote Anne Bridge and Susan Lowndes in the late 1940s. 'Of little towns and villages, church-bejewelled and castle-crowned, set on their hills so far from one another, with such vast sweeps of brown soil and green cork-woods rolling between that their distant whiteness reminds him of sails on a lonely ocean; most of all, perhaps, of the solitary figures of shepherds, motionless in their hooded cloaks, standing guard over their flocks miles from anywhere, immobile as pillars in the desert.'

All is not as desolate as might at first be thought, as novelist Douglas Goldring had observed some ten years earlier: 'Portuguese honey, especially the honey from Alentejo, is admirable, and in the region most of the familiar kinds of fruit, and some varieties not often seen in England, grow to perfection. I have seldom seen a greater abundance of delicious-looking peaches, and a basket of pears given

us by a Portuguese acquaintan[ce] out of his own garden were th[e] most delicious I had ever taste[d]

The most famous exports of th[e] region are the sugar-plums of Elvas, a frontier town where th[e] Infantas of Spain or Portugal r[...] their bridegrooms from across the border. In the 1950s Marie Noele Kelly reported a thriving plum industry: 'Under the old aqueduct, plum orchards marched in serried ranks. We were too la[te] for the famous plums but we were promised iced ones for dinner. They are green, treated in spirit first, and covered with icing after, a very special plum indeed.'

Although the rural population lives among their fields and flocks i[n] the white farmsteads which dot the plains or tuck into the folds of the valleys, the region grew rich on trade with the Orient as well as the treasure of the New World. The money went to build handsome towns – many in the process of restoration three centuries after the Great Earthquake brought them tumbling down – where the citizen[s] can afford to eat more luxuriously than their country cousins. Rich[er] versions of old recipes appear in the towns; traditional cakes and egg-rich custards which were once the province of the convents became the work of professional pastry chefs whose clients could afford to sit in the sun and sip coffee with their cakes. In the towns too, the empanada, traditionally the fieldworker's midday piece-for-the-pocket, is made with buttery pastry rather than the plain flour-and-water doughs of the countryside.

Alentejan pigs, *porcos de montado*, oak-forest pigs, are descendants o[f] the semi-wild foraging herds which once roamed freely in the forest[s] of the Mediterranean littoral. Breeding and diet dictate the price of

Fields of wheat and poppies, Alentejo

each beast, which must, to achieve the highest price, be finished on acorns, a seasonal harvest in limited supply. The hams, when the pigs can be guaranteed to be properly fed and of the Ibérico race, fetch higher prices in the curing-factories of Spain than can possibly be achieved in the home market – although this is nothing new. The pig is a commodity like any other, and the swineherds of the Alentejo are accustomed to walking their charges across the border to the ham-curing town of Jabugo in Andalusia, or selling the pick of the crop to dealers from Salamanca – an interchange reflected in various subtle ways, including the use of leaf-coriander (rather than the parsley found throughout the rest of Spain) in the dishes eaten in the pig-curing farmsteads of the Serrania de Aracena, the mountain range which includes Jabugo.

The region also has good lamb and several excellent sheep's milk cheeses, of which the best-known are Evora, creamy and piquant when fresh, firm and biting when mature; Serpa, white and ripened under a crust of pimentão and olive oil; and Beja, buttery fresh and available only in the milking season, from February to June.

In rural Portugal – and the Alentejo is very rural – chickens are kept as egg-layers, providing a form of currency, corner-of-the-apron money for housewives who have no other income. The eggs are of very high quality, since hens which are allowed to glean in the maize and wheat fields after the harvest has been gathered lay wonderfully rich-yolked eggs of an astonishing brightness. Huge quantities of these eggs went to the monasteries and convents as rent, to be sold back to the congregations in the form of the delicate pastries and sweetmeats traditionally eaten on the feast days of female saints, including the Virgin Mary. The hen is doubly useful to the cook. When its egg-laying days are done and it is fit for nothing but the pot, its well-exercised joints make a good strong broth and provide the stuffing for chicken pasties, *empadas de galinha*.

Leftover-bread dishes include migas gatas, a soft bread porridge flavoured with garlic and oil – proportions roughly 450g (1lb) stale bread to 2 garlic cloves and 4 tablespoons best-quality olive oil – pan-fried until it forms a ball and served with fried fish or a finishing sprinkle of grilled, shredded bacalhau dressed with oil and vinegar. Migas a la alentejana are what the rest of Portugal would describe as an açorda, a cooked bread porridge, while the Alentejan açorda is a clear garlic-and-oil broth to which diced or torn bread is added without any additional cooking.

empadas de galinha de Beja
chicken pasties

In the town of Beja, the countryman's bread-dough turnover stuffed with a scrap of chewy boiling-pot hen becomes a delicate chicken filling enclosed in buttery puff pastry. Although a tough old egg-layer gives a good strong broth for the sauce, a free-range chicken can substitute and will need half the time to become tender. Traditional country recipes use the fat from the cooking broth to shorten the dough.

Makes about 20 little pasties

1 boiling fowl or chicken, jointed (include the back and the neck)
1 bacon knuckle
1 onion, quartered, or 1 leek, trimmed and cut into chunks
A Few parsley sprigs
1/2 teaspoon peppercorns
4 cloves
3 tablespoons white wine vinegar

The sauce
4 egg yolks
Juice and finely grated zest of 1 lemon
A handful of parsley, chopped
Freshly grated nutmeg
Salt and pepper

The pastry
225g (8oz) plain flour
1/2 teaspoon salt
200g (7oz) unsalted butter, chilled
About 2 tablespoons water

To finish
A little beaten egg, for gilding

The typical whitewashed, tiled farm buildings of Alentejo Alto

Put the chicken and the bacon in a roomy pot with enough cold water to cover generously. Bring to the boil and skim off the grey foam that rises. Add the aromatics: the onion or leek, parsley, peppercorns, cloves and vinegar. Bring back to the boil, turn down the heat and leave to simmer gently for about 2 hours, until the bird is perfectly tender (if using a tender young chicken, 1 hour is enough).

Lift out the chicken and the bacon. De-bone, skin, dice the meat and reserve. Strain the broth and measure it: you'll need 500ml (18fl oz) for the sauce. If there's too much, return it to the pan and boil it fiercely to reduce. Allow to cool, then lift off the fat. Whisk in the egg yolks, lemon juice and zest and return to a low heat, whisking until it thickens like a custard. Stir in the chopped meats, a generous handful of chopped parsley and season with a scraping of nutmeg, a little salt and plenty of pepper. Leave to cool.

Meanwhile, make the pastry in a very cool place. Take a large bowl and sift in the flour with the salt. Cut in a quarter of the butter with a sharp knife until you have a mixture like fine breadcrumbs. Mix in enough water to make a paste which does not stick to the fingers. Knead lightly. Set the dough

aside for 20 minutes, with the rest of the butter beside it so that pastry and butter reach the same temperature. Roll out the pastry to a thickness of about 5mm (1/4in) and dot it with small pieces of butter the size of a hazelnut, using about one third of the total remaining quantity. Then fold the pastry into three, as you would a napkin, and again into three, with the folds in the opposite direction. Set aside for 20 minutes. Go through the last process twice more, adding the same amount of butter each time. Set the pastry aside for 20 minutes after each process. Then leave another 20 minutes before you roll it out.

Preheat the oven to 190°C/375°F/gas mark 5.

Roll out the pastry to a thickness of about 3mm (1/8in), and use one large and one smaller tumbler to cut out enough discs to line and top 20 tart tins, 5cm (2in) in diameter. Drop a tablespoon of the filling into each lined tin, wet the edges and cover with the smaller discs, pressing to seal. Mark the edges horizontally with a knife to ensure an even rise and brush the tops with a little beaten egg.

Bake for 20–25 minutes, until the pastry is well-risen and golden.

favas com coentros
fava beans with coriander

A simple little summer salad of young fava beans tossed with spring onions and coriander – perfect with a slice of broa and a plate of Alentejan sausages: paios, linguiças, farinheiras.

Serves 4

900g (2lb) unshelled fava beans
Salt
2 garlic cloves, skinned and finely chopped
4 tablespoons olive oil
1 tablespoon white wine vinegar
3–4 spring onions, finely chopped
Small handful fresh coriander, roughly torn

Shell the beans and slip off the skins if the beans are mature. Cook briefly in salted water, drain thoroughly and toss with the garlic, oil and vinegar.

Allow to cool, then toss with the spring onions and coriander. Although traditionally served with grilled or roast pork, these are perfect as a starter – maybe with a bowl of new potatoes boiled in their skins or a handful of olives.

açorda alentejano
bread soup with garlic and eggs

In the Alentejo, an açorda, eaten at midday throughout the region by rich and poor alike, is always finished with a liberal amount of leaf-coriander, an oriental herb (a reminder of Portugal's maritime adventurings) which defines the cooking of the area. Additional refinements – eggs, fresh sardines, fried peppers, grapes, figs – vary according to season, purse and availability. Optional flavourings are pennyroyal, a mint which grows in every ditch, and a finishing sprinkling of olives for piquancy. Sometimes the soaking broth is the water used to soften salt-cod, though that is something of an acquired taste. The quality of the bread and the excellence of the oil determines the quality of the dish. Portuguese country bread, baked once or twice a week by rural housewives, is robust and chewy – somewhere between white and wholemeal. Bread made with stone-ground flour and a handful of semolina is a fair approximation.

Serves 4–6

A large bunch of fresh coriander
A small bunch of pennyroyal or mint (optional)
2–3 garlic cloves, skinned
1 teaspoon rough salt (rock salt rather than
   sea salt)
150ml (¼ pint) virgin olive oil
2–3 green peppers, de-seeded and cut into
   matchsticks (optional)
About 1.2 litres (2 pints) boiling water or broth or
   salt-cod soaking water
450g (1lb) hard country bread, torn into bite-sized
   pieces (or diced)

To finish
Coriander leaves or mint sprigs
Greeny-violet Portuguese olives
4 poached or hardboiled eggs

To accompany (optional)
Grilled or fried sardines
Ripe figs
Green grapes

Strip the leaves from the herbs and mash to a paste in a mortar with the garlic and salt, then work in the oil – or give everything a quick whizz in a liquidiser. Tip the oily paste into a warm soup tureen or deep serving bowl along with the strips of pepper, if using. Pour in the boiling water or broth (if you're finishing the dish with poached eggs, use the poaching water from the eggs). This is the sopa mestra (master of the soup), also known as sopa azeiteira or olive oil soup.

Drop in the bread pieces and leave for 5 minutes to swell. If you cover the tureen, the bread will be softer than if you leave it uncovered: it's a matter of preference. Ladle the soup into bowls, finish with an extra sprinkling of herbs and a few olives (you can hand these around separately if you prefer) and top each portion with an egg – quartered if boiled, whole if poached.

Each guest then stirs the soup with a slice of bread, tastes the broth and adds seasoning and whatever other accompaniments or toppings are on offer: grilled or fried sardines, quartered ripe figs (in spring and autumn), and green grapes if you've included strips of green pepper rather than mint leaves. Other possible embellishments include chopped tomato, small fried river fish, slices of linguiça, chouriço or farinheiro, a handful of purslane (a mustardy salad green), crumbly white cheese and plain-boiled potatoes.

Whatever the variations, bear in mind the distinguishing characteristics of the Alentejan açorda: the basic broth is clear, the enrichment is olive oil, the flavouring is garlic and coriander and the bread is soaked in the broth – as with the Andaluz gazpacho – rather than cooked as is the case with other regional açordas.

arroz a amarelo
golden rice with chicken

This wedding dish is made with rice grown in the riverine wetlands of the region, cooked with chicken broth, layered with bacon, chicken and chouriço, gilded with egg yolk and oven-baked until it forms a golden crust. The presence of egg yolk (a fertility symbol in all cultures), the rice (seeds) and gilding (a token of sunshine) are an encouragement to the young couple to do what comes naturally: make children. The everyday version, *arroz com galinha*, omits the chouriço, the gilding and the oven-baking. It's the first food a baby ever tastes and the last that old men remember.

Serves 6

1 boiling fowl or free-range chicken
1 bacon hock or thick rasher of streaky bacon
1 chouriço (optional)
1 onion, quartered
1 carrot, cut into chunks
A small bunch of parsley

1–2 bay leaves
$^1/_2$ teaspoon peppercorns
1 teaspoon salt
700g (1$^1/_2$lb) long-grain rice

To finish
2 egg yolks, mixed with a fork

Put the boiling fowl or chicken, bacon, optional chouriço, onion, carrot, parsley, bay leaves, peppercorns and salt in a large boiling pot, bring to the boil, skim off any grey foam that rises, turn down the heat, put the lid on and simmer until the meat is tender and the broth well-flavoured – 1–2 hours depending on the age of the bird.

Remove the meat and reserve. Strain the broth and measure 1.8 litres (3 pints) back into the pot. Return it to the boil while you wash and drain the rice. Stir in the rice, bring the broth back to the boil, put the lid on loosely and cook until the rice is just tender – 18–20 minutes.

Meanwhile, debone the chicken, reserving the meat, shred the bacon and slice the optional chouriço.

Preheat the oven to 200°C/400°F/gas mark 6.

Spread half the rice in the bottom of a gratin dish or ovenproof casserole and top with the chicken, shredded bacon and chouriço. Cover with the rest of the rice and brush with the egg yolks. Bake for 15–20 minutes, until the surface is crusted and golden.

Alentejan coastline

túberas com ovos
truffles with eggs

Oaks and truffles go together like, well, pigs and acorns. Cooked in pork lard and combined with egg yolks sharpened with lemon juice, the scented tubers were a meat substitute when times were hard.

Serves 4

350g (12oz) summer truffles
1 onion, finely chopped
2 tablespoons pure pork lard
Salt and pepper
4 perfectly fresh free-range egg yolks
Juice and zest of 1 lemon
1 tablespoon chopped parsley

Rinse and brush the truffles to remove the mud and sand. Peel them and cut them into thick slices. Fry the onion in the pork lard and add the truffle slices. Cook gently for 15 minutes, adding salt and pepper halfway through, until the truffles release their juices and begin to fry.

Meanwhile, whisk the egg yolks with the lemon juice, lemon zest and chopped parsley.

Stir the egg mixture into the truffles, lower the heat and turn the mixture gently until the eggs form soft curds – remove just as they begin to set. Pile on toasted bread – the crisp, sweet crumb of a cornmeal broa is perfect.

pastéis de santa clara
santa clara almond pasties

In Beja at Eastertime the pasticceria opposite the convent of Nostra Signora de la Consolacion, where the Portuguese nun wrote her *Five Love Letters to a French Cavalier*, used to be crowded with ladies who take coffee and cakes. The display of pastries in the glass cabinet that stretches the length of the shop would be crammed with sugary treats: *pastéis de Santa Clara* (a speciality of the Convento da Esperança), marzipan figs in little paper cases, *queijadas* (cheesecakes: paper-thin pastry shells filled with curd cheese, sweetened, set with very yellow egg), a yellow madeira cake (almondy, with a walnut on top), little castle-puddings, *pasteis de arroz* (rice pastries) and ring cakes, including a very dark honey cake, a butter cake and a nut cake. Awaiting collection by customers who had ordered in advance were the *folares de pascoa* (round breads of various sizes set with whole eggs) and a salamander-shaped bread of whose provenance no one seemed quite certain – perhaps because of an awareness that the origin was not quite as the church would have wanted.

Makes about a dozen little pasties

The filling
250g (9oz) sugar
125g (4¹/₂oz) ground almonds
75g (3oz) cooked chickpeas, mashed
6 large egg yolks and 1 egg white
125g (4¹/₂oz) butter
2 tablespoons pumpkin jam (see p. 209)
1 teaspoon ground cinnamon
¹/₂ teaspoon ground cloves

The pastry
350g (12oz) plain flour
2 large egg yolks
Salt
110g (4oz) butter

To finish
Icing sugar, for dusting

Bring the sugar gently to the boil in a heavy pan with 300ml (¹/₂ pint) water and boil steadily, stirring with a wooden spoon, until the syrup forms threads when you lift the spoon from the pan: the fine thread stage. Stir in the almonds and mashed chickpeas, bring back to the boil, remove from the heat and leave to cool.

Meanwhile, make the pastry. Sift the flour into a bowl and work it to a soft dough with the egg yolks and a tablespoon or two of warm, lightly salted water. Leave for 10 minutes, then, with a floured rolling pin, roll it out into a long thin strip on a floured board. Spread the butter on two thirds of the pastry, then fold the unbuttered section over to cover the middle third of the pastry. Fold the remaining third over to make a small parcel. Roll it out and fold it over again in the same way. Repeat. The pastry has now had three foldings. Leave to rest for another 10 minutes, then roll it out again thinly. Cut into rounds with a cookie-cutter or sharp-edged wine glass.

Finish the filling. Whisk the egg yolks with the egg white and stir into the cooled syrup. Bring it all back to the boil and stir in the butter, jam, cinnamon and cloves. Beat the mixture over the heat for 10 minutes or so, until it pulls away from the bottom of the pan. Allow to cool a little.

Preheat the oven to 200°C/400°F/gas mark 6.

Drop teaspoons of the filling on one side of each round of pastry, dampen the edges and fold over to make a half-moon. Transfer to a buttered baking tray and bake for 12–15 minutes, until puffed and golden. Dust with icing sugar and serve warm.

queijadas de requeijão de Beja
cinnamon cheesecakes

Cinnamon-flavoured cheesecakes, creamy and light, just as they like them in the prosperous town of Beja.

Makes about 12–18 tarts (depending on the size of the tart tins)

The pastry
275g (10oz) plain flour
1 large egg yolk
Salt
75g (3oz) butter

The filling
450g (1lb) fresh white curd cheese
2 whole eggs and 3 yolks
350g (12oz) sugar
50g (2oz) butter, melted

Make the pastry as in the recipe for Santa Clara almond pasties (see p.200) by mixing the flour to a softish paste with the egg yolk and a little warm salted water, then rolling it out and folding it over a layer of butter, followed by two more rollings and foldings – a technique very similar to that used to make puff pastry, though a little less laborious. Roll out very thinly, cut into rounds and use to line 12–18 little tart tins, fluted for preference. Prick the bases with a fork.

Preheat the oven to 190°C/375°F/gas mark 5. Bake the pastry cases for 5–6 minutes, until the surface turns white. Meanwhile, beat the filling ingredients together until well-blended and smooth – easiest in a processor. If mixing by hand, sieve the curd cheese before you work in the rest of the ingredients.

Spoon the filling into the cases and bake for 20 minutes or so, until the pastry is well-risen and the filling just set – it will cook more as it cools.

bolo podre rico
spice cake with almonds and raisins

Every pastry shop in Portugal has its own version of these spiced cutting cakes. Some include nuts and dried fruits, others are plain so that the housewife can add her own refinements, maybe a soaking of sugar syrup or a spoonful of oves moles and a hank of fios de ovos (very fine egg-threads poached in boiling syrup, available in all Portuguese cake shops). It is a deliciously moist cake, and a remarkably good keeper. Bake it well ahead for Christmas and keep it in a tin for a month to mature.

Serves 6

225g (8oz) plain flour
1 teaspoon powdered cinnamon
1/2 teaspoon powdered cloves
2 teaspoons baking powder
1/2 teaspoon salt
350g (12oz) raw cane sugar
50g (2oz) butter, softened
50g (2oz) lard
2 large eggs
2 tablespoons molasses or golden syrup
2 tablespoons blanched split almonds
2 tablespoons raisins, tossed with a little dry flour
2 tablespoons candied peel, tossed with a little
  dry flour
About 150ml (1/4 pint) milk

Sift the flour, spices, baking powder and salt into a roomy bowl. Beat the sugar, butter and lard together, then beat in the eggs one by one, adding a spoonful of flour between each addition. Work in the rest of the flour and the remaining ingredients, adding enough milk to give a soft mixture which drops easily from the spoon.

Preheat the oven to 160°C/325°F/gas mark 3.

Butter or oil a 1kg (2lb) loaf tin or line it with baking parchment. Tip in the cake mixture, smoothing the top and spreading it into the corners. Bake for 1 1/4–1 1/2 hours, until the cake is well-risen and firm to the finger, and has shrunk from the sides.

Wait for a few minutes before you tip it out of its baking tin, then transfer to a wire rack to cool. As with all rich fruitcakes, it is best stored in an airtight tin for a week or two before you cut it.

It is good as a simple dessert with a ripe fig or a slice of winter melon, with an infusion of lemon grass – an oriental weed which thrives along the stream and river banks of the Algarve and the Alentejo – to aid the digestion (see p. 207).

alentejan ham

The Portuguese ham cure is very different from that of the hams of Spain. Unlike the unsmoked, cellar-matured serrano and Ibérico hams, the hams of Portugal are smoked and the joint is rubbed with a protective crust of chilli and olive oil after the initial salting; the hams are then left to dry and develop their flavour hanging from an airy beam for the full turn of one year, and are not, as in Spain, permitted to develop a mould by cellaring. They are, too, semi-boned – only the blade-bone is left in – allowing the meat to be cut in thick slices against the grain rather than in thin slivers, as with Spanish hams.

In the days when people expected to be self-sufficient, an Alentejan rural household kept at least two pigs for their own consumption, of which only two hams were taken for smoking, with the rest going for sausages – affluence indeed, when you consider that in Tras-os-Montes one pig was usual and all four legs of the animal were needed for ham. Since the quality of the meat dictates the excellence of the sausages, the paios, farinheiras, chouriço and linguiça of the Alentejo became famous throughout Portugal. All are salt-cured, wind-dried and smoked – a sign, it must be admitted, that the climate is damp enough to warrant an additional method of conservation. Linguiças are made with lean pork flavoured with mashed garlic, salt and chilli, stuffed into the small intestine (self-evidently narrower than the large intestine). Paios (also known as painho or paiote) follow the same or a similar recipe, but the container is the large intestine. Paios brancos – white puddings – are seasoned with nothing but salt and are left unsmoked. Chouriços are all-meat sausages, made with the meat which is too fatty or chewy for the more delicate paois, stuffed into the larger intestine. Farinheiras, flour sausages, are, as their name suggests, more of a dumpling than a sausage: finely chopped pork belly, very rich and fatty, is mixed with a high proportion of wheat flour worked into a soft paste with boiling water, white wine and orange juice; the mixture is then seasoned with the usual garlic,

salt and chilli mix along with enough pimentão – paprika – to turn it appetisingly rosy. All can be sliced and eaten as they are, or sliced and fried, or grilled and eaten with bread or a dish of migas, or added to the boiling-pot.

algarve

Portugal's most southerly region is, naturally enough, the warmest. It's also the region whose culinary and domestic habit was most influenced by the Moors, the occupying power between 714 and 1147, and was nominally an independent kingdom until the nineteenth century. These days the Algarve is the main destination for sun-seekers, citizens of the northern regions of Portugal as well as tourists from elsewhere. Long white beaches fringe the coast, while the hinterland is undulating and fertile. Those slopes not occupied by tourist high-rises are clothed with almond trees and date palms, olive and orange groves, tall stands of maize with pumpkins and melons between the rows to keep down the weeds. Bees collect nectar in the orchards and scrawny chickens peck among the olive trees for grubs and worms, providing the raw materials for the egg sweets found in every other region, though most particularly those with a strong Moorish connection.

In the 1950s travel writer Marie Noele Kelly described the region as a jewel, 'a little kingdom full of brilliant reflexions: the light sapphire of its sky, the ruby tones of its geraniums lining the roads, the silvery rim of every olive leaf and the deep brassy tones of its unbelievable rocks: all hard and gleaming hues mercifully softened by the evanescent and pearly tones of almond blossom, so thick as to be compared to a fall of snow.' Until the fifteenth century, she continues, the Algarve earned its money from whaling. When the leviathan withdrew to deeper waters, the fishermen turned their attention to the migrating tuna fish – the arriving tuna in the spring being more prized than the returning tuna, spent after the spawning, in the autumn. There were, in the 1950s, more than fifty factories engaged in the tuna-canning trade. 'Fishing this monster, up to 400 pounds [180kg] in weight, is a great and not always safe

sport. More than one fisherman has had his back broken by its tail when the bull-fight of the sea, the copeja, is on. The fish has been previously lured by clever manipulations of the nets into barrage after barrage until in the last net he meets the fisherman hanging perilously by his left hand to a cord at the extreme edge of the boat. With his right he harpoons the tunny.'

The specialities of those with direct access to the sea are, naturally, fresh fish: tuna steaks for the grill, sea bass and conger eel for a fisherman's stew, sardines, thick sieved-fish soups, and almost anything cooked in the cataplana, a hinged copper pan which looks like a double wok – an instrument, it's thought, of Arab design. To counterbalance this somewhat suspect pedigree, the usual combination of foodstuffs cooked between its Moorish curves is shellfish and pork – both ingredients prohibited by the Prophet, a useful recipe for testing Christian allegiances.

In Faro, where a few fishing boats still land their catch in one corner of the harbour where the pleasure yachts crowd the harbour wall, the Club Náutico has a reputation for the excellence of its table and the freshness of its fish. At lunch on a Sunday in May – the day of rest, when the local population eats its fish somewhere other than at home – the little dishes which appear on the table automatically along with the basket of bread are not, as they would be in Spain, a free tapa, compliments of the house.

You choose and pay for what you eat, however tiny. On offer that day, and most other days in this part of Portugal at this time of year, are blood-red carrots, sliced, cooked soft and dressed with onion, cumin, vinegar; Sintra cheese – small, round, white and cut in horizontal slices; and a dish of purply-green olives, very mild and soft. The main event, chosen from the display just inside the door, is shellfish – Venus clams – opened in white wine with very little oil. Afterwards, a line-caught gilt-head bream, sparkling-eyed and bright

Boats on the River Gilao at Taveira, Algarve

of gill, split through the head and down one side of the backbone right to the tail, plain grilled and presented with steamed potatoes and more of the blood-red carrots. There'll never be a better bream: snowy flesh brushed with oil and flecked with grey salt. The unprotected side is crisp and golden with blackened bits around the head; the cheeks and tongue are the tidbits, delicious little morsels; the other side, protected by the bone, is white and soft as cream. To follow, comfort food – rice pudding with pumpkin jam.

Marie Noele Kelly also investigated the fig harvest: 'Faro has a great market for almonds and figs, bananas, oranges, dates; in fact quite an African crop. The figs, black, with unctuous yellow pulp, are called *figo de enchario*, *figo de bispo*, and *figo da toca*. Figs, if left to themselves, would fall before they are ripe; but if pierced by insects, they have their maturity hastened and are thus fit to be sold. When this is done artificially, it is called caprification, and it is the Greeks who no doubt taught this strange trick when coming here of old, to sell amber and spices. The wild and worthless *figo da toca* is cut and hung amongst the more valuable fig trees: the blastophaugus which infests the former in June then migrates to the latter which two months later are miraculously ripened before the figs fall. Boxed, after drying in the sun or in ovens, in charming ornate mat-weed esparto, they bring to sunless Europe that Virgilian fruit packed with sunshine and sugar.'

cataplana de mariscos
shellfish cooked with pork in a cataplana

Shore-gathered shellfish, live and kicking, cooked in a closed pot in their own fragrant juices: what could be more perfect? The success of this ancient dish – which, as with the Spanish paella, takes its name from the utensil in which it's cooked – depends on the possession of the right instrument, the cataplana: a double-sided, hinged copper pan with handles which snap together to keep it shut, allowing the whole thing to be flipped over on the heat source without spilling its contents. The contraption permits small pieces of same-sized foodstuffs – shellfish, white fish, tuna, swordfish, meat and potatoes – to cook evenly and quickly in their own steam. The ingredients are variable, though shellfish – clams, mussels – are the most common. A little ham or chouriço or fresh pork is advisable, though that depends on the means of the cook. The potatoes serve to absorb the sea flavours and provide a little bulk, particularly if the other (costlier) ingredients are in short supply. If you don't have a cataplana, use a heavy-bottomed pan equipped with a tight-fitting lid, and shake it regularly and thoroughly.

Serves 2 as a main dish, 4 as a starter

1.2 litres (2 pints) clams, cockles, mussels, razor-
  shells or any other bivalves, so long as they're
  alive and on the shell
1 large onion, finely sliced
2–3 tablespoons olive oil
2–3 mature yellow potatoes, peeled and cut into
  cubes
110g (4oz) pork, or 50g (2oz) presunto
  or chouriço, diced
Salt
2 tablespoons white wine

To finish (optional)
Parsley or fresh coriander, chopped

If using clams, cockles or razor-shells, put them to soak in fresh water for an hour or two to spit out their sand; if using mussels, scrub thoroughly, scrape off any barnacles and trim off their hank of beard (once bearded, they die – and fresh shellfish should always go live into the pot).

Meanwhile, make a refolgado: very gently fry the sliced onion until soft and golden in the olive oil in one side of the cataplana. Allow 25–30 minutes. When the onion is jammy and golden, add the potatoes and the pork, salt lightly and fry gently for 5 minutes. Add the shellfish and wine, then snap the lid shut. Cook on a gentle heat for 10 minutes, then flip the whole thing over and allow 10 minutes on the other side. If using a saucepan, put the lid on tightly and leave it on the heat for 20 minutes without lifting the lid – shake the pan every now and then to stop the contents sticking.

Sprinkle with parsley or coriander, if using, and serve straight from the cataplana, or eat it fisherman-style, directly from the pot, with chunks of rough bread for mopping and wiping fingers.

caldeirada
fisherman's stew

This is a variable feast of assorted fishes, though as with the French bouillabaisse) certain species, such as the rascasse (scorpion fish), are essential for the glueyness of their little bones and the body they give to the broth. Fresh sardines are included when the dish is made in the traditional way on board the fishing boat itself, but there's very little point in including them unless you are within sight of the fishing grounds. Buy them in cans instead and enjoy them with a glass of wine while the stew simmers on the hob. Portugal's canned sardines, salted and packed in olive oil as soon as they come out of the sea, are a delicacy worthy of caviar prices which, happily, they don't yet fetch.

Serves 6 as a main course

2.7kg (6lb) mixed soup-fish, including rascasse (scorpion fish), conger eel and dogfish; skate, monkfish, red mullet and sea bass are also possible
450g (1lb) sardines or 900g (2lb) shellfish on the shell: cockles, mussels, clams, razor-shells
150ml (¼ pint) olive oil
2 glasses white wine
1 tablespoon white wine vinegar
1 tablespoon mild pimentón (Spanish paprika)
1 tablespoon salt
900g (2lb) potatoes, peeled and thickly sliced
900g (2lb) ripe tomatoes, sliced
3–4 large onions, finely sliced
3–4 garlic cloves, skinned and crushed with a little salt
1 bay leaf, crumbled

Prepare the fish – scale, gut, behead and so on – and cut into thick steaks. (Use the debris to make a broth for a plain fish soup with soup noodles or rice – very traditional in the area.) Rinse the shellfish, if using, leaving them to soak and spit out their sand.

Have ready a roomy, deep-sided casserole. Mix the oil with the wine, vinegar, pimentón and salt until well blended. Starting with the shellfish (if using – if not, the potatoes go in first), layer the fish with the vegetables (including the onion, garlic and bay leaf) to create as many layers as is convenient for the shape of the pot. Pour in the oily dressing and leave to stand for an hour or two. Heat, put the lid on as soon as steam begins to rise and leave to simmer gently for an hour or so, until all is tender – or transfer to a preheated oven and bake at 170°C/325°F/gas mark 3. Check and add boiling water if necessary.

Allow to cool a little before serving. Push a spoon through all the layers so that each person gets a fragrant slice of everything, and serve with a bottle of piri-piri (see right) or whatever chilli sauce you please.

Use any leftovers to make a sieved fish soup: add water to cover, season and push thorough a sieve (easiest if you liquidise everything first). Boil it up and season to taste. Keep adding more fish debris and leftovers – as long as you boil it up every day, you can keep it going almost indefinitely.

homemade piri-piri

The standard table sauce of Portugal is available in every supermarket and corner store in the land. Failing that, a fiery blend of hot chillies and mild red peppers does the trick.

Makes about 300ml (½ pint)

225g (8oz) fresh red chillies (malagueta, for preference)
225g (8oz) mild red salad peppers
4 tablespoons rough salt
150ml (¼ pint) white wine vinegar

Hull and de-seed the chillies and peppers and cut into strips. Pack them into a sterilised jar with the salt. Seal and leave for a month, then liquidise with the vinegar and bottle up. Keep in a dark, cool corner and wait a week before you use it.

lemon grass tea

In the southern provinces – Algarve as well as Alentejo – reedy stalks of lemon grass grow wild along the river beds. It's known as the prince's herb, named for Henry the Navigator, who had a bad stomach and took an infusion of lemon grass for his health. To prepare, steep in boiling water, leave to stand for 10 minutes in a vacuum flask or well-insulated pot, and drink plain, without sugar, the way the Portuguese like their tea.

fatias douradas
golden slices

Poor knights, eggy bread: everyone's favourite instant dessert, attributed to the Minho but found everywhere else as well. Children love it – my own included. A traditional Christmas dessert as well as an everyday delight.

Serves 4

4–8 thick slices of dense-crumbed country bread (fluffy townie slices won't do)
300ml (½ pint) creamy milk
4–5 eggs (depending on size)
A pinch of salt
1 tablespoon sugar
Caster sugar and ground cinnamon, for dusting
Mild olive oil, for shallow-frying

Cut the bread into thick fingers or leave it whole, as you like; similarly, remove the crusts or not. Pour the milk into a soup plate and set it by the stove. In another soup plate, use a fork to mix the eggs with salt and the tablespoon of sugar. Have ready a dish of caster sugar mixed with powdered cinnamon.

In a frying pan, heat enough oil to submerge the bread slices. As soon as it's lightly hazed with blue, slip each finger or slice of bread into the milk and then through the egg (make sure it's well soaked) and drop it into the hot oil. Let it brown, then flip it over to cook the other side. Transfer with a draining spoon to kitchen paper and dust with cinnamon sugar. Continue until all are prepared.

This is particularly good soaked in a syrup made from orange-blossom honey melted with its own volume of orange juice, as I first had it when taking my four children on our annual adventure from our home in the rainy part of Andalucia into the spring sunshine of the Algarve. In some parts of the country the milk is replaced with wine, and the soaking syrup is made by boiling red wine with sugar and cinnamon. Suit yourself.

sonhos de laranja
orange fritters

Sweet dreams (sonhos) are crisp little fritters, Christmas and carnival favourites, for which there are as many different recipes as there are cooks. Older versions suggest you make them with bread dough – they're basically doughnuts; the modern alternative is a sophisticated choux paste, which produces something very light and delicate.

Serves 4–6

50g (2oz) butter
175g (6oz) plain flour
Juice of 3 oranges
4 medium eggs
6 tablespoons caster sugar
1 teaspoon finely grated orange zest
Oil, for deep-frying

In a heavy saucepan, bring 150ml (¼ pint) water to the boil with the butter, add the flour and beat with a wooden spoon until it forms a shiny, smooth dough which pulls away from the sides of the pan. Remove from the heat and beat in 1 tablespoonful of the orange juice. Allow to cool a little and then beat in the eggs one by one, making sure each is incorporated before you add the next. Stop when the paste begins to lose its shine.

Meanwhile make a dipping syrup: heat the rest of the juice, diluted with its own volume of water, with the sugar in a small pan. Let bubble gently for a couple of minutes, remove from the heat, stir in the orange zest and reserve.

Heat a panful of oil. As soon as it's hazed with blue, drop in marble-sized blobs of the choux paste: use 2 teaspoons and fry only a few at a time. Wait until they bob to the surface and puff up before you flip them over to cook the other side. (If the oil's too hot, the outside will burn before the inside is cooked; if it's too cool, they'll be oily and heavy. You'll soon get the hang of it.) Transfer to kitchen paper with a draining spoon and dip them in the syrup before you serve them. You can finish them with a drizzle of warm honey if you prefer – orange-blossom would be perfect. Or with a dusting of sugar and cinnamon. Dreamy.

Orange groves in southern Portugal, watered by irrigation hoses beneath the trees

doce de chila
spiced pumpkin jam

The pumpkin (also known as abobora) is a New World import which matures at the end of autumn and thrives in areas where maize can be grown. In fact, it's often used as a weed inhibitor between the rows, while runner beans are encouraged to skim up the stalks, producing three crops for the price of one. Winter squashes have the virtue of keeping well, making them doubly popular in rural areas: if you pop one on an airy beam, it will still be good in the spring, even in a centrally heated kitchen. Believe me – it works.

Makes 2.7kg (6lb)

1.7kg (4lb) pumpkin
2–3 cloves
1 short cinnamon stick
about 1.7kg (4lb) unrefined (golden) sugar

Peel the pumpkin, and scoop out and discard the wool and seeds (rinse off the latter and roast them in the oven for the children to enjoy). Cut the pumpkin flesh into chunks, stick the cloves and cinnamon into a piece of pumpkin for ease of retrieval and transfer to a heavy pan previously rinsed with cold water. Bring gently to the boil, shaking the pan so the watery juices make their own cooking steam, put the lid on and cook for 15–20 minutes, until perfectly soft and dry as can be – shake it uncovered over the heat for a moment or two to evaporate any visible moisture.

Discard the cloves and cinnamon, mash the pulp and weigh it. Return it to the pan, stir in its own weight of sugar and reheat, stirring steadily, until the sugar crystals have melted and the jam is transparent. Allow one big belch and remove from the heat. Pot up in sterilised jars, seal when cool, store and use as required – mostly in desserts, as a stuffing for tarts and as an extra level of thickening for sugar-and-egg-yolk custards (oves moles).

Madeira, the largest of Portugal's off-shore islands, lies southeast of Lisbon and, as the seagull flies, some 160km (100 miles) off the coast of Africa. Geography and latitude have blessed the island with year-round sunshine, volcanic soil and plentiful rainfall in which tropical fruits and flowers flourish – pineapples, bananas, orchids for the florists' trade. And in the elegant capital with its Mudejar cathedral, every garden, however modest, is bright with blossoms.

In the summer of 1953 poet Sacheverell Sitwell was captivated by the island's raw beauty, linking it to the legend of the Hesperides, source of the golden apples Hercules was sent to seek, the gardens of paradise which lay in the path of the setting sun. Flower-sellers with bouquets of frangipani awaited the visitors who disembarked

at the harbour of Funchal, filling the air with a subtle, ancient fragrance. His pleasure was all the greater because, he explained, there was no reason to visit it to look at churches or paintings since comparatively it has no past: 'The Ancients may have known of the Cape Verde and the Canary Islands, but no one had ever settled on Madeira. It was a virgin island. There were no aboriginal inhabitant to exterminate. It is an island to which you go for the flowers and the climate, seductive and captivating.'

The island's sugar industry was the main source of employment until the tourist trade swept all before it. Molasses, the treacly part of the sugar syrup which will not crystallise, was distilled into alcohol for the winemakers who used it to fortify their wines for th transatlantic trade.

Fields near Cabo Girao, Madeira

MADEIRA

Funchal

Contact with the New World brought yams, maize and sweet potatoes, while haricot beans joined the Old World chestnuts in the winter store cupboard.

For their cultural and domestic traditions, the islanders look to the mainland, particularly the province of Minho, which provided the early settlers. From Minho too comes the pattern for the crimson capes and brightly striped skirts the women of the islands wear on feast days: in Portugal, the beautiful embroideries and hand-knotted lace, each pattern telling of the wearer's origin, are worn not as fancy dress, but as a declaration of national pride. The dark, sweet wines of Madeira, pressed from grapes gathered from hardy little vines carefully sheltered from the seawinds, need no introduction. On the island they're a lady's treat, served with delicious little pastries and fritters made with sweet potato or pumpkin.

Sopa de trigo is an unusual main-course soup made with wheat kernels (sometimes replaced by chestnuts), haricot beans, pumpkin and sweet potato fortified with salt-pork or bacon, the sailor's staple. The açorda madeirense is made with diced wheat-bread and polenta porridge, and may or may not include shredded cabbage; the enrichment is olive oil and the flavouring is thyme and malagueta pepper, with poached eggs and roasted or baked sweet potatoes on the side.

The Azores, nine volcanic peaks in the path of the setting sun due west of the Portuguese mainland, lie like pearls in the vastness of the mid-Atlantic. They, too, were uninhabited until the ocean route to the Americas was opened up. Romantics will tell you they're all that remains of the great kingdom of Atlantis, lost for ever beneath the waves. Practically as well as philosophically the Azores form a bridge between the Americas and Europe, each island with its own culinary character. Beans, particularly dried fava, provide bulk. The capsicums – both sweet peppers and chillies, used dried in winter – added to the classic onion refolgado for colour and fire.

In the 1940s Anne Bridge and Susan Lowndes described the islands as 'beautiful, wild and strange', finding likenesses in the spirit and habit of the people to the inhabitants of another island, equally verdant but somewhat less exotic: 'The visitor familiar with the West of Ireland will be struck by many resemblances – the white-washed houses, the intense greenness of the grass, and above all the small stone-walled fields. On many of the islands one might imagine oneself in Connemara or Ennis, save for the fact that the main crop is not oats or potatoes, but pineapples!' Here, too, the dairy industry provided the inhabitants with a cash crop. 'There is a special breed of tiny pale coffee-coloured cattle, not unlike miniature Jerseys, which yield exceedingly good milk. Owing to the damp Atlantic and the constant sea mists, the pasturage in many of the islands is exceptionally good, and they have always been renowned for their dairy products. Indeed, in the early days of colonisation it is known that cattle and sheep were sent from Portugal, which multiplied so rapidly that soon numbers were being exported back to the mother country.'

The inhabited islands are São Miguel, Santa Maria, Terceira, Graciosa, São Jorge, Faial, Corvo, Flores and Pico. The islanders are frugal, making the best of what's available from land and shore as well as the sailor's staples of rice and dried chestnuts. Limpets, free for the gathering round the rocks and inlets, flavour the regional rice dish, afonso de lapas; on São Miguel wild fennel is used for sopa de funcho. Several excellent cheeses are made on the islands, particularly on São Jorge. Faial has good sweetmeats, Pico makes a deliciously light, flowery wine. Terceira has a stupendous beef hot-pot flavoured with mint and chilli. Spices – cinnamon and cloves – are used in soups and stews as well as in sweet things. On São Miguel a robust all-in stew is traditionally cooked by lowering the cauldron inside a crater in a volcanic lake at the heart of the island, Lagoa das Furnas. The islanders have the Portuguese sweet tooth: treats include curd puddings enriched with butter and eggs, walnut cakes and the full complement of elegant pastries rich with eggs, almonds and spices.

AZORES

CORVO
FLORES

GRACIOSA
SÃO JORGE
FAIAL   TERCEIRA
PICO
SÃO MIGUEL
Ponta Delgada
SANTA MARIA

milho frito a modo de madeira
polenta with cabbage

In Madeira they cook their cornmeal porridge (*xerem*) with finely shredded cabbage; here it's allowed to cool before being cut into bite-sized cubes and fried crisp in olive oil. Young fava (broad) beans can replace the cabbage.

Serves 6

450g (1lb) fine-ground cornmeal
50g (2oz) butter
1 teaspoon dried malagueta pepper, de-seeded and crumbled (optional)
1 teaspoon salt
About 450g (1lb) dark green cabbage, finely shredded
Olive oil, for frying

Mix half the cornmeal with 300ml (1/2 pint) cold water until smooth and free of lumps. Bring 2.4 litres (4 pints) water to the boil in a heavy pan with the butter, the optional malagueta pepper and the salt. Stir in the watered cornmeal and bring to the boil. Add the cabbage. Cook for about 10 minutes, until the cabbage is tender. Sprinkle in the rest of the cornmeal, bring back to the boil and stir over the heat for another 20–30 minutes (depending on how finely ground it is), until the mixture is thick and pulls away from the base of the pan. If you need extra water, make sure it's boiling.

Tip out onto a lightly oiled board or plate and leave to set and cool. Cut into bite-sized cubes and fry in shallow oil until crisp and golden. Good with a fried egg and piri-piri sauce.

chicharros de agraço com molho de açafrao
spring mackerel with sour grapes and saffron salsa

Mackerel (*chicharro*) is very plentiful around the islands at midsummer, when the grapes are forming on the vine. The fish is given a crisp cornmeal jacket – it has plenty of subcutaneous fat which melts into the coating – and dressed with a saffron-flavoured raw onion and pepper salsa sharpened with vinegar and a handful of unripe grapes. The traditional frying implement is an unglazed earthenware frying-cazuela, well-seasoned, which conducts the heat without burning the food. Use a heavy, black iron or non-stick pan (not a light, raw iron pan) instead.

Serves 4

4 fine fat mackerel
Salt
4 tablespoons cornmeal
Fresh pork lard or olive oil (or a mixture of both), for frying

The salsa
1 mild onion, chopped
2 garlic cloves, skinned and chopped
1 red pepper, de-seeded and diced
3 tablespoons wine vinegar
Salt
1/2 teaspoon saffron threads
6 tablespoons olive oil
1 tablespoon green grapes, halved and pips removed

First, make the salsa. Combine the chopped onion, garlic and pepper with the vinegar and a little salt in a small bowl and leave to marinate for the time it takes to cook the fish. Toast the saffron threads in a dry pan until they darken a little – don't let them burn – then crush them and add them to the sauce. Mix in the olive oil and add the grapes – sour or sweet, whatever you can find.

Rinse the mackerel, leaving them a little damp. Salt them on both sides, not forgetting the belly cavity. Spread the cornmeal on a plate and flip the fish through it, making sure all sides are well-coated.

Heat a little lard or oil – a tablespoon or two – in a heavy frying pan and fry the fish gently, turning once, until firm to the finger: 4–6 minutes a side, depending on the fatness of the fish. Serve the fish with the sauce handed around separately.

sopa de moganga
pumpkin soup with noodles

This main-course soup from Madeira is spoon food to be eaten with bread at midday. The pumpkin, like other members of the squash and marrow family, is a Central American native unknown in Europe until well after Christopher Columbus made landfall.

Serves 4

450g (1lb) stewing veal or beef, cut into bite-sized cubes
1 large onion, finely sliced
2 tablespoons butter

450g (1lb) plum tomatoes, scalded, skinned, de-seeded and diced
900g (2lb) pumpkin, peeled, de-seeded and thinly sliced
450g (1lb) sweet potatoes, peeled and diced
4 tablespoons shelled peas or baby fava beans
Salt
1 malagueta pepper, fresh or dried, de-seeded and chopped or crumbled
110g (4oz) vermicelli or other soup noodles

Put the meat and onion in a roomy casserole with the butter and fry gently until everything takes a little colour. Add the tomatoes and let bubble up until the flesh collapses a little. Lay in the pumpkin slices and let bubble up again. Put the lid on tightly and cook gently for about 20 minutes.

Add the sweet potatoes and peas or beans. Bring to the boil again, turn down the heat (adding a little water if necessary) and season with salt and the malagueta pepper. Put the lid on tightly and simmer gently for another 20 minutes, until all is tender.

Stir in the vermicelli, cook for another 5 minutes, then serve with bread and a handful of sweet grapes.

The typical terraced fields and scattered farmhouses of inland Madeira

espetada de espadarte
swordfish kebabs

Swordfish is one of only three fish firm enough to keep its shape on a skewer; the others are tuna and monkfish, the poor man's lobster, either of which can be substituted in this recipe. Espetadas (kebabs), bite-sized pieces of meat or fish threaded on sharpened sticks, are the fairground treat on Madeira. They're eaten with bread rolls (*bolos do caco*): yeast-raised baps the size of a dinner plate traditionally cooked on a bakestone (*caco*) made of basalt, the rock of which the island is formed – though in modern times, rather less romantically, the caco is made of concrete.

Serves 4

450g (1lb) swordfish steaks, cut into cubes

The marinade
2 tablespoon olive oil
3–4 garlic cloves, skinned and crushed
1 oregano sprig, crumbled
1 dried piri-piri pepper, crushed or 1 malagueta
   pepper, de-seeded and finely chopped
Rock salt

Thread the fish onto skewers and arrange them on a flat dish. Combine the marinade ingredients, pour over the kebabs and leave them for an hour or two to take the flavours. Remove from the marinade and drain thoroughly.

Heat a small barbecue or grill to maximum heat and grill the fish kebabs fiercely. Serve with white rice or soft cornmeal porridge (polenta).

escabeche de atúm
marinated tuna fish with baby onions

An escabeche, a light vinegar and oil pickle, began as a method for making a perishable catch last a little longer in the days when no one had fridges. It's customary to soak the tuna in cold water for a couple of hours to ensure no blood remains, though this applies only to very fresh tuna. If you mean to keep it in the fridge for longer than a couple of days, omit the baby onions.

Serves 4 as a main course, 6 as a starter

900g (2lb) tuna loin, middle cut, in one piece
450g (1lb) baby onions, skinned
150ml (¼ pint) olive oil
1 teaspoon dried thyme
1 tablespoon salt

To finish
4 tablespoons wine vinegar
2–3 garlic cloves, skinned and finely chopped
2 tablespoons chopped flat-leaf parsley

Put the tuna in a roomy casserole with the onions, olive oil, thyme and salt and add enough boiling water to come halfway up the fish. Bring to the boil, put the lid on and simmer gently for 20–30 minutes, until the fish is firm but still juicy. Remove and transfer to a deep dish, reserving the baby onions. Boil up the pan juices with the vinegar until you are left with a sticky spoonful. Return the onions to the pan, turn them in the sauce and transfer them to the tuna. Add a glass of water to the remaining juices, let them bubble up, then stir in the garlic and parsley and pour over the tuna. Leave to marinate overnight.

To serve as a starter, pull the fish into chunks with a fork, pile it on toasted bread and dress with the marinade, a sprinkling of chopped hardboiled egg and more freshly chopped parsley. As a main course, serve with quartered hardboiled eggs, chopped tomatoes and fingers of cooked, cooled polenta crisped in olive oil.

have some madeira?

Anne Bridge and Susan Lowndes investigated Madeira's most celebrated export in the 1940s. 'Madeira wine…was exported throughout the sixteenth century. In the latter part of the seventeenth, Charles II suddenly prohibited the import into the American colonies of any commodities save those shipped from English ports in "English bottoms", but made an exception in favour of the wines of Madeira and the Azores. English merchants, realising what this could mean, hurried out to Madeira and began to encourage the peasants to scrap their sugarcanes and grow vines instead. Ships calling at Madeira on their way to and from America or the East Indies took wine on board for the round trip, as well as for sale in America. In the absence of refrigeration, the health of passengers and crew alike depended on an ample supply of wine, the only anti-scorbutic available. The practice of fortifying the island wines with spirits began about the 1750s, but, unlike port, the alcohol is not now used to control fermentation at once, but is only added after this has been done by the application of heat. This dual process gives to Madeira an astonishing and unequalled resistance to age and climatic conditions – wines a hundred years old may, by the lucky, be drunk in Madeira, and are as bland, as delicate and virile at once, as vintage ports, which can rarely be drunk with satisfaction after forty years.'

recheios de batata-doce
sweet potato pasties

On Madeira, everyone's mother makes the best sweet potato pasties. Alternative stuffings are one of the dense-fleshed winter squashes, or with any other filling, sweet or savoury: prawns in béchamel sauce and salt-cod with onion and parsley are particular favourites. If the filling is savoury, the pasties are usually egg-and-breadcrumbed before being fried.

Makes a dozen

The filling
450g (1lb) small sweet potatoes
Salt
250g (9oz) sugar
3 egg yolks
1 teaspoon ground cinnamon

The pastry
About 225g (8oz) strong bread flour
1/2 teaspoon salt
150ml (1/4 pint) milk
25g (1oz) butter
1 teaspoon finely grated lemon zest

To finish
Olive oil, for frying
Sugar and ground cinnamon, for dusting

Boil the sweet potatoes in their skins in plenty of lightly salted water until tender: 20–30 minutes. Drain and skin as soon as they're cool enough to handle, then mash and return to the pan with the sugar. Beat well and cook until you have a thickish paste which pulls away from the base of the pan. Remove from the heat and beat in the egg yolks and cinnamon. If the mixture is not hot enough to cook the egg, return the pan to the stove and cook for a minute or two over a low heat.

Meanwhile, make the pastry. Sift the flour with the salt. Heat the milk and an equal volume of water in a pan with the butter and lemon zest. As soon it boils, beat in the flour – add it all at once. Beat thoroughly and cook until it forms a ball and a thin film sticks to the base of the pan and browns. Tip the dough out onto a floured board and knead until it cools. Roll it out into a long thin strip and drop teaspoons of the sweet potato filling along half the strip, leaving plenty of space between for a flap which will enclose the filling, as if for ravioli. Continue until you have at least a dozen little mounds. With a wet finger, dampen the space between each dab of filling and flip over the second half of the strip to enclose the filling. Use a pastry cutter or a wine glass to trim the edges of the envelopes to give you half-moon shapes.

In a heavy frying pan, heat enough oil to submerge the little pasties. When a faint blue haze rises, slip in the pasties a few at a time so the oil temperature doesn't drop. Fry, turning them once, until crisp and golden. Transfer to kitchen paper and dust with cinnamon and sugar.

Eat them with a cup of hot strong English tea – very Anglo-Madeiran – or a glass of sunny Madeira wine.

panquecas de abóbora
pumpkin, orange and cinnamon pancakes

This is one of the many ways in which pumpkins come in handy for treats and desserts on the island of Madeira. For a celebration tea, serve with broa de mel (Madeiran honey cake) and sweet potato fritters.

Makes about a dozen

450g (1lb) pumpkin, peeled, de-seeded and cut into chunks
Juice and finely grated zest of 1 small orange
450g (1lb) plain flour
1 teaspoon baking powder
1 teaspoon ground cinnamon
1 egg
Olive oil, for frying

To serve
Sugar and ground cinnamon, for dusting

Cook the pumpkin in the orange juice in a tightly lidded pan until perfectly tender: 10–15 minutes. Mash thoroughly, adding the orange zest.

Sift the flour with the baking powder and cinnamon and beat it into the mashed pumpkin. Beat in the egg to make a softish mixture which holds its shape when dropped from a spoon.

Heat a little oil in a heavy frying pan and fry spoonfuls of the mixture until deliciously browned and lightly risen, patting each one down to form a pancake and turning it once. Sprinkle with the sugar and cinnamon and serve with tea or a glass of Madeira wine. Delicious for breakfast American-style, with crisp bacon and maple syrup.

fartes de batata-doce
sweet potato and almond cookies

A speciality of Madeira: crisp little cookies made with mashed sweet potato and ground almonds, flavoured with orange zest.

Makes a dozen

450g (1lb) sweet potatoes
Salt
Juice and grated zest of 1 orange
450g (1lb) caster sugar
75g (3oz) butter
1 tablespoon plain flour
1 teaspoon baking powder
1 teaspoon bicarbonate of soda
3 eggs, lightly beaten
175g (6oz) ground almonds
Melted butter, for drizzling

To finish
Caster sugar
Chopped toasted almonds (optional)

Cook the sweet potatoes in their skins in lightly salted water until tender: 20–30 minutes. Drain and skin them as soon as they're cool enough to handle, and mash thoroughly with the orange juice, zest, sugar and butter. Return the pulp to the pan. Sift the flour with the baking powder and bicarbonate of soda and beat it into the sweet potato mixture along with the eggs and ground almonds. Stir over a gentle heat until the mixture is very thick and comes away from the bottom of the pan. Tip it out onto a floured board, smooth the surface and leave to cool.

Preheat the oven to 180°C/350°F/gas mark 4. Cut the cookie dough into any shape you fancy, transfer to a buttered baking sheet and drizzle with a little melted butter. Bake for 20–30 minutes until lightly browned – don't let them dry out. Dust them with sugar as soon as they come out of the oven and transfer to a wire rack. Finish with chopped toasted almonds.

Green fields occupy a valley floor on the island of São Miguel, Azores

broas de mel
honey cakes

Sugary treats are traditionally baked by Madeira's housewives to mark the feast days of the Virgin Mary.

Makes about 2 dozen

300g (10^{1}/$_{2}$oz) plain flour
^{1}/$_{2}$ teaspoon bicarbonate of soda
2 teaspoons ground cinnamon
A pinch of freshly grated nutmeg
250g (9oz) butter
200g (7oz) brown sugar
2 tablespoons honey

To finish
A handful of walnut halves
Demerara or unbleached cane sugar

Sift the flour with the bicarbonate of soda, cinnamon and nutmeg. Work in the rest of the ingredients, melting the butter with the warmth of your hand, until you have a soft smooth dough. Allow to rest for 30 minutes.

Preheat the oven to 190°C/375°F/gas mark 5.

Break off walnut-sized nuggets of the dough, pop a walnut half on each, sprinkle with sugar and arrange well apart on a buttered baking sheet. Bake for 15–20 minutes, until golden brown. Transfer to a wire rack to cool and crisp.

sorbete de pinho
pineapple sorbet

The perfect summer refreshment, this sorbet is very good with a slice of honey cake. There's no need to include an egg white to keep the sorbet soft: the pineapple is equipped with its own tenderising enzyme which prevents the juices from freezing hard.

Makes about 1 litre (1³/4 pints)

1 pineapple, peeled, cored and cut into chunks
1 tablespoon lime juice
275g (10oz) unrefined sugar
500ml (18fl oz) water

To finish (optional)
Chunks of fresh pineapple

Process all the ingredients together in a liquidiser, then strain and freeze. There's no need to allow it to soften before you serve it: just spoon it straight from the freezer into long, thin glasses. Good with chunks of fresh pineapple folded in among the scoops.

pudim de papaia
papaya pudding

The papaya, a post-Columbian import, native to the lowlands of Central America, thrives on the volcanic soil of the Atlantic islands and is eaten both ripe and unripe. When unripe it can be eaten raw in salads, or cooked, as in this elegant dessert.

Serves 4–6

1 green (unripe) papaya, about 900g (2lb)
4 eggs
225g (8oz) caster sugar
110g (4oz) butter, softened
75g (3oz) plain flour
150ml (1/4 pint) milk
1 teaspoon grated orange zest

The caramel
4 heaped tablespoons caster sugar

Cut the papaya into chunks and cook until soft in enough water to cover: about 20 minutes from the water boiling. Skin, de-seed and either push the pulp through a sieve or purée in a liquidiser.

Preheat the oven to 180°C/350°F/gas mark 4. Whisk the eggs with the sugar until light and white. Beat the softened butter, flour, milk and orange zest into the papaya pulp and fold in the whisked egg and sugar.

Make the caramel by melting the sugar gently in a heavy pan until it bubbles and browns (easier if you start with a very little water and stir throughout the process of caramelising), then tip it into your chosen mould and roll it around the sides to coat. You can make the caramel in the mould itself.

Pour the pudding mix into the mould and transfer to a bain-marie. Bake for 40–50 minutes, until it is firm to the finger. Allow to cool. Turn out of the mould and serve with a ripe papaya and passion fruit salad, or a handful of strawberries dressed with lemon or bitter orange juice.

index

acknowledgements

To thank everyone whose knowledge and expertise I have ransacked over fifty years – ever since I first set foot as a twelve-year-old schoolgirl on the high hot plains of Castile – would be an impossible task. I can only say that I owe a great debt of gratitude to all those natives of the ancient kingdoms who have set me straight over the years, but most of all to the people of the valley of the Gualmesi in the province of Cadiz, our family home for more than twelve years.

As always, I owe a debt of gratitude for heroism beyond the call of duty to my husband Nicholas for his willingness to accompany and entertain me during long, sometimes hazardous explorations of the byways and highways of the several kingdoms of Iberia – and for not complaining when the place was shut. To my beloved children, Caspar, Francesca, Poppy and Honey for their willingness to share what they learned during their schooldays in Andalusia and their tolerance and patience thereafter. To my sister-in-law Priscilla White and her husband Mark for guidance to the hidden corners of Asturias and northern Spain, and for the loan of their apartment in the beautiful port of Llanes. I am indebted, too, to Dun Gifford and Sara Baer-Sinnott of Oldways, Boston, and to María José Sevilla of Foods from Spain for opportunities to explore places and people I would never have been able to find on my own.

My thanks and admiration are also due to the brilliant Jean Cazals and Janie Suthering for their inspirational visual interpretation of the recipes. For unfailing support and unflappable enthusiasm during the production and editing to my editor and chief trouble-shooter Caroline Taggart, her right-hand woman Vicki Murrell, to designer Geoff Hayes, to Robina Pelham Burn for patient copy-editing, Ruth Baldwin for proof-reading and Sarah Ereira for the index. And, as always, to my friend and agent Abner Stein, who has looked after me for more years than either of us cares to count.

Sources quoted in the text:

Gerald Brenan, *South From Granada* (Hamish Hamilton, 1957)
Ann Bridge and Susan Lowndes, *The Selective Traveller in Portugal* (Chatto, 1949, new ed. 1967)
Samuel Chamberlain, (London, 1952)
Susan Plant Dos Santos, *Touring Rural Portugal* (London 1972)
Nina Epton, *Grapes and Granite* (Cassell, London, 1956)
Richard Ford, *Gatherings from Spain* (John Murray, London 1846)
Douglas Goldring, *To Portugal* (Rich & Cowan, London, 1934)
Tomás Graves, *Bread and Oil* (Prospect, 2000)
Ethel Hargrove, *Progressive Portugal* (London 1914)
Christina Gascoigne Hartley, *Spain Revisited* (Stanley Paul, London, 1911)
Thomas Hinde, *Spain: a personal anthology* (Newnes, London, 1963)
W. D. Howells, *Familiar Spanish Travels* (Harper, New York, 1913)
Gerald Howson, *The Flamencos of Cadiz Bay* (Hutchinson, London, 1965)
Maria de Lourdes Modesto, *Cozinha Tradicional Portuguesa* (Verbo, Lisbon 1982)
Sacheverell Sitwell, *A Traveller in Portugal* (London, 1953)

Photographic acknowledgements
All food photography by Jean Cazals.

page 9 Michael Busselle/CORBIS; 10 Archivo Iconográfico, S.A./CORBIS; 13 Royalty-free/CORBIS; 15 Torleif Svensson/CORBIS; 16 Geoff Hayes; 19 Still Life with a Bowl of Chocolate, or Breakfast with Chocolate, c.1640 (oil on canvas), Juan de Zurbaran (1620-49) (attr. to)/Musée des Beaux-Arts et d'Archéologie, Besançon, France, Lauros/Giraudon/Bridgeman Art Library; 20 Mark A. Johnson/CORBIS; 23 Two Children Eating a Melon and Grapes, 1645-46 (oil on canvas), Bartolome Esteban Murillo (1617-82)/Alte Pinakothek, Munich, Germany; 24 Geoff Hayes; 26 Patrick Ward/CORBIS; 27 Geoff Hayes; 29 Valencian Fisherwomen, 1915, Joaquín Sorolla y Bastida, (1863-1923)/Museo Sorolla, Madrid, Spain/Bridgeman Art Library; 30/31 Preparing the Dry Grapes, 1890 (oil on canvas), Joaquín Sorolla y Bastida, (1863-1923)/Musée des Beaux-Arts, Pau, France, Giraudon/Bridgeman Art Library; 35 Michael Busselle/CORBIS; 38 Michael Busselle/ CORBIS; 39 Nik Wheeler/CORBIS; 45 Jim Sugar Photography/CORBIS; 48 Nik Wheeler/CORBIS; 50/51 Carmen Redondo/CORBIS; 52 Stephanie Maze/CORBIS; 53 Jose Fuste Raga/CORBIS; 55 Michael Busselle/CORBIS; 58 Jack Hollingsworth/CORBIS; 62 Francesc Muntada/ CORBIS; 63 Quince, Cabbage, Melon and Cucumber, c.1602, Juan Sanchez Cotan (1560-1627)/© San Diego Museum of Art, USA, Gift of Anne R. and Amy Putnam; 64 Michael Busselle/CORBIS; 65 Yann Arthus-Bertrand/ CORBIS; 69 Ron Watts/CORBIS; 75 The Pilgrimage to the Basque Country, José Arrué (1890-1977)   /Museo de Bellas Artes, Bilbao, Spain/Bridgeman Art Library; 81 Michael Busselle/CORBIS; 84 Owen Franken/ CORBIS; 86 Ted Spiegel/CORBIS; 88 Michael Busselle/ CORBIS; 92 Diego Lezama Orezzoli/CORBIS; 95 Elisabeth Luard; 98 Archivo Iconografico, S.A./CORBIS; 99 Still Life with Golden Bream, 1808-12 (oil on canvas), Francisco José de Goya y Lucientes(1746-1828)/© Museum of Fine Arts, Houston, Texas, USA, Museum Purchased with Funds from Alice Pratt Brown Fund/Bridgeman Art Library; 102 Michael Busselle/CORBIS; 109 Francesc Muntada/CORBIS; 111 Michael Busselle/CORBIS; 119 Michael S. Yamashita/CORBIS; 121 Geoff Hayes; 125 Owen Franken/CORBIS; 126 Jim Zuckerman/CORBIS; 133 Geoff Hayes; 135 Paul Almasy/CORBIS; 141 Ingrid Rasmussen; 145 David Forman; Eye Ubiquitous/CORBIS; 147 Diego Lezama Orezzoli/CORBIS; 148 Geoff Hayes; 150/1 Douglas Peebles/CORBIS; 152 George W. Wright/CORBIS; 154 Torre dos Clerigos, Oporto, Portugal, 1837 (oil on canvas), James Holland (1799-1870)/© Yale Center for British Art, Paul Mellon Collection, USA/Bridgeman Art Library; 156 Charles O'Rear/CORBIS; 163 Tony Arruza/CORBIS; 164 Geoff Hayes; 168 Tony Arruza/CORBIS; 171 Tony Arruza/CORBIS; 177 Tony Arruza/CORBIS; 179 Tony Arruza/CORBIS; 183 View of Coimbra, Portugal, James Holland (1799-1870)/Christie's Images, London/Bridgeman Art Library; 188 The Harbour, Lisbon,Charles Henry Seaforth (1805-c.1853)/The Fine Art Society, London/Bridgeman Art Library; 195 Tony Arruza/CORBIS; 196 Tony Arruza/CORBIS; 198 Geoff Hayes; 203 Geoff Hayes; 205 Tony Arruza/CORBIS; 208 Andrew Brown/CORBIS; 210 Hubert Stadler/CORBIS; 213 Jonathan Blair/CORBIS; 217 Bob Krist/CORBIS.